The Empire Abroad and the Empire at Home

African American Literature and the Era of Overseas Expansion

JOHN CULLEN GRUESSER

The University of Georgia Press   Athens and London

© 2012 by the University of Georgia Press
Athens, Georgia 30602
www.ugapress.org
All rights reserved
Set in Minion by Graphic Composition, Inc.
Manufactured by Thomson-Shore
The paper in this book meets the guidelines for
permanence and durability of the Committee on
Production Guidelines for Book Longevity of the
Council on Library Resources.

Printed in the United States of America
16 15 14 13 12 P 5 4 3 2 1

Library of Congress Cataloging-in-Publication Data

Gruesser, John Cullen, 1959–
    The empire abroad and the empire at home : African American
literature and the era of overseas expansion / John Cullen Gruesser.
        p. cm.
    Includes bibliographical references and index.
    ISBN 978-0-8203-3434-9 (hardcover : alk. paper) — ISBN 0-8203-3434-0
(hardcover : alk. paper) — ISBN 978-0-8203-4406-5 (pbk. : alk. paper) —
ISBN 0-8203-4406-0 (pbk. : alk. paper)
    1. American literature—African American authors—History and criticism—
Theory, etc. 2. Imperialism in literature. 3. Literature and globalization.
4. African Americans—Intellectual life. I. Title.
    PS153.N5G785 2012
    810.9'896073—dc23   2012017908

British Library Cataloging-in-Publication Data available

Contents

Acknowledgments   vii

Introduction: Empire at Home and Abroad   1

Part 1. African American Literature and the Spanish-Cuban-American War

Chapter 1. Cuban Generals, Black Sergeants, and White Colonels: The African American Poetic Response to the Spanish-Cuban-American War   19

Chapter 2. Wars Abroad and at Home in Sutton E. Griggs's *Imperium in Imperio* and *The Hindered Hand*   39

Part 2. African American Literature, the Philippine-American War, and Expansion in the Pacific

Chapter 3. Black Burdens, Laguna Tales, and "Citizen Tom" Narratives: African American Writing and the Philippine-American War   63

Chapter 4. Annexation in the Pacific and Asian Conspiracy in Central America in James Weldon Johnson's Unproduced Operettas   96

Coda: Pauline Hopkins, the *Colored American Magazine*, and the Critique of Empire Abroad and at Home in "Talma Gordon"   113

Notes   127
Works Cited   139
Index   153

Acknowledgments

My thought process, research, and writing have been significantly shaped and greatly enriched by my participation in the activities of several professional associations and scholarly communities. These include not only large organizations such as the American Literature Association (led by the indefatigable Alfred Bendixen) and the Modern Language Association but also regional and more specialized groups such as the New Jersey College English Association, the Collegium for African American Research, the Association of Graduate Liberal Studies Programs, the Society for the Study of Southern Literature, and the Poe Studies Association, as well as small, narrowly focused intellectual communities and initiatives such as the Pauline Hopkins Society, the Sutton Griggs Project (organized by Ken Warren and Tess Chakkalakal), the 1990 NEH summer seminar on the problem of race in American and Afro-American literature from 1860 to 1930 held at UC Berkeley and directed by Eric Sundquist, the 1994 NEH summer seminar on literary history in theory and practice held at Princeton University and directed by Earl Miner, and the 2007 NEH summer seminar on hemispheric American literature held at Columbia University and directed by Rachel Adams and Caroline Levander. Over the past five years, parts of this book have been presented in sessions and symposia organized under the aegis of the ALA, MLA, NJCEA, CAAR, AGLSP, SSSL, and the Griggs Project, and I have greatly profited from audience responses to these panels. What follows is very much a partial list of the people I have been fortunate enough to get to know through and in some cases work closely with in these scholarly associations and communities during the past two decades: Elizabeth Ammons, Claudia Tate, Jennie Kassanoff, Lois Brown, Jill Bergman,

Richard Yarborough, Maryemma Graham, Daylanne English, Stephen Knadler, Jonathan Eburne, Houston Baker, Paul Lauter, Mary Balkan, Kelly Shea, Burt Kimmelman, Susannah Chewning, Ed Shannon, John Wargacki, Claude Julien, Isabel Soto, Tish Crawford, Kim Phillips, Ira Dworkin, Cindy Hamilton, Jean Yellin, Martyn Bone, Keith Cartwright, Holly Stave, Beth Sweeney, Kelly Ross, David Schmid, Kate Nickerson, Susan Amper, Barbara Cantalupo, Jerry Kennedy, Scott Peeples, Richard Kopley, Alisha Knight, Eric Gardner, Dorri Beam, Mary Frances Jiménez, Carla Peterson, Tanya Clark, April Logan, John Ernest, Giulia Fabi, Carole Doreski, Joe Alvarez, and Aldon Nielsen. I am grateful to Jennifer James and Keith Wailoo for their helpful advice and to Rudolph Byrd, the researchers at the U.S. Army Military History Institute, and the librarians at Yale University's Beinecke Library and the U.S. Army War College Library at Carlisle Barracks for answering my questions. The people at the Nancy Thompson Library and many fellow faculty members at my home institution, especially Richard Katz, Mia Zamora, Bert Wailoo, Alan Robbins, Holly Logue, Carole Shaffer-Koros, and Terry Golway, have been very supportive. I owe a profound debt to Colleen O'Brien, Nirmal Trivedi, Ira Dworkin, Hanna Wallinger, and Paula Seniors for reading parts of the manuscript and to John Ernest, Ken Warren, and MJ Devaney for reading all of it and offering sage advice for improving it. Some of the material in this book appeared in different form in *American Literary History* and *Revue Afram: Publication Semestrielle du Cercle d'Etudes Afro-Américaines et Diasporiques*, and in the section on Frank R. Steward in chapter 3, I draw on the ideas and in some places the eloquence of Gretchen Murphy with whom I collaborated in editing and writing an introduction to Steward's Laguna stories, published in the May 2011 issue of *PMLA*. Beth Snead, Jon Davies, and the amazing Nancy Grayson at the University of Georgia Press and my most patient and generous e-mail correspondents Malin Pereira and Hanna Wallinger offered me much appreciated encouragement during the whole course of this project. By no means can I fail to mention the support of my old friends Mike, Phil, Joe, and Tim, my in-laws the Spilmans, various Cullen and Fandel cousins and uncles, my parents John and Eileen, my sister Jenny, my son Jack, my daughter Sarah, and, most of all, my wife Susan.

Empire at Home and Abroad

When the United States learns that justice should be blind as to race and color, then may it undertake to, with some show of propriety, expand. Now its expansion means extension of race hate and cruelty, barbarous lynchings and gross injustice to dark people.
—Lewis H. Douglass, "Black Opposition to McKinley"

The older idea was that the whites would eventually displace the native races and inherit their lands, but this idea has been rudely shaken in the increase of American Negroes, the experience of the English in Africa, India and the West Indies, and the development of South America. The policy of expansion, then, simply means world problems of the Color Line. The color question enters into European politics and floods our continent from Alaska to Patagonia.
—W. E. B. Du Bois, "The Color Line Belts the World"

Best known for the role it plays in the "Forethought" to *The Souls of Black Folk* (1903), W. E. B. Du Bois's famous declaration "The problem of the twentieth century is the problem of the color line" (100) originally appeared three years earlier in "The Present Outlook for the Dark Races of Mankind." In this speech he delivered at the third annual meeting of the American Negro Academy in Washington, D.C., in March 1900, Du Bois makes the statement in the context of the "new imperial policy" (53) the United States was implementing in the wake of its victory over Spain and amid the ongoing Philippine-American War: "Indeed a survey of the civilized world at the end of the 19th century but confirms the proposition with which I started—the world problem of the 20th century is the Problem of the Color line—the question of the relation of the advanced races of men who happen to be white to the great majority of under-developed or half developed nations of mankind who happen to be yellow, brown, or black" (54). Du Bois goes on to link the empire abroad and the em-

1

pire at home explicitly: "We must remember that the twentieth century will find nearly twenty millions of brown and black people under the protection of the American flag, a third of the nation, and that on the success and efficiency of the nine millions of our own number depends the ultimate destiny of Filipinos, Porto [*sic*] Ricans, Indians, Hawaiians, and that on us too depends in large degree the attitude of Europe toward the teeming millions of Asia and Africa" (53). Beyond asserting that the actions of U.S. blacks ("nine millions of our own number") will determine the future not only for peoples in the nation's newly acquired territories but for colonized peoples everywhere, this passage indicates how profoundly African American public intellectuals such as Du Bois engaged with U.S. expansion at the turn of the twentieth century.

Like Du Bois in "The Present Outlook," his contemporary Pauline E. Hopkins connects the fate of inhabitants of the nation's new overseas empire with that of U.S. blacks in "Some Literary Workers," published in the Boston-based *Colored American Magazine* in 1902. However, whereas Du Bois emphasizes the impact the latter will have upon the former, Hopkins stresses the opposite. In this essay, the fourth of her eleven-installment Famous Women of the Negro Race biographical series, she contends,

> The observant eye can trace the impress of Divinity on sea and shore as He, in mighty majesty, protects the weak in the great battle that is now on between the Anglo-Saxon and the dark-skinned races of the earth. . . . The increasing gravity of our situation in relation to the body politic, and the introduction of new peoples who must live under the same ban of color that we are forced to endure, may operate to our advantage by bringing about desirable changes in the future of our race. . . . The subjugation of Cuba, Porto [*sic*] Rico and the Philippines . . .—all is but the death knell of prejudice, for the natural outcome of the close association that must follow the reception of these peoples within our Union, will be the downfall of cruel discrimination solely because of color. In this way malice defeats itself. (140)

Hopkins by no means endorses what she terms the "subjugation" of the "new peoples who must live under the same ban of color that we are forced to endure," associating it with "malice." However, she believes that U.S. blacks ("our race") will benefit from what she sees as the inevitable "downfall of cruel discrimination solely because of color" resulting from the influx of these nonwhites into the nation state. This argument to some extent echoes the one she makes in her short story "Talma Gordon," published in the *Colored American Magazine* in October 1900 and now widely available in the second edition of the *Norton Anthology of African American Literature*. Critical discussions of this text, Hopkins's first, most all-encompassing, and in many ways most profound response to empire, which is the focus of the coda to this book, have avoided or minimized the subject of imperialism, reading the tale as something less than a condemnation of U.S. expansion.

In general, the subject of the African American response to late nineteenth- and early twentieth-century expansion has received short shrift. On the one hand, discussions of imperialism have tended to ignore or marginalize the responses of African Americans. On the other hand, studies of these years by scholars of U.S. black history, culture, and literature have devoted scant attention to the relationship between the empire at home and the empire abroad. Adopting a focus limited in time but broad in scope, this book strives to establish that at the end of the nineteenth and the beginning of the twentieth century U.S. black writers made connections between and responded extensively and idiosyncratically to overseas expansion and its implications for domestic race relations. Specifically, *The Empire Abroad and the Empire at Home* aspires to (1) make the case that African American responses to imperialism should be an integral part of the study of turn-of-the-twentieth-century U.S. black literature and culture, (2) show that in their responses to expansion African Americans were consistently more staunchly committed than most whites to addressing the domestic problem of race, and (3) bring African American literary studies to the study of political history rather than simply bring political history to African American literary studies. In doing so, this project builds on Willard B. Gatewood's, George P. Marks's, and Daniel B. Schirmer's pioneering work on U.S. imperialism in the 1970s and has been influenced by discussions, published during the last twenty years, about the relationship between literature and empire by scholars such as Donald Pease, Amy Kaplan, Kevin Gaines, Frederick Wegener, Michele Mitchell, and Ifeoma Nwankwo. It also participates in the current transnational turn in literary and cultural studies epitomized by Caroline F. Levander and Robert S. Levine's collection *Hemispheric American Literature* (2008) and shares the emphases on race and empire at the heart of literary scholar Gretchen Murphy's *Shadowing the White Man's Burden: U.S. Imperialism and the Problem of the Color Line* (2010) and recent historical studies such as Jackson Lears's *Rebirth of a Nation: The Making of Modern America, 1877–1920* (2009) and James Bradley's *The Imperial Cruise: A Secret History of Empire and War* (2009). Moreover, it draws on and responds to recent scholarship devoted to Pauline Hopkins, Sutton E. Griggs, and James

Weldon Johnson and reads the texts of lesser-known writers, including James Ephraim McGirt, Frank R. Steward, and F. Grant Gilmore, as well as heretofore unexamined archival material by Johnson written in conjunction with his brother J. Rosamond Johnson and with his brother and Bob Cole.

Unlike publications that discuss late nineteenth- and early twentieth-century African American writing in connection with a specific region in the United States, such as the South, or a particular domestic topic, such as lynching, *The Empire Abroad* addresses poetic, fictional, and dramatic texts about the Caribbean, Asia, the Pacific islands, and Latin America, as well as the United States and its borderlands, published by African Americans during a single, pivotal generation. In relation to historical events, the era it focuses on extends from the early 1890s to the mid-1910s. The former date roughly corresponds with the closing of the American frontier, the onset of an aggressive pursuit to establish a U.S. overseas empire, the southern push to rewrite state constitutions in a manner designed to deny blacks the vote, and the North's abandonment of efforts to reverse the tide of disenfranchisement. The latter date corresponds roughly with the administration of Woodrow Wilson, the first southern-born president since the 1860s, who sent U.S. troops to Haiti, resulting in a twenty-year occupation of the hemisphere's oldest black-run nation; screened D. W. Griffiths's *The Birth of a Nation*, based on *The Clansman* by his longtime friend Thomas Dixon, at the White House; and mandated the segregation of federal offices in Washington. Examinations of U.S. imperialism during this period of approximately twenty-five years have tended to treat black responses to the empire abroad as adjuncts to rather than as distinct from the debate among whites on the subject even though, as Christopher Lasch established over fifty years ago, white imperialists and white anti-imperialists in the late 1800s and early 1900s wholeheartedly subscribed to the scientific racism and social Darwinism of the day. To be sure, U.S. blacks such as Du Bois were influenced by the ideas about race current at the time, as Kwame Anthony Appiah has pointed out (28–46), yet in their responses to expansion African Americans differed profoundly from their white counterparts because they rejected racist assumptions and insisted on the salience of the country's founding documents, which whites, in embracing the negrophobia and xenophobia of the era, considered null and void in connection with U.S. blacks, Chinese immigrants, Puerto Ricans, Hawaiians, and Filipinos.

For the most part, recent critical examinations of African American literature and culture, like their predecessors, continue to pay little or no attention to the engagement with late nineteenth- and early twentieth-century imperialism, as evidenced by books such as Barbara McCaskill and Caroline Gebhard's collection *Post-Bellum, Pre-Harlem: African American Literature and Culture, 1877–1919* (2006). The postbellum, pre-Harlem years have long been a terra incognita for African Americanists, who have characterized the period in strictly domestic and frequently transitional terms. To this day there is little consensus as to what the era's significance is, how it should be regarded, the specific dates that define it, and what it should be called.[1] Surprisingly, especially in the light of current scholarly trends, McCaskill and Gebhard's volume does not address the dawn of U.S. overseas expansion and its ramifications, the relationship between African Americans and people in Latin America, Haiti, Asia, and Africa, or the transnational forces at work in various locations within the borders of the United States. Similarly, anthologies of African American writing, such as Henry Louis Gates and Jennifer Burton's *Call and Response: Key Debates in African American Studies* (2010), tend to avoid the topic. Gates and Burton devote none of their fifty key debates to U.S. imperialism, nor do any of the hundreds of individual selections in their twelve-hundred-page textbook address it.

Recent readings of individual authors that do grapple with empire, such as those devoted to Griggs and James Weldon Johnson, have sought to extrapolate the writer's position on expansion from a single text rather than examining the full range of the author's writings that engage imperialism. Despite publishing more novels than any other African American during the period, three of which directly engage U.S. expansion, the Southern Baptist minister Griggs has seldom been the subject of serious critical attention. Although articles by Stephen Knadler and Levander addressing Griggs and empire suggest that the process of rediscovering and reevaluating the writer may finally be getting under way, these readings, perhaps not surprisingly, concentrate on his best-known novel, *Imperium in Imperio* (1899). As for Johnson, given the recent scholarly attention devoted to the relationship between cultural productions and imperialism, it is not surprising that this key literary figure, U.S. diplomat in Latin America, and prominent race activist has been one of the few African American authors whose views on and links to expansion have been the subject of scholarly scrutiny. However, these readings have tended to focus on his lone novel, *The Autobiography of an Ex-Colored Man* (1912), without addressing his poetry and his produced and unproduced dramatic texts. The scholars who have published recent articles on Johnson, moreover, have sought to place him in either the pro- or anti-imperialist camp, in some cases faulting him for failing to adhere to what they deem to be a consistent or appropriate stance on expansion.

In *Race over Empire: Racism and U.S. Imperialism, 1865–1900* (2004), Eric T. L. Love challenges the standard reading of the relationship between race and imperialism in the late 1800s, contending that ideas about race either proved to be a hindrance to U.S. expansion or played a less significant role than is commonly believed. Specifically, he characterizes "the relationship between the imperialists of the late nineteenth century and the racist structures and convictions of the time" as "antagonistic, not harmonious" (xi). In doing so, he rebuts the assumption prevalent among historians that in the late nineteenth century racist science and social Darwinism bolstered, if not created, the impetus for the United States to acquire an overseas empire. In support of this larger argument, he makes three subsidiary points. First, in chapters devoted to successful and unsuccessful U.S. initiatives to annex Santo Domingo, Hawaii, and the Philippines, he asserts that racial considerations outweighed those relating to empire in the years prior to 1898 and that, in contrast to the widely accepted narrative about the era, this did not change in the years 1898 to 1902 (xii). Second, because of the continued preeminence of prejudice against color in the North as well as the South, proimperialists avoided rather than emphasized race and thus—again in contrast to the prevailing scholarly assumption—they deemphasized rather than touted Darwinism, benevolent assimilation, Anglo-Saxon superiority, and white man's burden rhetoric to promote the annexations of 1898 and 1899.[2] Third, in connection with white U.S. policy makers, Love states, "the evidence demonstrates that the line between imperialist and anti-imperialist was blurry more often than not and that it could shift, wildly and unpredictably, from person to person, incident to incident, and even within the same person during the same incident" (12). Building in part on Love's important reassessment of the relationship between race and empire in the United States, *The Empire Abroad* contextualizes and analyzes the responses to expansion by African American literary artists and public intellectuals at the end of the nineteenth and the beginning of the twentieth century.

The chapters that follow establish three points about the African American engagement with U.S. imperialism during this period. First, race consistently trumped empire for U.S. black writers. Whether they promoted, opposed, and/or equivocated over expansion abroad, these writers invariably adopted the positions they did based on the effects they believed an empire overseas would have on blacks at home. Second, given the complexity of the era's debates over expansion, the unique and precarious position in which U.S. blacks found themselves, and the rapidity with which events in the Caribbean and the Pacific unfolded in the 1890s and early 1900s, it should come as no surprise that African American writers often did not adopt and maintain a fixed position on the subject of imperialism. The stance of individual authors depended on several factors, including the foreign location in question, the presence or absence of African American soldiers within the text, the stage of the author's career, and the text's relationship to specific generic and literary traditions. Third, no matter what their disposition toward imperialism, the fact of U.S. expansion allowed and in many cases compelled these writers to grapple with empire, and they often use texts about expansion to address directly or obliquely the situation facing blacks at home during a period in which their citizenship rights and very existence were increasingly in jeopardy. The following section tells the story of two prominent U.S. families, one white and southern, one black and northern—the Blounts of Georgia and the Stewards of New Jersey. Revealing key differences between the white and the African American engagement with empire, the histories of these families intersected at key moments and members of both clans were intimately connected with and thoughtfully responded to U.S. expansion and its connections to domestic race relations.

Theophilus G. and Frank R. Steward, Black Participation in the U.S. Military, and the African American Response to Expansion

African Methodist Episcopal (AME) minister, U.S. Army chaplain, Wilberforce professor, prolific author, and outspoken defender of his people, Theophilus Gould Steward (1843–1924) built an AME church in Macon that still bears his name during his 1866 to 1871 sojourn in Georgia. As his biographers William Seraile and Albert G. Miller have both noted, Steward's subsequent beliefs were shaped by his years in the South during Reconstruction. His experiences convinced him of the need to use military force to achieve justice in certain circumstances. Steward faced death threats by the Ku Klux Klan and other groups when he called on President Grant to send troops to stamp out anti-Union dissent in Georgia (Andrews 27). During the 1880s, he became the widely respected pastor of the Metropolitan AME Church in Washington, D.C., developing friendships and alliances with influential African Americans, including Frederick Douglass. In 1891 he became chaplain for the Twenty-Fifth (Colored) Infantry regiment and a decade later served in that capacity in the Philippines, where he was also a military superintendent of schools during the occupation. In addition to writing a book about black participation in the U.S. military, *The Colored Regulars in the United States Army* (1904), Steward published articles about conditions in the Philippines in the leading black journal of the day, Boston's *Colored American Magazine*.

His son Frank R. Steward (1872–1931), who graduated from Harvard College in 1896 and Harvard Law School in 1899, served in Cuba at the rank of lieutenant in the Eighth Volunteer Infantry shortly after Spain's surrender in 1898. He was appointed captain in the Forty-Ninth Infantry, a volunteer black regiment that was stationed and saw action in the Philippines, and in 1901 became a military judge in San Pablo in the province of Laguna. In addition to contributing a chapter about black officers to his father's book, he published three short stories about the U.S. occupation of the Philippines in the *Colored American Magazine* in 1902 and 1903, which I examine in chapter 3. These stories indicate the younger Steward's awareness of the ambiguities and iniquities of his country's—and his own—presence in the Philippines. Raising subtle and unsettling questions about the U.S. occupation specifically and about expansion generally, Steward's stories appeared during Pauline Hopkins's tenure as the magazine's literary editor and may have contributed to her dismissal from it.

He begins "Colored Officers," the appendix to *The Colored Regulars*, by describing "the commission ranks" of the armed services as the "stubbornest" of the "avenues to American citizenship" to "yield to the newly enfranchised" (299). Citing specific battles during the Civil War, as well as the Haitian and Cuban revolutions, he proceeds, at some length, to refute the notion that officers of color cannot lead black soldiers, a belief that was held, as chapter 1 shows, by Theodore Roosevelt, among others. In the process, he applauds the War Department's reversal of past practice by appointing blacks—including himself—as line officers in the volunteer regiments in the Philippines. Urging that military academies and promotion opportunities be opened to the "capable" of the race, he closes the chapter with the assertion that the black soldier "lays claim to no prerogative other than that of a plain citizen of the Republic, trained to the profession of arms. The measure of his demand—and it is the demand of ten millions of his fellow-citizens allied to him by race—is that the full manhood privileges of a soldier be accorded to him" (327). Articles by and about Steward in black publications such as the *Colored American* newspaper out of Washington, D.C., present his educational achievements, captain's commission, and provost judgeship in a like manner as important contributions to the struggle to attain full citizenship rights at home, thereby aligning him with his fellow Harvard alumnus Du Bois's talented tenth.[3]

Like Frank R. Steward, James H. Blount Jr. (1869–1918) was an Ivy League–trained lawyer, an army officer during the Spanish-Cuban-American and the Philippine-American wars, a judge during the occupation of the Philippines, and a writer who raised concerns about the U.S. role in the archipelago. He was the son of James H. Blount (1837–1903), a Civil War veteran, wealthy planter, and longtime chair of the House Committee on Foreign Affairs. In 1892, the elder Blount retired after nearly twenty years as a U.S. congressman representing the district that included Macon. The following year President Grover Cleveland named him special commissioner of American affairs in Hawaii charged with investigating the recent revolution in the islands. The result was a document that criticized the actions of the United States during the overthrow of the native government and that led Cleveland to reject the request of the revolutionaries in Hawaii for the admission of the territory into the union. Tennant S. McWilliams suggests that, similar to T. G. Steward but from an opposing perspective, Blount's experiences during Reconstruction, especially what he resentfully viewed as the federal occupation of Georgia, may have caused Blount, who in the House was consistently anti-imperialist, to sympathize with the Hawaiians. In 1894, the Senate's Morgan report, named after powerful, pro-imperialist Alabama U.S. senator John T. Morgan, largely repudiated the Blount report, and four years later, in July 1898, the United States annexed Hawaii at a time when its troops were at war with the forces of Spain. An honors graduate from the University of Georgia like his father, the younger Blount earned a law degree from Columbia University in 1891, practiced as an attorney in Macon, and served in the army in Cuba in 1898 and in the Philippines from 1899 to 1901 at the rank of lieutenant. He was then appointed a civil judge in the archipelago, a position he held for three and a half years until poor health (according to some accounts) or his political views (according to others) resulted in his return to the United States.[4] In 1907 Blount published two articles in the *North American Review* advocating self-determination for the Filipinos, and five years later *The American Occupation of the Philippines, 1898–1912* appeared. Extensively documented, this 655-page book provides a chronological history of the U.S. presence in the islands that criticizes the occupation as wrongheaded from the start and calls for an independent Philippines by July 4, 1921.

Despite the striking similarities between them, Blount never refers to Frank R. Steward in *The American Occupation of the Philippines*. Given his white Georgian family's beliefs about African Americans, it would be surprising if he did. Taking pains to distinguish Asiatics (and thus Filipinos) from Africans (and hence U.S. blacks), Blount recounts the following about himself and a fellow southern white army officer turned judge: "We instinctively resented any suggestion comparing the Filipinos to negroes. We had many warm friends among the Filipinos, had shared their generous hospitality often, and in turn had extended ours. Any suggestion as that indicated implied that we had been doing something equivalent to eating, drinking, dancing, and chumming with negroes. And we resented such suggestions with an anger quite as cordial and intense as the canons of good taste and loyal friendship demanded" (364). Here Blount takes pains to deny that he had crossed what he perceived to be a global color line. He goes on to make a statement reflecting the widely held belief among whites during this period in the different levels of development among the races that was clearly inflected by Blount's experiences with blacks in the South: "I really believe that the southern men in the Philippines have always gotten along better with the Filipinos than other Americans out there.... [T]he American from the South out there is a guarantee that [the educated Asiatic] shall never be treated as if he were an African. The African is aeons of time behind the Asiatic in development" (365). Whether or not his family's experiences as members of an occupied people during Reconstruction predisposed the younger Blount favorably toward the Filipinos, as it apparently did his father toward the Hawaiians, it certainly informed his dismissive and disdainful attitude toward U.S. blacks, even those who had achieved as much as, served their country as extensively as, and addressed expansion as profoundly as Theophilus G. and Frank R. Steward.

U.S. Blacks and the Spanish-Cuban-American and Philippine-American Wars

In a thoughtful essay entitled "Telling War Stories: The Civil War and the Meaning of Life" (2011), Drew Gilpin Faust addresses the profound, complex, and intimate connection between literature and war:

> We have been telling and hearing and reading war stories for millennia. Their endurance may lie in their impossibility; they can never be complete, for the tensions and contradictions within them will never be eliminated or resolved. That challenge is essential to their power and their attraction. War stories matter.... Wars decide; they change rulers, governments, societies—and the human beings swept up in them. They accelerate and concentrate change in ways that make it vivid and visible.

Wars are turning points, in individual lives and in national histories. Stories of wars are infused with the aura of the consequential.

Jennifer C. James in the introduction to *A Freedom Bought with Blood: African American War Literature from the Civil War to World War II* (2007) accounts for the large number of U.S. black texts that tell war stories as follows: "The destabilizing effects of war—in which allegiances are made and broken, geographical boundaries crossed, countries renamed, and territories redistributed; in which women become heads of households and neighbors become adversaries; in which the oppressed may rise up against domination—have the power to disrupt even the most deeply ensconced notions of national, racial, and gender identity. The use of war as a narrative context allows black writers to seize these moments of historical rupture to assert newly formed notions of a black 'self'" (9–10). The Spanish-American War, as the conflicts in the Caribbean and the Pacific at the turn of the twentieth century are collectively known in the United States to this day, may have appeared to the vast majority of the nation's whites to be, as secretary of state John Hay declared it, "a splendid little war," but, as Du Bois, Hopkins, and other African American public intellectuals argued, the Spanish-Cuban-American and Philippine-American wars had wide-ranging domestic as well as international ramifications. The war against Spain served as a vehicle for reconciliation between the North and the South because it was the first conflict fought against a foreign nation since the Mexican-American War. Although the southern-led campaign to rewrite the Civil War as a noble struggle and a national tragedy that had little or nothing to do with the abolition of slavery had been under way for some time, the conflict with Spain came to be seen as a defining moment of heroic cooperation between the two sections, and U.S. blacks did not fit easily into this picture. The African American press and public took a keen interest in the actions of U.S. black soldiers abroad, their portrayal in the mainstream media, and their treatment by the government because the wars in the Caribbean and the Pacific appeared to present opportunities for African Americans to demonstrate their patriotism and bravery by directly participating in the conflict. For this reason, Theodore Roosevelt's accusations of black cowardice in his account of the Battle of San Juan Hill, as well as his assertion that African American fighting men are necessarily dependent on white officers in the April 1899 issue of *Scribner's*, generated considerable resentment and, as subsequent chapters demonstrate, provoked rebuttals by U.S. black combatants and literary artists.

Officially, the war with Spain lasted a mere four months, from April 21, 1898, when the United States declared war, until August 14, 1898, when hostilities were formally suspended (Torruella 107). There were two major naval battles, both decisively won by the United States, which largely determined the outcome: the Battle of Manila Bay on May 1 and the battle at Santiago, Cuba, on July 3 (Torruella 104). The most famous land engagement of the war was the much publicized, highly controversial, and ultimately legendary Battle of San Juan Hill on July 1, in which Theodore Roosevelt and his volunteer regiment of "Rough Riders" participated. When the Spanish forces at Santiago surrendered on July 16, the war was effectively over. In the subsequent peace negotiations, Spain gave up all claims to Cuba and the United States acquired Puerto Rico and Guam and purchased Spanish rights to the Philippines. Just as many historians believe that the standard name applied to the conflicts involving Cuba, Spain, the Philippines, and the United States—that is, the Spanish-American War—lacks precision by focusing too much on the United States, preferring the combination of the Spanish-American-Cuban War and the Philippine-American War, which is used here, there are problems with regarding the conflict as one that lasted for only a few weeks in 1898.[5] Cubans fought for independence throughout much of the 1800s and these efforts intensified in the last third of the century. The Ten Years' War, which ended in 1878, was followed a year later by the Little War, which was, in turn, succeeded by the War of Independence (1895–98), in which José Martí and Antonio Maceo were killed. In the 1880s and 1890s, Cubans and Puerto Ricans in New York and Florida, including Martí and Arturo Alfonso Schomburg, founded organizations in support of the independence movement, several of which attempted with lesser and greater success to supply the rebels with arms.[6] In February 1896, the United States declared that a state of war existed between Spain and Cuba and urged the former to recognize the latter's independence. Two years later, in response to riots in Havana, the United States dispatched the battleship *Maine* to the island, where it exploded under mysterious circumstances in Havana Harbor on February 15, 1898 (Pérez, *The War* 57–80). Just as armed struggle long predated the U.S. entry into the war in April 1898, fighting was by no means over in August of that year. The United States occupied Cuba until 1902 and, under the terms of the 1901 Platt amendment, it reserved the right to intervene militarily in the newly independent nation and maintain control over Guantánamo Bay (Pérez, *The War* 33–34), which, as recent events have reminded us, it retains to this day. Although the Platt amendment led to resentment among Cubans, it did not result in open hostilities, as did the U.S. annexation of the Philippines. Between fifteen thousand and forty thousand members of the Army of Liberation, led by Emilio Aguinaldo, did battle against approximately twenty thousand U.S. troops in and around Manila. There were two phases to the war. The conventional part of the conflict lasted from February through November 1899, when it was succeeded by eighteen months of guerrilla warfare (Welch 25, 32). In the words of Juan Torruella, the result "would be a dirty three-year war of 'pacification,' in which American casualties would exceed by several thousand those suffered by the United States in the entire Spanish-American War proper, and in which the losses on the Filipino side would rise into the tens of thousands and large areas of the Philippines and its economy would be destroyed" (134). For years after the official end of the Philippine-American War, sporadic fighting continued between U.S. forces and Filipinos. Thus, the time span of the conflicts involving Cuba, Spain, the United States, and the Philippines stretches, at a minimum, from 1895 through 1902.

In June 1898, a month after the U.S. defeat of the Spanish navy in the Battle of Manila Bay, an anti-imperialist league opposed to the annexation of the Philippines had begun to form in Boston that would eventually include William James, Andrew Carnegie, Charles Francis Adams, Mark Twain, and Jane Addams among its members. Four months later, in the wake of the U.S. victory in Cuba and Luzon, President William McKinley decided to annex the islands, and in December the U.S. purchase of the rights to the archipelago for $20 million from Spain, which had ruled it for over three centuries, became a provision of the Treaty of Paris. Convinced that annexation would result in considerable bloodshed, the wealthy industrialist Carnegie reportedly met with McKinley while the treaty was pending, offering to pay the full amount for the islands himself so that Filipinos could have their independence but to no avail ("Offered"). Following a raucous debate on the Senate floor that commenced in January 1899, the treaty passed—but only just barely—because of a series of closed-door deals and because U.S. troops provoked a fight with Aguinaldo's forces that ignited what would become the long and devastating Philippine-American War (Love 159–95). Just as the perception and media portrayal of Cubans as noble freedom fighters underwent a radical change when U.S. forces journeyed abroad and engaged an opposing army in the Caribbean in 1898 (Levander, "Confederate" 832), a year later Filipinos, as Jennifer James remarks, would undergo "a radical metamorphosis from ally to enemy. As the 'enemy,' the Filipinos were 'othered' to the point of being unrecognizable. They were 'part-Spanish,' 'niggers,' 'Malays,' and 'Mongols'; [Theodore] Roosevelt referred to them as Apaches and Oceala. One report declared that Filipinos were 'spotted' and 'striped'" (151).[7]

Some African American veterans of the Cuban campaign, aware of the discrimination and harsh treatment they would face upon returning to the United States, volunteered to participate in the pacification of the Philippines, where they joined "colored" regulars already stationed there.[8] Such men saw military service abroad as a means for personal advancement and citizenship status unavailable at home. Letters from black fighting men in the Philippines, however, several of which appeared in the African American press, commented with disgust on their white counterparts' use of the word "nigger" in reference to Filipinos, and some lamented the atrocities perpetrated on native soldiers and civilians. Moreover, a handful of black soldiers deserted from the U.S. Army and joined the opposing forces, the most notable among them being David Fagen, who hectored U.S. forces for several months (Gatewood, *"Smoked"* 287–90, James 125–66, Ngozi-Brown, Robinson and Schubert, Ontal). Although the majority of the black press had supported the war against Spain, there was significant opposition to the annexation of the Philippines and the war it engendered, as evidenced by the formation of the National Negro Anti-Expansion, Anti-Imperialist, Anti-Trust, and Anti-Lynching League in Cairo, Illinois, in 1899, the founding of the Black Man's Burden Association late that same year, and a proposal for the anti-imperialist National Afro-American Party sent to the editor of *Howard's American Magazine* in June 1900 (S. Miller 127; Gatewood, *Black* 184; "National" 209).[9] The election of 1900 became a referendum on U.S. imperialism generally and the effort to subjugate the Filipinos specifically. Having staunchly supported the party of Lincoln since the Civil War, African Americans who were allowed to vote could cast their ballots for the proexpansionist Republican incumbent McKinley, who had done little to protect the rights of blacks, or the anti-imperialist Democrat William Jennings Bryan, who unabashedly advocated white supremacy. Faced with this difficult choice, most blacks regarded McKinley as the lesser of two evils. A notable exception was Baptist minister and novelist Sutton Griggs, the focus of chapter 2, who in November 1900 urged the readers of the *Indianapolis World* to support the Democrats because of the administration's policy in the Philippines (Gatewood, *Black* 249–50).

In May 1899, AME bishop Henry McNeal Turner, whom Lincoln had appointed as the first U.S. black army chaplain in 1863, angrily denounced African American enlistment in the Philippine war. Citing in particular the violence and intolerance directed at black soldiers during and in the wake of the war with Spain, Turner said that although he had once been proud of the U.S. flag he now regarded it as "a worthless rag": "It is a symbol of liberty, of manhood, sovereignty and of national independence to the white man, we grant, and he should be justly proud of it, but to the colored man that has any sense, any honor, and is not a scullion fool, it is a miserable dirty rag" ("The Negro" 184–85). Nearly a year and half later, Turner denounced the ongoing conflict in the Philippines as an "unholy war of conquest" against "a feeble band of sable patriots, not white, on their native soil, surrounded by their homes and the graves of their sires, maintaining a heroic but pitifully unequal struggle for their God-given rights and for their liberties" ("Philippine" 186). He charged McKinley with endorsing slavery in part of the archipelago—a reference to the treaty signed between a U.S. representative and the ruler of the Moro people known as the sultan of Sulu—and with violating and subverting the U.S. Constitution by subjecting Filipinos and Puerto Ricans to taxation without representation. Turner directed some of his strongest language, however, at U.S. black troops in the archipelago: "I boil over with disgust when I remember that colored men from this country that I am personally acquainted with are there fighting to subjugate a people of their own color and bring them to such a degraded state. I can scarcely keep from saying that I hope the Filipinos will wipe such soldiers from the face of the earth" ("Philippine" 186–87). In sharp contrast, as discussed in chapter 3, African American writers of the period stress the bravery and patriotism of black fighting men in the Philippines and rarely denounce U.S. military action in the islands.

The body of this book comprises two sections, one about the African American literary response to the Spanish-Cuban-American War and another concerning the U.S. black literary engagement with the Philippine-American War and expansion in the Pacific. Each section has two chapters, the first addressing several texts relating to the specific theater of war or site of expansion and the second devoted to the texts of a particular literary figure who addresses empire in an extensive, compelling, and unique manner. Chapter 1, "Cuban Generals, Black Sergeants, and White Colonels: The African American Poetic Response to the Spanish-Cuban-American War," examines verse about the Cuban Revolution and the participation of U.S. white and black soldiers in the war against Spain and its aftermath, paying particular attention to expressions of solidarity between African Americans and Cubans (and/or New World blacks generally), refutations of Theodore Roosevelt's accusations of black cowardice in the war in Cuba, and counterdiscursive responses to plantation fiction's portrayal of black subservience and white southern patriotism. Chapter 2, "Wars at Home and Abroad in Sutton Griggs's *Imperium in Imperio* and *The Hindered Hand*," reads the southern minister's best-known novels in relation to the Spanish-Cuban-American War and U.S. expansion. The climactic events of *Imperium in Imperio* (1899), in which a secret black organization plans a mass African American immigration to and takeover of the state of Texas and later votes to go to war against the United States, occur between the sinking of the USS *Maine* and the declaration of war on Spain, and the novel closely links these events to the ensuing conflict. *The Hindered Hand* (1905) chronicles the fates of three black servicemen who return from the Cuban campaign to confront economic hardship, political disenfranchisement, mob violence, and racial insanity in the South; moreover, it features a plot to devastate the white population of the South by infecting the water supply with yellow fever germs. Chapter 3, "Black Burdens, Laguna Tales, and 'Citizen Tom' Narratives: African American Writing and the Philippine-American War," begins by discussing parodic and nonparodic U.S. black verse responses to Rudyard Kipling's widely read poem "The White Man's Burden: The United States and the Philippine Islands" (1899) and then analyzes fictions that address the Philippine-American War by Griggs, Frank R. Steward, James Ephraim McGirt, and F. Grant Gilmore. Drawing extensively on archival materials, chapter 4, "Annexation in the Pacific and Asian Conspiracy in Central America in James Weldon Johnson's Unproduced Operettas," examines libretti that Johnson wrote between 1899 and 1914, either in conjunction with his brother J. Rosamond Johnson or with his brother and Bob Cole, for comic operas set in the Pacific and Latin America that directly confront expansion and U.S. attitudes toward nonwhite peoples. This book concludes with a coda that reconsiders Pauline Hopkins's stance on imperialism, particularly in connection with "Talma Gordon," arguing that this short story published in *Colored American Magazine* in 1900 exposes the greed, racial intolerance, and hypocrisy at the heart of expansion and thereby calling into question the long-standing reading of Hopkins and other turn-of-the-twentieth-century U.S. black writers and public intellectuals as effectively proimperialist because of their support of uplift ideology and the civilizing mission.

PART ONE

African American Literature and the Spanish-Cuban-American War

CHAPTER ONE

Cuban Generals, Black Sergeants, and White Colonels

The African American Poetic Response to the Spanish-Cuban-American War

Flag images—such as the iconic 1945 photo of Iwo Jima—deeply influence patriotism especially in times of war and political change. No flag has an inherent meaning—such as duty, honor, and comradeship—but those who understand how to use flags are capable of inspiring great deeds. Thus in the American Civil War, for example, when a battle standard fell because its bearer had fallen, it was a point of honor for other soldiers to seize that banner immediately, keeping it from the enemy.
—*National Geographic Visual Atlas of the World*

Q. How are they [the people] worked up to such a degree of Assinity [to fight in wars]?
A. A lay figure, known as Patriotism, is inflated and carried on a pole up and down the land; it works a charm like that of the Pied Piper.
—James Weldon Johnson, "The War Catechism"

In *The Anarchy of Empire in the Making of U.S. Culture* (2003), Amy Kaplan sees "a battle raging over the interconnected representations of race, manhood, nation, and empire" (125) in the conflicting black and white representations of what she refers to as the "legendary" events on San Juan Hill.[1] She notes that Theodore Roosevelt's account of the battle ends not with "a cathartic shoot-out with Spanish soldiers, but with a sustained confrontation with African American soldiers that caps the horizontal narrative, throughout the report, of the increasing intermingling of blacks and whites" (126). By depicting himself threatening to shoot retreating black troops, Roosevelt, claims Kaplan, "reestablished the reassuring order of the domestic color line in a foreign terrain" (127). In "Where Did the Black Rough Riders Go?" Christine Bold asserts that Roosevelt, writing his account of the war in Cuba in 1899 as U.S. troops were engaging Aguinaldo's dark-skinned forces in the Philippines, "realized the perils of welcoming black Americans into what Richard Slotkin calls the 'mythic space' of the frontier" and thus it became "crucial that Roosevelt relegate blacks to servile dependency on white authority, and he increasingly whitened the rough rider image to that end" (277, 278). She goes on to observe that despite such efforts to suppress the story of African American heroism, it has nevertheless functioned as a persistent countermyth to tales of white preeminence in the Cuban campaign such as Roosevelt's.[2]

Bold points out that the figure of the black sergeant has served as the focal point of this alternative myth. As she explains, "The rank of sergeant had particular meaning for black soldiers, for whom it was the highest rank available in the regular army and in which position several won fame" (282–83). In 1897, a statue by Augustus Saint-Gaudens commemorating the black Fifty-Fourth Massachusetts regiment, led by the white Colonel Robert Gould Shaw, was unveiled on Boston Common. At the indoor portion of the festivities, held at Music Hall, which Booker T. Washington describes at length in *Up from Slavery* (1901), Sergeant William Carney appeared with the flag he bore in one of the most famous battles of the Civil War, holding it up at a key moment to deafening cheers. In the charge against Fort Wagner, Carney, a free black man from New Bedford who was born a slave in Virginia, threw away his rifle, seized the regiment's banner from the fatally wounded color bearer John Wall, carried it up the hill, planted it on the parapet, and then brought it back with him when retreat was ordered, despite being wounded in two or more places. To a member of the (white) One Hundredth New York who offered to carry the flag for him, Carney reportedly replied, "No one but a member of the 54th should carry the colors" (Reef 62). When he finally relinquished the flag upon reaching the field hospital, Carney, according to several accounts, declared, "Boys, the old flag never touched the ground" (Hopkins "Sergeant"; Reef 62). Whereas white writers in the 1860s and then again following the unveiling of Saint-Gaudens's monument tended to celebrate the white colonel Shaw, who gave his life helping blacks achieve freedom, African American authors such as William Wells Brown celebrated the actions of the black sergeant Carney (Smethurst 171, 177).

In "The Return of the Sergeant," published in *Harper's Weekly* in September 1900, William Huntington Wilson provides a vivid illustration of white fears of the mythic figure of the heroic African American sergeant through his effort to discredit it. In the short story, a group of backward small town blacks hold a feast in honor of one of their own who claims to have been wounded in battle in Cuba only to learn that his tale is false, "de Sargent" having stolen the clothes of a white soldier while working as a bellhop in Charleston. The son of a long-serving West Virginia Democratic U.S. congressman, Wilson, as Gretchen Murphy remarks, "goes one step further [than Roosevelt] in denying black heroism by mocking the very idea that blacks could even *leave* home, replacing them spatially and temporally back into the South—in Possum Hollow, a mythical village untouched by modernity" (78). In creating Possum Hollow and its buffoonish denizens, Wilson draws liberally from plantation fiction, a powerful engine of white mythmaking to which several African American writers at the turn of the twentieth century felt compelled to respond.

In the same year that Roosevelt's account of the Battle of San Juan Hill appeared in print, Herschel V. Cashin et al. published *Under Fire with the Tenth U.S. Cavalry*.[3] Designed to counteract "the tendency of the average historian to either entirely ignore or grudgingly acknowledge the courage, valor, and patriotism of a so-called *alien* race, in their efforts to court the favor and the patronage of the influential and the popular" (iii), this "purely military narrative" (iv) was compiled largely from the eyewitness testimony of U.S. black soldiers who served in Cuba. Christine Bold and Jennifer James observe that by invoking Thomas Nelson Page's 1884 story "Marse Chan," Major-General Joseph Wheeler's introduction undermines the stated intentions of the book's editors.[4] Wheeler attests to the participation—but not the leadership—of African American soldiers in the "heroic charge" and "gallant fight" at Las Guasimas and the capture "under a murderous fire" of the Spanish entrenchments on San Juan Hill and the artillery support that proved indispensable during that battle, as well as noting the unanimous commendation of black soldiers by their white commanders. He goes on to suggest that Cashin's book offers hope for a solution of the nation's race problem by demonstrating that blacks can elevate themselves morally and intellectually through "education, discipline, and judicious training" (xiv). However, Wheeler closes by remarking that southerners know that "a loyalty touching in its beauty and simplicity" characterized "the old Negro slave," adding, "who has not seen a thousand times the counterpart of Sam in 'Marse Chan,' a story so touchingly true to life that one can scarcely read it with dry eyes" (xv). As James observes, in this passage the general "accomplishes what Roosevelt did—he is able to write white male officers into their master-full command, forcing a text bursting with black masculine self-assertion to submit to his authority" (139). Despite his prediction of brighter days ahead, Wheeler in this passage reverts to the past, albeit a fictional one, reducing the contributions of African American soldiers in Cuba to truckling submissiveness.

African American poems about the war against Spain in Cuba, including those about the role of African American soldiers in the conflict, respond to specific poetic and literary traditions related to armed conflict at home and abroad, often making reference to the role of U.S. blacks in previous wars. Moreover, such verse relates to and in some cases builds explicitly or implicitly on U.S. black poems that address the Cuban Revolution, some of which invoke a pantheon of New World black warriors. Additionally, many of these poems serve as ripostes to Roosevelt's published accusations of black cowardice during the Battle of San Juan Hill and to attempts by southern white writers such as Page to mock African American soldiers and appropriate tropes and symbols associated with military heroism and patriotism in the ongoing efforts to rewrite the Confederacy's role in the war between the states and reconcile northern and southern whites at the expense of U.S. blacks.

African Americans, Cuba, and Revolution

Long before the U.S. declaration of war on Spain, African Americans identified with Cubans. Prior to 1898, U.S. white writers, notably Joaquin Miller, expressed sympathy for the plight of the Cubans, frequently depicting them as freedom fighters oppressed by a cruel and corrupt colonial regime; however, the disposition toward the rebels quickly changed when U.S. troops joined Cubans in the fight against Spanish forces.[5] As Caroline F. Levander explains, "Once a movement explicitly anticolonial, antislavery, and antiracist came under the influence of a nation then inventing Jim Crow segregation and acquiring a far-flung empire, U.S. soldiers, officers, journalists, and cartoonists propagated images of Cuba as a land of inferior indigenous racial others in order to assert the superiority of whites as rulers" ("Confederate" 832). In contrast, the views of U.S. blacks, who tended to regard Cubans as persons of color and as victims of oppression like themselves, largely remained consistent. In the 1860s and 1870s, leading African Americans, including Henry Highland Garnet, John Mercer Langston, Frederick Douglass, and William Wells Brown, committed themselves to the abolition of slavery in Cuba and independence for the island, and during the next two decades U.S. black sympathy for the rebels intensified. Whereas African Americans opposed U.S. intervention in Hawaii because it foreclosed the self-determination of the native people, they supported it in Cuba because they believed it would result in an independent black nation. The mulatto revolutionary general Antonio Maceo Grajales (1845–96), known as the "bronze titan" or the "hero of bronze," whom the U.S. black press covered extensively, became the focal point of African American identification with Cubans (Gatewood, *Black* 16–17). In the words of José Yglesias, Maceo "was not and is not known by Americans—but he was known by blacks in the terrible Reconstruction years, particularly by Southern blacks who had few safe opportunities to express pride in themselves. They named their boys Maceo and gave it the American pronunciation: May-see-oh. This was a secret pleasure and today there are American blacks who do not know how they have come to be named Maceo" (108). Particularly after 1896, the Cuban Revolution and Maceo appear in texts by African Americans.

The small black community in St. Paul, Minnesota, provides a vivid example of the African American identification with Cuban revolutionaries generally and Maceo in particular. Following the February 1898 murder of black U.S. postmaster Frazier Baker and his daughter by a lynch mob in Lake City, South Carolina, and the lack of efforts by federal and local authorities to prosecute those responsible for the crime, blacks in St. Paul established the American Law Enforcement League. To raise money for the league's efforts, they organized an ambitious four-act pageant entitled "Cuba—A Drama of Freedom," in which three hundred African Americans performed. The show, which included depictions of Maceo leading the revolutionists as well as the defeat of the Spanish by Cuban and U.S. forces at Santiago, was performed several times in St. Paul and Minneapolis in November of that year. According to Dave Riehle, the climax of the pageant was a speech delivered by leading African American attorney and activist Frederick McGhee "in the character of General Maceo, who 'recounted the wrongs of his country, and called upon his followers to avenge them'" (17).[6] The Cuban Revolution, moreover, plays a brief but notable role in James Weldon Johnson's *The Autobiography of an Ex-Colored Man*. Although most of this novel, begun before 1906 and originally published in 1912, is set in the North, first in the protagonist's childhood home in Connecticut and later in New York City, chapter 5 depicts Florida, and Johnson's hometown of Jacksonville in particular, as a transnational space. When the protagonist sojourns in Jacksonville, he spends much of his time with Cubans, getting a job at a cigar factory and acquiring their language. As a result of a depression that hit Cuba in the mid-1880s, many cigar factories closed and production declined steeply. By the early 1890s, thirty-five thousand cigar makers had lost their jobs. A significant number of them moved to cities in Florida, including Jacksonville, where cigar production was on the rise (Pérez, *Cuba* 132–33). Working in a "trade in which the color line is not drawn" (67), Johnson's main character learns "to smoke, to swear, and to speak Spanish" (72). By conversing with his landlord and co-workers and by reading Cuban newspapers, the protagonist becomes fluent in the language and gains knowledge about the Cuban independence movement and its leaders, including Antonio Maceo.

Following the lead of Elijah W. Smith, whose "Song of the Liberators" appeared in the revised edition of William Wells Brown's *The Rising Son: The Antecedents and Advancement of the Colored Race* (1876), African Americans in the late 1890s and early 1900s published poems attesting to their identification with Cubans fighting for independence.[7] Prior to the U.S. declaration of war against Spain, George Hannibal Temple wrote "The Cuban Amazon," included in *The Epic of Columbus' Bell and Other Poems* (1900), in honor of the women who took up arms in the revolution. A year after the death of "el titan de bronce," Frank Barbour Coffin's "Maceo—Cuba's Liberator" appeared in *Coffin's Poems with Ajax's Ordeals*, published in Little Rock in 1897. Two years later, chaplain W. Hilary Coston of the Ninth Infantry printed Stella A. E. Brazley's "The Colored Boys in Blue," which invokes Maceo twice, in *The Spanish-American War Volunteer* (1899). The same year, in *Avenging the Maine, A Drunken A. B., and Other Poems*, James Ephraim McGirt published "The Memory of Maceo," and in 1900 Frances Harper's "Maceo" appeared in the expanded version of her *Poems*, first published in 1895.[8]

The fifty-four-canto title poem of Temple's collection concerns a large bell, reputed to have once hung in the Alhambra, that was given to Columbus by Queen Isabella, transported to South America, and, according to a story the poet recounts in a note, eventually ended up in an African Methodist Episcopal church in Hayleyville, New Jersey.[9] The volume also includes poems about West Africa, Samoa, Harriet Beecher Stowe, and Crispus Attucks's heroics during the Boston Massacre in 1770. Thus, this book by a Reading, Pennsylvania, chair caner has a broad historical and geographic sweep, linking inhabitants of the United States, and African Americans especially, to people from earlier eras and other parts of the world. "The Cuban Amazon," as a note by Temple explains, "was written in 1897 during the Cuban revolution, at which time quite a number of Cuban women took part in the battles fought for independence. They fought with a bravery and determination equal to the men, and not a little of the credit for the successful termination of the war is due to the valor of their arms" (78).[10] Identified as being of African descent through her "crisped locks" (9), the "martial maid" (2) must decide whether to withdraw from the field of battle or face the possibility of being led "dishonored like the vilest slave" (21) in "cruel chains" (19) to a Spanish prison in a reverse Middle Passage:

> Perchance to Afric's distant clime,
> Be borne across the wave,
> And deep in Ceuta's dungeon thrust,
> To die a penal slave. (25–28)

Heedless of this and other dangers, she chooses to fight on so that

> Cuba shall soon see,
> The tyrant driven from her shores,
> And her proud mountains free! (38–40)

At the poem's conclusion, she aims her broadsword at a Spaniard who

> humbly bites the dust,
> And surely pays, with dearest life,
> The forfeit of his lust. (54–56)

The Amazon and her foe function as allegorical figures for Temple and his African American readers—she embodies not simply Cuba but also the black woman fighting for her freedom and her chastity; meanwhile, Spain and white patriarchal power are represented as seeking to shackle and exploit her sexually and economically.

Rather than focusing on an anonymous female figure, the poems by Coffin, Brazley, McGirt, and Harper eulogize the renowned black freedom fighter Maceo. An Arkansas pharmacist and a college graduate, Coffin, citing the pressing need for black literature at the turn of the twentieth century, asserts in the preface to his collection that "now the black man must write for the black man" (6).[11] Appearing among tributes to Stowe, Frances Harper, Anna Julia Cooper, Bishop Daniel Payne, Frederick Douglass, and Abraham Lincoln, "Maceo—Cuba's Liberator" contrasts the Caribbean island's long history of colonial oppression with U.S. independence through its references to the Revolutionary War, the War of 1812, the Mexican-American War, John Brown's raid on Harpers Ferry, and the Civil War. In the figure of Maceo, however, the poem asserts that Cubans' calls for freedom were finally answered:

But God who's here with men,
Had him a man in store;
And at the heights of Spanish sins,
He called forth Maceo. (25–28)

By ambushing and killing Maceo, who had committed himself to Cuban independence, beat back the Spaniards, and galvanized the people, the Spanish transformed him into a martyr comparable to "Christ" (58), medieval Czech priest and proto-Protestant "John Huss" (63), and "Abr'am Lincoln" (65). Like these forerunners, Maceo did not die in vain, for now,

the world's in sympathy;
It says that foul act [of killing Maceo] implores
That Cuba must be free. (70–72)

Thus, Coffin's speaker tells Cubans in the poem's final lines, "Thy Maceo without a fear, / Has died to set you free" (79–80). Whereas Temple's poem links colonial rule in Cuba to slavery in the United States, the juxtaposition of "Maceo—Cuba's Liberator" with several other poems in Coffin's volume denouncing lynching underscores the connection between Cuban independence and agitation for African American citizenship rights.

A North Carolina native and college graduate who published three books of poetry and a collection of short fiction, McGirt moved to Philadelphia, where from 1903 through 1909 he edited *McGirt's Magazine*, in which the texts of many of the day's leading U.S. black writers and public intellectuals appeared. His brief "The Memory of Maceo" appears in a volume featuring several poems about the participation of U.S. troops in the war against Spain. In the first ten lines, the speaker addresses the "men of Cuba, patriots all" (1), urging them to tell their children about "the wonderful general who's fallen asleep" (4) and to erect a monument in his honor. The last two lines, addressed to Maceo himself, depict him much as Coffin's poem does—as a martyr in the cause of freedom: "Dear Maceo, our hearts pine for thee! / For whom thou died, can say we are free" (11–12). The lack of clarity of these lines may arise from the author's refusal to address the implications of expansion during an era in which U.S. blacks saw their citizenship rights being stripped away. A supporter of the wars in Cuba and the Philippines in his poems and fiction, McGirt uneasily conflates Cubans and U.S. blacks in the closing couplet. Presumably it is the "hearts" of both groups of people that "pine" for Maceo, but "for whom" did he die, and who is the "we" that can be said to be free? Maceo may have given his life for not only Cubans but oppressed people everywhere, particularly oppressed blacks; however, in contrast to the inhabitants of newly independent (although still occupied) Cuba, African Americans at the turn to the twentieth century, as Coffin emphasizes in his collection, can hardly be described as "free."

In "The Colored Boys in Blue," which she sent "as a token of friendship" to Henry O. Franklin, a second lieutenant in the Ninth U.S. Infantry (the only one of the four black "immune" regiments actually to reach Cuba) as he departed for the island, Brazley links Maceo not only to African American soldiers past and present but also to the black military leader who liberated Haiti. The thirty-six line, six-stanza poem calls on U.S. blacks to "be the warriors you are" (5) by joining their Cuban "kinsmen" (13) who have "fought for many years / The sanguinary hosts of Spain" (8–9) in "freedom's cause" (14) and thereby have "won the world's applause" (16). Not only should African American men "go seek the spot where Maceo fell / And strike his slayers" (19–20) but the ghost of Lincoln urges them to "Renew the prestige of your sires" (32). In doing so, they will

win the place
Where glory flames with radiant fires,
With those great heroes, brave and pure,
Men like Maceo, Touissaint L'Ouverture. (33–36)

Particularly with its call to "purge and clear" the Spanish from "the occidental hemisphere" (23–24), Brazley's poem makes reference to a pantheon of heroic New World black warriors, well established in the minds of African Americans, whose bravery U.S. black soldiers en route to Cuba should emulate.

A poem about the Cuban leader by an African American writer who produced a substantial body of poetry over a long career, Harper's "Maceo" uses the death of its subject as the occasion for an extended appeal to God to bring about the day when people will embrace Christ and follow his example. Although the poem resembles those of Coffin and McGirt by portraying Maceo as a heroic figure who fell fighting for his people's independence, at heart it is a lament for humankind's failure to embrace freedom, which makes martyrs such as Maceo necessary. Only the first three of the poem's fifteen quatrains explicitly concern Maceo. Lines 1–3 register the speaker's sorrowful response to the general's death and the closing line of the initial stanza emphasizes his manhood. Stanzas 2 and 3 stress his deft leadership of the Cubans and unwavering commitment to their liberation. Maceo

held the cause for which he perished
    With a firm, unfaltering hand.
On his lips the name of freedom
    Fainted with his latest breath.
Cuba Libre was his watchword
    Passing through the gates of death. (7–12)

Associating Maceo with the adjectives "fearless," "brave," "earnest," "true," and "strong" (21, 24) without specifically mentioning him, stanzas 4 through 7 ask why such "heroes" (23) must die to bring about freedom and why people do not see and embrace God's plan. Moving even further away from the man who inspired the poem, the final eight quatrains beseech God to usher in "the reign of our Redeemer" (31), put an end to war and crime, "lead us from the paths of madness" (43), and guide humankind to "the balmy rest of peace" (53). In addition to its profound religious sentiment, Harper's "Maceo," like several of her other poems, especially "'Do Not Cheer, Men Are Dying,' Said Capt. Phillips in the Spanish-American War" (1898), laments the effects of war. Yet she does not criticize Maceo for taking up arms for Cuban freedom; rather, she decries the misguided beliefs and un-Christ-like behavior that deny people freedom, thereby necessitating war and martyrdom. The poem's repeated references to the lack of freedom in the world and the resulting misery had, of course, particular relevance for U.S. blacks in 1900.[12]

The African American poems about the Cuban Revolution published at the end of the nineteenth century link U.S. racial oppression past and present to Spain's colonial subjugation of Cuba. They also advocate self-determination for native peoples and equal treatment for racial minorities. Moreover, they posit a New World pantheon of black military freedom fighters that includes Haiti's Toussaint, African American soldiers in the Civil War and other conflicts, and Cuba's Maceo.

African American Poetry and U.S. Blacks in the Cuban Campaign

Several African Americans published poems about U.S. troops in the war against Spain. Some, such as James T. Franklin's "Battle of Manila" (1900) and McGirt's "The Siege of Manila" and "Siege of Santiago," simply celebrate the victories. The majority, however, concern the participation of black soldiers, often referring directly or indirectly to, or dwelling on, the battles that occurred in the vicinity of Santiago in which African Americans played a pivotal role, most notably the assault on San Juan Hill.[13] Unlike the U.S. black poetry about the Cuban Revolution, which frequently decries colonial tyranny and advocates independence for colonized peoples, the verse about the Cuban campaign tends to adopt a narrower focus, relating the actions and treatment of African American soldiers to domestic race relations. Poems such as minister and Oberlin graduate B. A. Imes's "Sergeant Berry" (1899), about the standard bearer of the Tenth Cavalry credited with leading the charge up San Juan Hill while carrying the flag of his own black regiment and that of the white Third Infantry, memorialize specific heroic acts by African American fighting men. Others, including Paul Laurence Dunbar's "The Conquerors: The Black Troops in Cuba" (1898) and McGirt's "Avenging the Maine," celebrate black heroism in the Cuban campaign in a more general way. The primary purpose of such poems is to commemorate the professionalism, patriotism, and courage of the African American soldiers. Another set of poems, including novelist, playwright, essayist, and poet Katherine Davis Chapman Tillman's "The Black Boys in Blue," published in her 1902 collection *Recitations*, links African American military service in Cuba to that by black soldiers in previous conflicts. A revision of her 1898 "A Tribute to Negro Regiments" (1898), Tillman's "Black Boys" refers to African American participation in the Battle of Bunker Hill, the War of 1812, the Civil War, and the campaigns against Native Americans before concluding that

> ne'er should the love of their country wane
> For the black boys who sank in the gallant Maine
> Nor the heroes who charged with such good will
> And saved the Rough Riders at San Juan Hill. (13–16)

Other examples of this type of poem include Twenty-Fifth Infantry member John Henry Allen's "Rings upon the Pike" (1899) and Lena Mason's "A Negro in It" (1902). Like Brazley's "Colored Boys in Blue," these poems point to an established history of U.S. black military heroism deserving of commendation by the nation.

Dunbar's "The Conquerors" relates to another group of poems in which African American soldiers who fought in Cuba receive neither the recognition nor the treatment their service merits, of which Samuel Alfred Beadle's "Lines: *Suggested by the Assaults on the Negro Soldiers as they passed through the south on their way to and from our war with Spain*," appearing in his collection *Sketches from the Life in Dixie* (1899), stands out as the most striking example.

According to his great-grandson Michael A. Middleton, Beadle was a former slave who taught himself about the law and, in 1884, was admitted to the Mississippi bar after a rigorous examination. Addressing the country he loves, the speaker of "Lines," a returning black soldier, states that he has "carried your flag to the front / Through pestilence, battles, and storms" (17–18),

> and gone with you down to the death,
>> With the thorns of caste on my head;
> Defended your home and your health
>> And wept o'er the bier of your dead. (21–24)

Linked to Christ through the painful crown of racial stigmatization 1890s U.S. society has forced him to wear, he has nevertheless committed himself fully to the nation's welfare. Yet, in spite of such devotion and even though Spain has surrendered, he can find no peace:

> As the smoke of the fight goes by,
>> And the bugle calls to repose,
> By my countryman's hand I die,
>> As well as by the hands of foes. (25–28)

Returning from Cuba, the soldier finds that nothing has changed: he faces another war, a racial one, that still rages at home.[14]

Bearing the Flag and the Stigma of Race

Along with Imes's poem about George Berry and Beadle's "Lines," McGirt's "The Stars and Stripes Shall Never Trail the Dust" and James Weldon Johnson's "The Color Sergeant" belong to a set of poems honoring African American flag bearers. McGirt conflates William Carney's actions during the July 18, 1863, assault on Fort Wagner with the exploits of black soldiers in Cuba. Set at the White House, McGirt's poem depicts a blood-encrusted black soldier, battle flag in hand, declaring,

> Uncle Sam, here is Old Glory,
> That you trusted to my care,
>> Through th' hottest I have ever held my trust;
> Though shells have rent my body,
> Yet I can truly say,
>> The Stars and Stripes have never trailed the dust. (13–18)

Uncle Sam takes the flag from him and then decorates him, stating, "My son you're black, but still you're a man" (27). Explaining that he "knows no color" (31) and issued a call to arms "simply for the brave" (33), Uncle Sam adds,

> I saw you negroes bear the flag
> Through shells up San Juan Hill,
> I saw the Spaniards from your valor flee. (37–39)

In stark contrast to poems such as Beadle's, "The Stars and Stripes Shall Never Trail the Dust" amounts to a fantasy in which an unnamed but representative black fighting man receives recognition for his heroism, patriotism, and manhood from the personification of the nation. Nonetheless, McGirt must indirectly acknowledge the persistent specter of race prejudice. Although the poem tells "a colored captain's story" (1), the third line, "He was mustered out because the war was o'er," attests to the restrictions preventing blacks, in all but the rarest cases, from serving in the regular army at a rank higher than sergeant. Following Spain's surrender, several African American soldiers received promotions to the rank of officer in volunteer regiments for their actions during the war; however, when these units were disbanded shortly thereafter, these men lost their commissions.

In "A Weapon of My Song: The Poetry of James Weldon Johnson" (1971), Richard A. Long observes that "The Color Sergeant" along with Johnson's other "early verse was a species of propaganda, designed sometimes overtly, sometimes obliquely, to advance to the reading public the merits and grievances of blacks" (374). In "Afro-American Literature of the Spanish-American War" (1985), James Robert Payne reads the poem somewhat differently. He asserts that whereas texts such as Dunbar's "The Conquerors" and the poems collected in U.S. black veteran Charles F. White's *Plea for the Negro Soldier* (1908) "are characterized by a strong, direct response to the war" of either "extreme idealism" or "disillusionment" (31), others, notably Johnson's "The Color Sergeant," "present a more distanced response to the war," going "beyond immediate idealistic or disillusioned responses in order to focus on the preservation and conveyance of essentials of an emerging tradition of the Black Spanish-American War experience" (27, 31). Although Payne's approval of Johnson's purportedly "distanced" response to the war derives in part from his New Critical assumptions and methodology, the 1917 publication date of the poem may also have played a role in this reading, perhaps having led the critic to assume that in composing the poem Johnson was looking back on the conflict nearly two decades after the fact. However, archival evidence indicates that Johnson likely wrote the poem in 1898, not long after the white and black presses published accounts of what occurred on the battlefield.[15] In contrast to Payne, I contend that "The Color Sergeant" engages the historical and racial controversies exacerbated by and emerging from the war in Cuba and participates in the turn-of-the-twentieth-century literary battle between white southern and African American writers over slavery, the Civil War, and their legacies. In the poem's twenty lines, Johnson explicitly and implicitly incorporates five key themes appearing in the poetry concerning the Cuban Revolution and the verse about African American participation in the Cuban war: bravery in the face of enemy fire, a professional military pedigree, battlefield martyrdom, racial stigmatization, and U.S. black flag bearing. In contrast to the poems about the Cuban Revolution and thus similar to other poems about U.S. black soldiers who served in Cuba, "The Color Sergeant" eschews specific references to empire and hemispheric black solidarity.

The main title of Johnson's five-ballad-stanza poem serves to identify its subject as a noncommissioned officer who bears both the flag (similar to Berry and Carney)—that is, the colors—and the skin tone—that is, the color—of his race and with it (like Beadle's soldier in "Lines") the stigma U.S. society unjustly attaches to it. The opening quatrain leaves no doubt as to the sergeant's fate: along with other fallen "comrades" (2), the unnamed "trooper" (3) lies fatally wounded in the scorching sunlight of the Cuban battlefield. The next eight lines recount the acts of bravery that have cost him his life. Line 5, "First in the charge up the fort-crowned hill," suggests that he, as "guidon" bearer (6), has led not only his company but all of the U.S. forces against the Spanish. The last two lines of the second stanza underscore his courage: heedless of the consequences, "He had rushed where the leaden hail fell fast, / Not death nor danger fearing" (7–8). Stanza 3 describes the circumstances of his wounding: the color sergeant has been struck down while still in the "front where the fight grew fierce" (9), thus proving himself "faithful" (10) until the end. The penultimate quatrain portrays the flag bearer, dutiful even in the act of dying, shutting his eyes and "present[ing] arms"—in other words, lowering the colors to a horizontal position—"to his Maker" (16), a sentiment echoed in the final stanza in which he is described as "true, in death, to his duty" (20).

Building on the racial meaning of the word "color" in its main title, the poem thrice refers to the African American identity of its subject. The first stanza terms him a member "of the sable Tenth" (3), one of four "colored" regiments in the regular U.S. Army, all of whom participated in the Battle of San Juan

Hill. Lines 11 and 12 term the sergeant's skin "black" and "yet his heart as true / As the steel of his blood-stained saber" (11–12), emphasizing through the word "true" both his fidelity to the nation and his competence as a professional soldier. The closing quatrain drives home the poem's racial message:

> There he lay, without honor or rank,
> But, still, in a grim-like beauty;
> Despised of men for his humble race,
> Yet true, in death, to his duty. (17–20)

Not merely unnamed and unheralded but treated as an object of derision, the fallen color sergeant nevertheless possesses a terrible beauty. His martyrdom functions as Johnson's homage to the anonymous African Americans who lost their lives in service of their country and, implicitly, by extension, to the pantheon of New World black military figures who died in the cause of freedom, including Attucks, Toussaint, and Maceo, explicitly invoked by poets such as Brazley and Tillman. His service unto death eloquently rebuts the beliefs of a society that regards him and his race as morally, physically, and intellectually inferior, a retort that is crystallized in the repetition of the word "true."

Black Sergeants, White Officers, and Mythic Battles

The subtitle of Johnson's poem—"On an Incident on San Juan Hill"—locates the color sergeant in a specific place and historical moment—the battlefield outside of Santiago, Cuba, on July 1, 1898. However, it also situates him in a mythic space, San Juan Hill, which, like Fort Wagner before it, quickly became the stuff of legends in the minds of both U.S. whites and blacks. The use of the word "on" reinforces the mythic qualities of the poem to follow, indicating that it is based on actual events but not limited by them. In this mythical dimension, Johnson's poem uses the figure of the valiant black sergeant to counter race prejudice generally as well as attempts to exclude or marginalize the contributions of African American soldiers in the Cuban campaign specifically. Although likely written first, Johnson's poem has come to serve as an enduring counterpunch to Theodore Roosevelt's published account of the Battle of San Juan Hill questioning the courage of black soldiers.

Unlike their white counterparts, U.S. blacks who wished to join the war effort in the Caribbean were barred from doing so by Jim Crow policies in several states. Thus, with some exceptions, African Americans who saw action in Cuba were regular army men, members of the Twenty-Fourth and Twenty-

Fifth Infantry and the Ninth and Tenth Cavalry, regiments that had served in the Civil War and, after being reorganized, had fought Native Americans in the West (James 133; Washington, Wood, and Williams 23–36). Conflicting reports by journalists and combatants, both black and white, about what happened on San Juan Hill began appearing in the U.S. press immediately as part of what was also known as the Correspondents' War (Kaplan 130). Eyewitness accounts by white reporters and by black soldiers, some of whom supplied articles for financially strapped black newspapers, attested to the integral role played by African American troops in the Cuban campaign. These included reports that the Ninth and Tenth rescued the Rough Riders at Las Guasimas on June 24, 1898; that it was Private T. C. Butler of the Twenty-Fifth who tore down the Spanish flag in the Battle of El Caney on July 1, although he was forced to surrender all but a small piece of it to white soldiers; that a black sergeant and not a white officer issued the call for and led the charge resulting in the capture of San Juan Hill; and that an African American color guard, Sergeant George Berry of the Tenth, as already mentioned, planted the flag of his regiment and that of the white Third Infantry atop the hill—reports that spread throughout the black community and initially gained some currency in the mainstream press.[16]

Roosevelt's published account in *Scribner's* of what happened during the battle tells a very different story, however, accusing some black soldiers of shirking their responsibilities. He claims that when he observed these men going to the rear he had to threaten to shoot them if they did not remain on the front lines:

> None of the white regulars or Rough Riders showed the slightest sign of weakening; but under the strain the colored infantrymen (who had none of their officers) began to get a little uneasy and to drift to the rear, either helping wounded men, or saying that they wished to find their own regiments. This I could not allow, as it was depleting my line, so I jumped up, and walking a few yards to the rear, drew my revolver, halted the retreating soldiers, and called out to them that I appreciated the gallantry with which they had fought and would be sorry to hurt them, but that I should shoot the first man who, on any pretence whatever, went to the rear. (150–51)

As Booker T. Washington, N. B. Wood, and Fannie Barrier Williams note in their celebration of black soldiers in *A New Negro for a New Century* (1900), this assertion contradicted some of Roosevelt's own public statements about the battle. Six months earlier, in a speech before a mixed audience at New York's Lenox Lyceum when he was running for governor, he called the black soldiers he fought with "brave men, worthy of respect" and stated,

I remember hearing my Rough Riders say, "The Ninth and Tenth are all right; they can drink out of our canteens." I recall when we were lying in reserve at San Juan and we got our orders to move forward, we struck the Ninth Cavalry as we charged up Kettle Hill, and the Ninth and the Rough Riders went up absolutely intermingled, so that no one could tell whether it was the Rough Riders or the Ninth who came forward with greater freedom to offer up their lives for their country. ("Roosevelt")[17]

Roosevelt's description of the battle in *Scribner's* was quickly disputed in the black press by African American soldiers, most notably by Sergeant Presley Holliday in the *New York Age*, who referred to the accusation of cowardice as "uncalled for and uncharitable, and considering the moral and physical effect the advance of the Tenth Cavalry had in weakening forces opposed to the Colonel's regiment . . . , altogether ungrateful," resulting in "an immeasurable lot of harm" (96).[18] When Roosevelt ran as the Republican candidate for vice president the following year, his accusations of black cowardice became a campaign issue, endearing him to some white voters and alienating him from African Americans (James 137; Gatewood, *Black* 241–43). Although he refused on more than one occasion to retract what he had written, Roosevelt did, in the face of lingering black anger, offer a somewhat different account of what happened during an October 1900 interview with the *Chicago Daily News*, placing the blame for the rearward movement of some black soldiers on their white commanding officer and stating that the victory in the battle belonged to the black fighting men "as much if not more than any other soldiers there" (qtd. in Gatewood, *Black* 244).

Christine Bold observes that Roosevelt and the eastern establishment were largely successful in popularizing their version of what happened during the Cuban campaign and in muzzling tales of heroic African American military service. Most of the U.S. black texts and images relating to the conflict, she notes, are long out of print and difficult to locate (293). Frequently anthologized in recent years, Johnson's "The Color Sergeant," providing a potent countermyth to the widely circulated story of the Rough Riders, stands as a prominent exception.

Wrapped in the Flag

The first epigraph to this chapter reminds us that, in addition to the symbolic significance with which flags are invested, bearing the colors meant leading men into battle—and consequently serving as a conspicuous and prized target for enemy fire. Along with his brother J. Rosamond Johnson and Bob Cole,

James Weldon Johnson in 1901 wrote a popular tune dedicated to Sergeant William H. Carney of the Fifty-Fourth Massachusetts entitled "The Old Flag Never Touched the Ground" (later used as the finale to Cole and Johnson's *The Shoo-Fly Regiment*, a production that reached Broadway in 1907, which included scenes set during the Philippine-American War). Composition of this song clearly indicates Johnson's familiarity with and participation in the mythmaking that had taken place in connection with the carrying of flags in battle.[19] By choosing a color guard as the subject of his poem, Johnson not only evokes the countermythic lore associated with U.S. blacks and flags in Cuba and the Civil War but also challenges the appropriation of a battle standard in Page's "Marse Chan," an influential text in the campaign of southern plantation writers to whitewash antebellum society, the Civil War, and Reconstruction.

Literary historians identify "Marse Chan: A Tale of Old Virginia," published in the April 1884 issue of *Century Magazine*, as one of the pivotal texts of plantation fiction, even though some of the hallmarks of such writing appear in earlier stories, such as Edgar Allan Poe's "The Gold-Bug" (1843).[20] However we fix its origins, plantation literature typically features nostalgia for the antebellum era, a quasi-familial but rigidly stratified relationship among slaves and their owners, chivalrous white southern males and virtuous white southern women, faithful blacks who speak in an exaggerated dialect and pine for a return to the days when their masters cared for them, and a dysfunctional society resulting from the devastation of the Civil War and the depredations of Reconstruction. As the story begins, not only is Marse Chan gone but his whole class has died out, his parents passing within a year of his death and his lifelong love interest Anne succumbing to a combination of fever contracted while working as a nurse and a broken heart. Set in 1872, the fiction clearly implies that had the Civil War never taken place, the beautiful, orderly plantations would still be intact, honorable and principled men and women like Marse Chan and Anne would still be in charge, and blacks would have whites to provide them with direction and a purpose in life. "Marse Chan" illustrates the dependent nature of blacks through the figure of Sam, whose current occupation seems to consist largely of looking after his deceased master's dog. Page not only depicts Sam lifting fence rails for the aged canine and admitting to spoiling him with "sweet 'taters" (938) but concludes the story by having Sam ask his wife, "Have Marse Chan's dawg got home?" (942). Clearly the point is to equate Sam and the hound as loyal, subservient beings lost without their master.

In her analysis of white and black accounts of the war in Cuba, Amy Kaplan underscores the tendency of white writers to reduce African Americans to purely servile roles. She seizes on a passage in journalist Richard Harding Davis's *The Cuban and Porto Rican Campaigns* (1898) describing the gravely wounded Lieutenant Roberts of the Tenth Cavalry flanked by a group of injured black soldiers "crouching at his feet like three faithful watch-dogs," each "with his eyes fixed patiently on the white lips of the officer," fiercely protective of their white superior whose critical condition makes it impossible to move him (qtd. in Kaplan 143). As she remarks, on the surface this appears to be a picture of "national consolidation between whites and blacks, bonded by shared wounds and sacrifice"; however, "this tableau reinscribes the racial hierarchy out of which national unity is forged, not only in the explicit racist images of the blacks as 'watch-dogs' or the fact that they, in contrast to the white officer, remain unnamed, but in the way in which the heroic white body is intimately constructed out of black bodies in several hybrid configurations" (143). Although Kaplan does not mention Page's immensely popular story, it certainly provided a precedent for the linking of blacks and dogs operative in this passage.[21]

In "Marse Chan," Sam recounts and highlights his owner's honorable qualities—his fearlessness, his sense of duty, his restraint, his deference to his elders, his respect for women, and his loyalty to the rebel cause in the war. Unlike Sam, who "wuz so skeered [he] couldn't say nuthin'" when his master fights a duel (938) and who "used to be pow'ful skeered sometimes" (940) when he accompanies Marse Chan to the front during the Civil War, the title character never exhibits any trepidation when his life is in jeopardy. To establish his gallantry, manliness, and devotion to his section, Page literally wraps Marse Chan in the flag, first on the battlefield and then in death. Sam describes his master eagerly picking up the fallen colors of his regiment and recklessly leading the charge against superior forces before being struck down by Yankee gunfire:

> An' dey said, "Charge 'em!" an', my king! Ef ever you see bullets fly, dey did dat day. Hit wuz jes' like hail; . . . our lines sort o' broke an' stop; de cun'l was kilt, an' I believe dey wuz jes' 'bout to brek all to pieces, when Marse Chan rid up an' cotch hol' de flag an' hollers, "Foller me!" an' rid straining up de hill 'mong de cannons. I seen 'im when he went, . . . de whole regiment right arfter 'im. (941)

Finding his master "onder one o' de guns wid de fleg still in he han', an' a bullet right th'oo he body," Sam picks him "up in my arms wid de fleg still in he han's," carries him off the battlefield, makes a pine coffin, "wrap[s] Marse Chan's body up in de fleg," and brings him back to the Channing plantation (941). After the body lies in state in the parlor of the ancestral home and his loved ones pay their respects, Marse Chan is buried "in de ole grabeyard, wid de fleg wrapped roun' 'im" (941). Aside from ascribing several other supposedly white virtues celebrated during the post-Reconstruction era to the title character, with no fewer than five references to the flag Marse Chan carries and which enshrouds him, Page emphasizes the southern scion's patriotism, even if the standard in question is the Stars and Bars rather than Old Glory.

The parallels between "The Color Sergeant" and the battle scene in "Marse Chan" are striking. Sam finds his master dead amid his fallen comrades, whom he fearlessly led into battle, similar to the black standard bearer in stanza 1 of the poem. In addition, Johnson's phrase "where the leaden hail fell fast" (7) echoes Sam's description of the bullets flying "like hail" in the story. More important, both figures serve as emblems for a "race"—a term used by both Page (932) and Johnson (19)—of people who suffer an undeserved fate despite possessing a host of noble qualities the literary texts take great pains to associate with them. As do the authors of other African American texts in which flags figure prominently, Johnson in "The Color Sergeant" clearly stresses the fidelity of U.S. blacks to the Stars and Stripes, invoking their long history of service in war, including the conflict against those whites who betrayed that flag by seceding from and seeking to destroy the union.

"The Color Sergeant" reflects key elements that appear in U.S. black poems about the Cuban Revolution and the participation of African Americans in the war against Spain, namely bravery, military heritage, martyrdom, racial stigmatization, and flag bearing. Building on the double meaning of its main title, Johnson's poem emphasizes the carrying of both the battle standard and the burden of race. Thus, although it lacks overt references to previous black warriors in the United States and the Western Hemisphere generally, it does, in some senses, epitomize the African American literary response to the Spanish-Cuban-American War. By placing the storied figure of the black color sergeant in the mythic space of San Juan Hill, it provides a countermyth to Roosevelt's narrative of white male predominance in Cuba and wrests the flag—and the patriotism it represents—from southern white plantation writers, challenging their program to reconcile whites North and South at the cost of African American citizenship rights.

Wars Abroad and at Home in Sutton E. Griggs's *Imperium in Imperio* and *The Hindered Hand*

What to that redoubted harpooner, John Bull, is poor Ireland, but a Fast-Fish? What to that apostolic lancer, Brother Jonathan, is Texas but a Fast-Fish? And concerning all these, is not Possession the whole of the law?
—Herman Melville, *Moby-Dick*

It is the weakened position of the Negro, not his strength, that is to be feared. The putrid body of a dead man lying at the bottom of a reservoir can poison the water of a city and thus slay more people than if the man were alive, dashing wildly though the streets of that city firing on the right and on the left.—Sutton Griggs, *Wisdom's Call*

Between 1899 and 1908, Sutton E. Griggs (1872–1933) published five long works of fiction, making him the most prolific late nineteenth- and early twentieth-century African American novelist. For a variety of reasons, these texts about black and white southerners have frustrated attempts by critics to arrive at definitive interpretations. In contrast to his more famous contemporaries Paul Laurence Dunbar and Charles Chesnutt, whose books, brought out by mainstream northern publishers, were marketed to white readers, Griggs "spoke primarily to the Negro race" (Du Bois, "Negro" 318), using his own Nashville-based Orion Publishing Company to print all but the first of his novels. Not only do individual texts by Griggs alternate between gloom and hope but his fiction taken as a whole follows a similar pattern with each book following *Imperium in Imperio* (1899)—his best-known novel and the only one currently in print—serving as a response or counterpoint to the previous one, as is suggested by their titles: *Overshadowed* (1901), *Unfettered: A Novel* (1902), *The Hindered*

Hand; or, The Reign of the Repressionist (1905), and *Pointing the Way* (1908).[1] Complicating matters, his first and fourth novels not only have open-ended conclusions but also give nearly equal time to coprotagonists with contrasting worldviews and political agendas. As Arlene Elder observes, the rival main characters in these books "have names beginning with the same letters because Griggs conceives them not so much as individuals but as alter egos, symbols of the opposing impulses within the new generation of blacks" (101).[2] The idiosyncrasies, ambivalences, and ambiguities of Griggs's texts, coupled with the tendency of critics to read them in binary terms, have resulted in widely diverse and in some cases starkly discrepant responses to the author. These include characterizations of Griggs as a militant (Gloster, Tucker, Lamon), radical black Baptist (Frazier), accommodationist (Bone), black nationalist (Gayle, Moses, Gillman), black chauvinist (Logan), marginal (Fullinwider), transitional (Elder), melodramatic sentimentalist (Rampersad), near-futurist (Tal), black utopian (Fabi, Winter, Kellman), and sensationalist (Knadler) novelist, who, in the eyes of some scholars, admired Booker T. Washington and supported his political program and, according to others, criticized and satirized the era's most influential black leader.[3]

In his novels, Griggs portrays U.S. blacks driven to desperation as a result of widespread disenfranchisement, unchecked white-on-black violence, and discriminatory justice.[4] In response to these conditions, his African American characters seriously contemplate or actively pursue various options, most notably amalgamation, emigration, and armed resistance. Since the early 1800s, U.S. black leaders had debated the pros and cons of both assimilation into the white race and relocation to Africa or other places beyond the borders of the United States. However, the possibility of organized violence was seldom, for obvious reasons, openly discussed during the antebellum period, nor was it explicitly raised in the decades immediately following emancipation. Thus, the proposals made and actions taken in Griggs's novels to respond to the denial of black citizenship rights with armed revolt represent a significant departure from the writings of his African American precursors and contemporaries, and critics have, understandably, regarded them as one of the most striking features of his fiction. Yet because of the reluctance until quite recently to address the relationship between U.S. expansion and literary texts, particularly those by African Americans, scholars have for the most part failed to situate Griggs's novels within the larger political context of the era, typically reading them exclusively in the light of U.S. race relations.

Griggs raises the option of warfare, both conventional and biological, in fiction that was composed during and immediately following and that explicitly grapples with the imperialistic wars at the turn of the twentieth century, the first major conflicts since the Civil War. In *Imperium*, *Unfettered*, and *The Hindered Hand*, Griggs addresses the Cuban Revolution, African American military service in the conflict against Spain, the frustrations of black war veterans, the controversy over the annexation and subjugation of the Philippines, and the connections between U.S. imperial policy overseas and domestic race relations.[5] Whereas *Imperium* explicitly thematizes the prelude to the war with Spain, *Unfettered* and *The Hindered Hand* address different aspects of its aftermath. Linking national electoral politics directly with expansion and comparing the status of newly annexed Filipinos to that of U.S. blacks during and after slavery, *Unfettered* raises legitimate concerns about the consequences of imperialism, both abroad and at home. Acting on a behest from the 1903 National Negro Baptist Convention in Philadelphia to respond to Thomas Dixon's 1902 race-baiting novel *The Leopard's Spots: A Romance of the White Man's Burden, 1865–1900* (Damon 781–83), in *The Hindered Hand* Griggs depicts the often harrowing experiences of three African American veterans of the Cuban conflict on their return to the South.

The first section of this chapter examines Griggs's perspicacious linking of empires abroad and at home in *Imperium in Imperio*, a novel about contrasting main characters, Bernard Belgrave and Belton Piedmont, who play key roles in a widespread, well-funded, and clandestine black organization called the Imperium that initially advocates mass African American migration to and the political takeover of Texas and that later approves a plan to make war on the United States in conjunction with foreign powers so as create a Texas-based black empire.[6] The second section, devoted to *The Hindered Hand*, addresses Griggs's depiction of the bitter disappointments that followed in the wake of African American military service in the war against Spain and teases out the wide-ranging implications of a key scene in which a sinister character attempts to use Dixon's anti-Negro campaign to convince a leading African American to participate in a plot to wipe out white southerners by introducing yellow fever germs into the water supply.

Imperial and Racial Battles in Imperium in Imperio

Although unquestionably a work of speculative fiction, Griggs's first novel looks less fantastic and bizarre than several critics have claimed when read in the context of, first, actual and proposed nineteenth-century black immigration to and emigration from Texas; second, the sometimes outlandish proposals that were put forward at the turn of the twentieth century by southern politicians, northern publications, and some leading African American figures to ship large numbers of African Americans from the South to such places as the southwestern United States, northern Mexico, Hawaii, Cuba, and the Philippines; and, third, U.S. expansion—especially the Spanish-Cuban-American War—and its domestic and international ramifications. Given Texas's liminal location and transnational history, Griggs's choice of the Lone Star State as the site for the Imperium has resonances that reach far beyond the "Negro question" within the United States that he addresses in his fiction and nonfiction and that has often been the focus of critical readings of his novels. Caroline F. Levander remarks in a recent article on *Imperium* entitled "Sutton Griggs and the Borderlands of Empire" (2010) that to think only in terms of a North/South divide within the United States or to regard the Rio Grande as a white/brown dividing line is to "oversimplify the racial contours of the nation and overemphasize the ease of its imperial reach. Both endpoint and access point, the territory comprising what is now the state of Texas functioned as a fluid, multidirectional, multiracial grid—a dynamic field through which Mexican-, Anglo-, and African-American groups crossed, recrossed, and blended with each other" (59). She adds that to frame "the question of African-American rights as a choice between assimilation within the nation or emigration from it overlooks the complex logics and opportunities inhering in the nation's blurry edges. Adjacent to and embedded within the United States, the region featured in *Imperium* offers Griggs a new territorial coordinate from which to rethink U.S. racism during the age of empire" (79). Although Griggs received a divinity degree in Virginia and spent the vast majority of his career as a Baptist minister in Tennessee, he was born and raised in and had an intimate knowledge of Texas, where his father, the Reverend Allen Griggs, who had been a slave in Georgia, founded numerous churches, a religious academy, Dallas's first black high school, and four colleges, including Bishop College, from which the younger Griggs graduated in 1890 (Coleman vii, 13, 18).[7] The widely read Sutton Griggs had a firm grasp on the history of his native state, which remained in his thoughts despite the years he spent away from it, as indicated by his act of "affectionately" dedicating his 1911 nonfiction tract *Wisdom's Call* to "the imperial state of Texas" (v).[8]

The influx of African Americans into as well as their departure from Texas during the 1800s constitutes less "a single great migration," as Levander observes, than "an ongoing oscillation of people" ("Sutton" 80). In accordance with an agreement worked out with Spain in 1820, Stephen Austin eventually led three hundred white families and their slaves into what is now Texas. Mexico, which won its independence from Spain in 1821, rejected repeated offers from the United States to buy Texas, outlawed slavery in 1829 (which the so-called Old Three Hundred circumvented by converting their slaves into indentured servants), and banned the immigration of U.S. citizens into Texas in 1830 (Barr 15; Douglass 118). Five years later, Texans revolted against Mexico, and within six months the Republic of Texas was born. Although some Texans supported continued independence, Sam Houston lobbied for annexation by the United States, finding support among a coalition of Northern expansionists and proslavery southerners. As Neil Foley explains, "Texas, it was supposed, would become a safety valve for attracting both slaves and freed blacks to the doorstep of Latin America, where they could cross the border and become mingled with Mexicans. Annexation, then, would facilitate the relocation of blacks from the South to the 'dumping ground' of the far-western frontier and hasten . . . the 'natural emigration' of blacks to Mexico and the equator" (20), thereby solving the supposed problems posed by free African Americans. Early in 1845 Congress passed a bill authorizing the annexation of Texas, which President John Tyler signed; it became effective at the end of that year. In the interim, Texans voted in favor of a state constitution legalizing slavery.

In a January 2, 1846, speech delivered in Belfast, Ireland, entitled "Texas, Slavery, and American Prosperity," Frederick Douglass, who, like other antislavery advocates, had vehemently opposed annexation, expressed his disgust and disappointment over these developments: "Two years ago, I had hoped that there was morality enough, Christian-mindedness enough, love of liberty enough, burning in the bosoms of the American people to lead them to reject for ever the unholy alliance in which they have bound themselves to Texas" (118).[9] His efforts and those of other abolitionists in the North were not successful in preventing what he termed a "most deep and skillfully devised conspiracy—for the purpose of upholding and sustaining one of the darkest and foulest crimes ever committed by man" (118). And indeed Douglass's worst fears did come to pass. The cotton industry brought so many immigrants and slaves to Texas that by 1860 there were close to two hundred thousand bondmen and bondwomen, roughly one-third of the entire population, an exponential rise from the total of five thousand slaves in 1836 (Barr 17).

Early in 1861, Texas seceded from the union and joined the Confederacy, and during the Civil War it supplied a significant number of soldiers to the rebel cause. On Juneteenth, June 19, 1865, federal troops landed at Galveston to take control of the state and liberate the slaves. Although there were notable exceptions, as Levander notes, for the overwhelming majority of black Texans, the postwar era brought economic hardship and political disenfranchisement rather than opportunity and prosperity. Indications of their desperation can be seen in various emigration movements and schemes. Over twelve thousand blacks left Texas for Kansas in 1879 in response to reports that free land could be found there, others migrated to Oklahoma when this option became available, and, beginning in the late 1870s, there was considerable interest in emigration to Liberia; moreover, in 1880 a Boston philanthropist secured the endorsement of an African American convention in Dallas for a black colony in northwest Texas, which never materialized (Lears 123–24; Barr 96, 97). Summing up his discussion of late nineteenth-century African American emigration, Alwyn Barr states, "Though the exodus never included more than a small percentage of black Texans at any time, only the costs of emigration or total despair held back thousands of others" (98). Griggs's use of Texas as the location of the Imperium's headquarters and the focal point of the plan for mass African American immigration should thus be seen, at least in part, in connection with the many actual and proposed movements of blacks to and from Texas from the 1820s through the 1890s.

Besides paying homage to U.S. black migration into and out of his home state, Griggs implicitly addresses proposals at the turn of the twentieth century to ship large numbers of African Americans abroad, which the federal government did not take steps to implement but was nevertheless forced to study and contemplate. Southern Democrats, editorial writers for mainstream publications, Republican legislators and policy makers, and U.S. black leaders proposed and debated schemes for the mass emigration of African Americans. Such suggestions were, of course, nothing new, as back-to-Africa initiatives date from the early part of the nineteenth century. What was new, however, was the nation's acquisition of an overseas empire—the annexation of Hawaii (as well as Guam, American Samoa, and Puerto Rico), the occupation of Cuba, and the takeover and bloody pacification of the Philippines. These new territories made it possible for influential Alabama U.S. senator John T. Morgan and others to propose transporting blacks from the South not to Africa but to the newly acquired lands in the Pacific and the Caribbean where they would be removed from the continental United States but still subject to the nation's control.[10]

Recalling earlier Confederate schemes, late 1890s and early 1900s expansionist ambitions included plans to take over sovereign nations within the Western Hemisphere, reflected in *Harper's Weekly*'s proposal that the United States purchase part of northern Mexican as the site for the resettlement of southern blacks ("Elihu Root"). In February 1903, this mainstream northern publication, responding to—and greatly misrepresenting—a speech by secretary of war Elihu Root to the Union League in New York ("The Union League Club"), floated a relocation plan of its own. The magazine recommended that the U.S. government pay Mexico $200 million for Chihuahua and two or three other sparsely populated northern states to be used for the voluntary resettlement of African Americans: "If the northern section of the Mexican Republic could be bought and erected into a Territory for the exclusive benefit of our colored people, and if it were distinctly understood that they not only would receive grants of land and cattle, but would enjoy educational facilities and a monopoly of political privileges, it is by no means incredible that a large body of negroes might be inclined to migrate thither" (307). *Harper's Weekly* cites as a precedent the relocation of Native Americans to lands acquired as a result of the Louisiana Purchase, an arrangement that, the magazine asserts, "neither the Indians nor we have had cause to regret" (307). Envisioning the extension of U.S. territory further south, this Mexican relocation scheme dovetailed perfectly with the expansionist furor of the era.

Furthermore, prominent African American leaders, including Bishop Turner, educator William Saunders Scarborough, and newspaperman T. Thomas Fortune, as well as lesser-known figures, such as Bishop Lucius H. Holsey of the Colored Methodist Episcopal Church and the Baltimore Baptist minister Harvey Johnson, advocated the relocation of U.S. blacks. Holsey urged the federal government to establish a black state in the Indian Territory of New Mexico (Bacote 493–94). Meanwhile, Johnson proposed a scheme whereby the U.S. government would buy up the entire state of Texas by means of eminent domain and then sell parcels of land to African Americans so that they could establish a separate black state within the union.[11] In *Imperium* Griggs responds to the era's many emigration schemes, some of which were no less far-fetched than his own Texas-takeover scenario. His fictional vision of a black-run Texas serves in part to highlight the absurdity of actual proposals to remove as many as five million blacks from the continental United States that were endorsed by whites as well as blacks.

In addition to implicit and explicit allusions to and commentary on nineteenth-century black migrations to and from Texas and turn-of-the-twentieth-century proposals to relocate large numbers of African Americans, references to imperialism generally and the run-up to the war against Spain specifically abound in *Imperium*. The narrative early on refers with apparent approbation to African American aspirations for "freedom, equality, and empire" (44). However, in the light of post-Reconstruction era conditions, U.S. blacks constituted not only a nation within a nation but also an "empire," in the sense of a colonized people, within the larger American empire, as Bernard Belgrave explicitly states in a speech to the Imperium's legislative body: "They have apparently chosen our race as an empire, and each Anglo-Saxon regards himself as a petty king, and some gang or community of negroes as his subjects" (147). Griggs, moreover, entitles chapter 17, in which the Imperium debates the possibility of war against the United States, "Crossing the Rubicon," a reference to Julius Caesar's irrevocable decision in 49 BCE to violate the law on imperium and take the battle to Rome, the seat of empire, itself.

The event that brings the Imperium to its moment of crisis in the final chapters of the novel is a white mob's murder of U.S. postmaster Felix Cook (based on the February 1898 lynching of Frazier Baker in Lake City, South Carolina), which happens around the same time as the sinking of the *Maine* in Havana Harbor.[12] In a rousing speech, Belgrave, the privileged, light-skinned, Ivy League–educated, newly elected president of the Imperium, reviews the history of white atrocities against blacks in the United States and calls upon the organization's legislators to take some decisive course of action. Quickly rejecting amalgamation into the white race and emigration to Central Africa, the Imperium seems to have only one option: an official declaration of war on the United States roughly coinciding with Congress's proclamation of war on Spain. At this key moment, however, the novel's other main character, a dark-skinned man of humble origins and the speaker of the Imperium's legislature, rises to address the assembly. Espousing views on patriotism closely resembling those that Griggs expresses and directly connects to *Imperium* at the start of his autobiographical sketch *The Story of My Struggles* (1914), Belton Piedmont makes an impassioned plea for the organization to continue to try to work within the union. He offers a spirited defense of American ideals, enumerates the benefits that U.S. blacks have gained from their association with white southerners, and proposes that the Imperium reveal its existence to the rest of nation and give the United States four years to restore to African Americans their constitutional rights. If the Imperium's demands are not met by the end of this period, then U.S. blacks shall all, says Piedmont, "abandon our several homes in the various other states and emigrate in a body to the State of Texas, broad in domain, rich in soil and salubrious in climate. Having an unquestioned majority of votes we shall secure possession of the State government" (163). Once lawfully in charge of the state, African Americans will defend to the death their newly acquired rights, and, as Piedmont puts it, "sojourn in the State of Texas, working out our destiny as a separate and distinct race in the United States of America" (163–64). His plan thus attempts to straddle both loyalty to the race and fealty to the nation.

Piedmont's resolution passes; however, it gives Belgrave an idea for a more radical scheme, which, after lining up support from key members of the organization, he proposes to the Imperium the next day. It calls for the takeover of Texas by the Imperium, the mutiny of strategically placed black sailors in the U.S. Navy, and the declaration and prosecution of war—in conjunction with foreign powers—on the United States. These actions will secure the Imperium's sovereignty in Texas and result in the ceding of newly captured Louisiana to the Imperium's foreign allies, thereby providing a buffer state for the Imperium. Belgrave's ultimate goal, in contrast to that of Piedmont, who wants to reform the United States but not break from it, is to lead a Texas-based African American empire. Here I must take issue with Levander's contention that Piedmont's and Belgrave's proposals constitute "two plans to secure the entire territory of Texas for the black empire" (62). Unlike Belgrave, Piedmont consistently makes clear that he wants the Imperium to remain a part of the United States—either with blacks enjoying citizenship rights throughout the country or at a minimum in Texas where they will have vast numerical superiority and control the organs of political power. Belgrave's scheme links the Imperium to the Confederacy, which not only seceded from the Union and appealed to European powers to assist it in remaining separated but also envisioned the establishment of an empire based on slavery comprised of territories acquired beyond the borders of the United States.[13] It also looks ahead to Marcus Garvey's dream of founding a black empire that he expounds in such writings as "African Fundamentalism."[14] As Addison Gayle observes, "Marcus Garvey probably never read Sutton Griggs' *Imperium in Imperio*, but had he done so, he might have been accused of plagiarism. For the Imperium that Garvey desired to establish on African soil was established here in America in this novel by a virtually unknown nineteenth-century Black writer" (75).[15]

Housed under the guise of Thomas Jefferson College in Waco, Texas, the organization's ruling body is modeled on that of the United States; however, it requires that all decisions be unanimous, and any dissent is ruthlessly punished. Thus, Piedmont's decision to resign from the Imperium in protest over the approval of the radical plan for war carries with it, according to the organization's laws, a sentence of death. In his provocative, multilayered reading of *Imperium*, first published in 2007 and reprinted in revised form in *Remapping Citizenship and the Nation in African-American Literature* (2010), Stephen Knadler argues that Griggs uses Piedmont to satire Booker T. Washington's accommodationist policies. He asserts that in the wake of the war against Spain "many African American leaders" invoked "the long history of romantic racist imagery, from Harriet Beecher Stowe's *Uncle Tom's Cabin* to the more recent plantation fiction of Thomas Nelson Page, to portray African Americans as patriotic 'Citizens Toms'" (*Remapping* 144). During the late 1890s and early 1900s when flag-waving rituals reached a peak in part as a response to the influx of immigrants, the figure of the naturally loyal and dutifully obedient "Citizen Tom" made it possible for U.S. blacks to participate in the "sentimental patriotism" of the era (144), which Knadler contends Griggs seeks to unsettle "traumatically" through a series of sensational scenes involving Piedmont (145). Similar to Pauline Hopkins in *Contending Forces* (1900), Griggs does indeed create opposing characters who resemble Washington and W. E. B. Du Bois in Piedmont and Belgrave—the former being a man who rises from southern poverty to become a college president, regards slavery as a kind of fortunate fall for U.S. blacks, and in the end places his country ahead of his race and the latter being a Harvard graduate who chooses race over country, at times advocates vengeance against U.S. whites, and dreams of a black empire.[16] Yet, despite the novel's description of Piedmont in the final chapter as "the last of that peculiar type of Negro heroes that could so fondly kiss the smiting hand" (175), Knadler, in associating Piedmont with Washington's accommodationism and "sentimental patriotism," overlooks the resistance that Griggs's character frequently offers to white oppression and minimizes both the duration and the depth of his commitment to the Imperium. At all-black Stowe University, Piedmont forms a "secret organization" with the password "Equality or Death" (44) that protests the segregation of the school's lone black professor from other faculty members during meals. When the astonished white teachers wave "the white flag," the student body celebrates its victory by holding up "a black flag" and, significantly, by singing "John Brown's Body" (46). This act of resistance orchestrated by Piedmont not only indicates that the "cringing, fawning, sniffling, cowardly

Negro which slavery left, had disappeared, and a new Negro, self-respecting, fearless, and determined in the assertion of his rights was at hand" (46) but also inspires similar "combinations" involving "one hundred thousand students" throughout the country (47). Piedmont's actions against white oppression, moreover, do not cease upon graduation, for he founds a popular newspaper that boldly exposes "frauds at the polls" before it is shut down (87). The protest at Stowe also portends the pivotal role that he will play in the Imperium: "Remember that this was Belton's first taste of rebellion against the whites for the securing of rights denied simply because of color. In after life he is the moving, controlling, guiding spirit in one on a grand scale" (47). It must also be noted that Piedmont, "a member for years" (133), invites Belgrave, who knows nothing about the Imperium, to join the organization and oversees the harrowing loyalty test that his friend must pass to gain admittance.

At the end of *Imperium*, Belgrave's plan to make war on white America does not come to fruition because Berl Trout, the Imperium's secretary of state and a member of the firing squad that kills Piedmont, as well as the novel's main narrator, betrays the organization to white authorities. Trout explains that he does so because, with the execution of Piedmont, "the spirit of conservatism in the Negro race died," and, without anyone capable of tempering the President's militancy, Belgrave "was a man to be feared" (175). Trout's action must therefore be seen in connection with the dynamic relationship between Belgrave and Piedmont that structures the entire book (and links it in particular to *The Hindered Hand*, in which a mulatto likewise struggles with a more conservative man of darker hue for hearts and minds of his people). Although Trout begins the book with the words "I am a traitor" (5), he declares he is also "a patriot" (6) and concludes the narrative with the assertion that he did what he did "in the name of humanity" (176). As Knadler notes (*Remapping* 160), Griggs in the final chapter complicates the conflict between allegiance to race and allegiance to nation by introducing another alternative in the form of what might be called global or universal patriotism. Trout also issues the plea that "all mankind will join hands and help my poor downtrodden people to secure those rights for which they organized the Imperium," adding, "I urge this because love of liberty is such an inventive genius, that if you destroy one device it at once constructs another more powerful" (177).

Some controversy surrounds when and how Trout betrays the Imperium. Levander suggests that the novel itself—which in the prefatory "To the Public," someone signing himself "Sutton E. Griggs" claims, after defending Trout's "strict veracity," to be merely "editing," and "giving . . . to the public" (3–4)—constitutes Trout's betrayal: "Trout has been identified as a traitor because he gives the story that we are about to read to Sutton E. Griggs to publish, and thereby destroys the secrecy upon which the Imperium depends for success" ("Sutton" 73). In other words, Levander contends that the United States first learns about the Imperium—and then presumably takes action against it—through the narrative. The use of the present tense in the second half of Trout's statement—"I decided to prove traitor and reveal the existence of the Imperium that it might be broken up or watched. My deed may appear that of a vile wretch, but it is done in the name of humanity" (176)—may seem to suggest that the betrayal has not yet occurred and that the text is itself the act of betrayal. However, the next sentence—"Long ere you shall have come to this line, I shall have met the fate of a traitor" (176–77)—indicates that the betrayal has already taken place and Trout has, consequently, paid the price for it. Moreover, simply revealing the existence of the Imperium, which is exactly what Piedmont proposed doing and what the Imperium's legislators initially unanimously agreed to do, would not in and of itself amount to an all-out "betrayal" of the organization. Thus, Trout must have specifically exposed Belgrave's plan to make war on the United States.

Imperium ends on neither a clearly positive nor a clearly negative note. On the one hand, Trout's betrayal of the organization means that a bloody race war has been averted, which Griggs certainly regards as a good thing. On the other hand, the future for U.S. blacks seems particularly bleak. Therefore, I cannot concur with M. Giulia Fabi's upbeat reading of the novel's conclusion in *Passing and the African American Novel* (2001): "Th[e] spirit of self-determination and self-reliance, which gave birth to the Imperium in the first place, survives and is even kindled by Belton's death and the dismantlement of the organization. The possibility and explicit threat of constructing an even 'more powerful' organization are reiterated at the very end of the novel and sustain the utopian vision of unstoppable black empowerment and liberation Griggs projects" (55). However, Trout actually uses the word "device," which is less concrete than Fabi's "organization"; moreover, with the venerable, well-funded, and puissant Imperium dismembered and their most dynamic leaders presumably jailed or executed, disenfranchised U.S. blacks find themselves entirely at the mercy of an increasingly violent and intolerant white population with little or no hope of protection from the nation's discriminatory justice system.

In a sense Griggs's novel offers his black readers a chance to indulge momentarily their revenge fantasies and dreams of power—and even empire—but also shows them that they must be rejected. Piedmont's dissension from and especially Trout's betrayal of the Imperium can thus be seen as actions designed to deflect African Americans—and by extension the country as a whole—from such fantasies so as to address soberly and constructively the situation here (and for Griggs this always meant the South) and now. He has a different message for white southerners. He vividly imagines the potentially nightmarish consequences of the continued oppression of blacks but then defuses the incendiary scenario he so powerfully envisions in order to persuade white southerners to abandon their own fantasies—either of continuing to rule over African Americans as an empire or of ridding the land of blacks through mass emigration—so that they, too, will realistically face the here and now. The plan to take control of Texas legally proposed by one of the novel's protagonists and then radicalized by the other can be read as a warning—work with the Piedmonts or create and later face the Belgraves.

Seen within the context of nineteenth-century black migration to and away from Texas and the chaotic and deadly serious combination of black disenfranchisement, mob violence, rigidly enforced segregation, mass African American emigration schemes, and overseas expansion at the turn of the twentieth century, Griggs's vision of a black-run Texas in *Imperium* becomes far less fantastic than it originally appears. Beyond engaging with the empire abroad through the parallels it draws to the war with Spain, the novel underscores and expands the notion of an empire at home by comparing U.S. blacks to colonized people and by imagining a black empire existing within and on the borders of the nation.

Biological and Literary Warfare in The Hindered Hand

In "The Danger of an Unprotected Spot," the first chapter of his nonfiction tract *Wisdom's Call* (1911), one of the last books to be brought out by his Nashville-based Orion Publishing Company, Griggs writes about a medical discovery that, a decade earlier, had brought under control a disease that had ravaged the United States and Cuba: "It is now well known that the epidemics of yellow fever which in times past disorganized the business of states and nations, and converted whole cities into one great funeral procession, were organized and conducted by such tiny beings as mosquitoes which flew from the swamps and carried the disease from man to man" (12). This statement appears as part of an extended analogy Griggs draws between the seeming insignificance of insects and the supposed desirability of stripping African Americans of citizenship rights and legal standing:

> There are some who seem to be of the opinion that the complete adjustment in the South of what is called the race question will immediately follow the repeal or annulment of the Fifteenth Amendment of the Constitution of the United States. Their cry is, deprive the Negro of all political power; cause him to be absolutely helpless so far as affecting the situation one way or another is concerned; reduce him to the position of a governmental insect, and, they assert, our troubles will all be over. But small things, we have just seen, can give trouble. . . . The Negro, though reduced to a position of utter helplessness will be a source of unending trouble to the white South and the nation. (12–13)

After making clear that the country has nothing to fear from U.S. blacks in terms of physical violence, Griggs goes on to assert, in a passage that serves as the second epigraph to this chapter, that a rotting corpse infecting a community's water supply can kill more people than a gunman intent on shooting down anyone he sees (13). These references to yellow fever and infected water would have sounded hauntingly familiar to those who had read *The Hindered Hand*, published six years earlier.

Although some scholars have maligned Griggs's skills as a novelist, even his harshest critics have acknowledged his ability to create audaciously sensational scenes. Reprinted in the *Norton Anthology of African American Literature* and elsewhere, one such scene in *The Hindered Hand* describes the torture, burning, and mutilation of an innocent black couple in excruciatingly vivid detail, emphasizing the eager participation of young white children in the lynching. Comprising the chapters "Mr. A. Hostility" and "Two of a Kind," a second scene in the same novel depicts a "cadaverous looking white man" (201) who hopes to boost his pan-Slavic movement by gaining Ensal Ellwood's help in ending Anglo-Saxon supremacy. Refusing to divulge his true name and nationality, he states that the A in his nom de guerre "stands for Anglo-Saxon, the God-commissioned or self-appointed world conqueror. I am the incarnation of hostility to that race" (202). Highlighting the conflict between allegiance to the race and allegiance to the nation that plays a key role in *Imperium*, Ellwood asks whether the topic of their discussion will be treason, to which Hostility retorts, "Are you a part of the American nation or a thing apart? I can prove that you are a thing apart" (204). He strives to enrage Ellwood about the current state of U.S. race relations by pointing to a book from the pen of a negrophobic southern writer and by asserting that "over seventy-five thousand Negroes have been murdered in the south since your Civil War" (208). When Ellwood asks, "What are we to do," Hostility claims that U.S. blacks can "take what is your curse and make it your salvation" (209), adding by way of explanation that

> the pigment which abides in your skin and gives you your color and the peculiar Negro odor renders you immune from yellow fever.[17] This bottle here is full of yellow fever germs. Organize a band of trusted Negroes, send them through the South, let them empty these germs into the various reservoirs of the white people of the South and pollute the water. The greatest scourge that the world has ever known will rage the South. The whites will die by the millions and those that do not die will flee from the stricken land and leave the country to your people. The desolation wrought will for a time disorganize this whole nation and the Pan-Slavists will have more time to plan for the coming struggle. (210)

Hostility makes clear that he has as his ultimate goal worldwide Slavic domination, telling Ellwood that once the Anglo-Saxons have been brought low through the devastations of yellow fever "we will have you Negroes to fight in the last contest" (210). Through Hostility's scheme, Griggs addresses the often bizarre and at times genocidal and apocalyptic notions about race current at the time, including fears about not only a Slavic movement but also, in response to the Japanese victory over Russia in 1904, a "yellow peril" rising up to rival the international dominance of Anglo-Saxons.[18]

Rather than being an anomalous moment in the novel, this scene addresses subjects that figure prominently in Griggs's fiction and turn-of-the-twentieth-century African American writing generally, namely the domestic implications of U.S. military action in the Caribbean and the Philippines, African American loyalty to the nation, and the need to respond forcefully to defamatory statements about U.S. blacks published by white authors. Given the role that the war with Spain and the nation of Cuba played in the successful efforts by U.S. Army doctors to determine how yellow fever is transmitted from person to person and to prevent further outbreaks, it seems clear that the scene with A. Hostility refers to this conflict and U.S. imperialism. It appears in a novel in which the participation of three African American characters in the Cuban campaign strongly influences their lives in Almaville, the southern city, based on Nashville, to which they return. Griggs uses the military service of these men to highlight African American patriotism, which he contrasts with white southern disloyalty through the links between Confederate germ warfare plots and

Hostility's yellow fever scheme. Moreover, Griggs describes race literature in martial terms not only in this scene by explicitly equating the deadly virus Hostility would use to infect the southern water supply with "the venomous assault on" African Americans (206) that Thomas Dixon disperses in homes throughout the United States via his fiction but also in the appendix to the third edition of the novel by emphasizing "the essentially *barbarous* character of Mr. Dixon's method of warfare" (306), against which, in a manner similar to that of the poets discussed in chapter 1, he uses his novel as a form of counterattack.

The war the United States waged against Spain in Cuba led directly to the solution of the long-standing mystery of how yellow fever is spread. Yet as historians have suggested, it might also be said that yellow fever made U.S. military intervention in Cuba all but inevitable. Having been brought to the island by slave ships, the disease had been endemic in Havana and its environs for more than two centuries. Those who had not been exposed to yellow fever in childhood were highly susceptible, as evidenced by the thousands of Spanish soldiers who died of it during the Ten Years War (1878–88) and the sixteen thousand Spanish troops in Cuba who came down with the disease between 1894 and 1898 (Espinosa 2, Crosby 103). Because yellow fever originating in Cuba continued to pose a deadly threat to millions of people in United States, many believed that the nation should take action. In *Epidemic Invasions: Yellow Fever and the Limits of Cuban Independence, 1878–1930* (2009), a book about the profound impact yellow fever had on the relationship between the United States and Cuba, Mariola Espinosa explains,

> The southern United States, just across the Gulf of Mexico from Cuba, frequently suffered yellow fever epidemics during the second half of the nineteenth century, and nearly all of these epidemics had been traced to the island. Many other diseases routinely caused greater mortality, but because yellow fever killed in such a horrific fashion and could take thousands of lives in just a few short weeks, word of an outbreak often triggered mass panic. . . . Faced with repeated invasions of epidemic yellow fever from Havana in the southern states, the U.S. government confronted Cuba with the prospect of an epidemic of invasions of their island by U.S. troops. (3)

Robert Desowitz puts things even more bluntly: "An undercurrent of opinion had long held that the United States should take over Cuba for medical reasons, a yellow fever cleansing. The sinking of the *Maine* was just the ticket to do so" (qtd. in Crosby 97).

There was a distinctly racial dimension to the relationship between the war in Cuba and yellow fever that has particular relevance to *The Hindered Hand.* Mr. A. Hostility, Ellwood in the first edition of the novel, and Griggs himself in the appendix to the third edition echo what was once the prevailing—and erroneous—belief that people of African descent possessed a natural immunity to yellow fever.[19] In late April 1898, after the declaration of war against Spain, President McKinley asked the secretary of war to raise ten so-called "immune" regiments, comprised of men thought to be resistant to tropical diseases, to supplement volunteers in state regiments and U.S. Army regulars. Four of these units were composed of black soldiers, only one of which, the Ninth Immunes, actually made it to Cuba (Cunningham). U.S. blacks were troubled by the scorn and violence to which African American soldiers in these units were subjected when they were stationed in the South and as they traveled north through Nashville and other cities following Spain's surrender. As noted in the introduction, Bishop Turner, reflecting on the resentment and violence that greeted black troops following Spain's surrender, termed the U.S. flag a "worthless rag." The decision to have white officers command the black "immune" regiments organized to fight in Cuba likewise upset many African Americans.[20] In what Roger D. Cunningham describes as "a small but important step in the advancement of the race, not only in the Army, but within society as well," when the military organized two black volunteer regiments to fight in the Philippines in September 1899, these units, the Forty-Eighth and Forty-Ninth U.S. Volunteer Infantry, had black captains, one of whom was Frank R. Steward, a member of the prominent family profiled in the introduction, whose short fiction set in the Philippines I examine in chapter 3.

The devastating effects of diseases on U.S. soldiers during the 113-day war with Spain, in which fewer than four hundred men were killed in combat but nearly three thousand died of illness, added urgency to the search by military doctors for a cure, especially as fifteen thousand U.S. men and women would remain in Cuba during the ensuing occupation (McSherry; Crosby 97, 121). For this reason, the U.S. surgeon general established the Havana-based Yellow Fever Board under the direction of Walter Reed to find the cause of the disease. Although others had speculated that an insect might be responsible for transmitting yellow fever, it was a Cuban doctor, Carlos Finlay, who in 1881 hypothesized that a mosquito was the culprit and correctly identified the specific species, now known as *aedes aegypti.* However, because he was unaware that this mosquito only becomes infectious after an incubation period of several days, Finlay was unable to prove his theory. At the end of 1900, Reed conceived of and oversaw the tests establishing that the bite of an infected *aedes aegypti* and not soiled linens transmitted yellow fever, but this was only after a member of his team, Jesse Lazear, had successfully used mosquitoes to infect a human being with the disease in experiments that cost Lazear his life (Espinosa 56–58). Acting on the findings of Reed's team, Major William C. Gorgas succeeded in all but eradicating yellow fever in Havana by managing the mosquito population. A few years later he was sent to Panama to control insects there, an effort that played a major part in enabling the United States to build a canal in a location where an earlier French team had failed (Crosby 203–5; Espinosa 120).

The Spanish-Cuban-American War plays a strategic role in the storyline of *The Hindered Hand*, establishing the patriotism, along with the valor, of U.S. black fighting men that contrasts with white southern disloyalty, which Griggs connects to Hostility's yellow fever cabal. Gus Martin and the coprotagonists Ensal Ellwood and Earl Bluefield find it difficult to adjust to the oppressive conditions in the South after having distinguished themselves in Cuba. Echoing the poems by Beadle and others discussed in the previous chapter, these men fail to receive recognition for their military service and are exposed to harsh treatment when they return home.

The trio took part in the war's most famous and, as noted in chapter 1, controversial land engagement: "These three were present at the Battle of San Juan Hill, and Gus, who was himself notoriously brave, scarcely knew which to admire more, Ensal's searching words that inspired the men for that world-famous dash or Earl's enthusiastic, infectious daring on the actual scene of conflict" (37). Back in the United States, Bluefield's efforts to "secure promotion upon the record of his service in battle" prove fruitless because of the "disinclination of the South to have Negro officers" (37).[21] Embittered by such ingratitude and believing that the nation has betrayed the black men who fought for the American flag, Martin dismisses it as an empty symbol, colorfully declaring, "The [U.S.] flag aint any more to me than any other dirty rag. I fit fur it. My blood ran out o' three holes on the groun' to keep it floatin', and whut will it do fur me? Now jes' tell me whut?" (37–38). In doing so, he echoes Bishop Turner's notoriously incendiary statement made in the light of the violence directed at African American troops organized to serve in Cuba. Moreover, this passage appears to identify him as a flag bearer, thereby affiliating him with William Carney and George Berry (as well as the unnamed subject of Johnson's "The Color Sergeant"). Martin's sense of betrayal proves more than justified later when, after killing an apparently white minister for taking liberties with a black woman and then finding himself besieged by an angry white mob, he appeals in vain all the way to the White House for governmental protection from the mob of white vigilantes intent on murdering him.

Although they are friends, the novel's two main characters, like Piedmont and Belgrave in *Imperium*, disagree over how to secure "the ultimate recognition of the rights of the Negro as an American citizen" (48). Bluefield plans to lead a force of five hundred men in an assault on the state capitol and a federal building, justifying his plot by making reference to what he learned in the war: "Look at Cuba. A handful of men stayed in the field and kept up a show of resistance until our government intervened. It is within the power of the Negro race to bring out intervention any time it is willing to pay the price" (145). Rejecting the sword in favor of the pen, Ellwood writes and widely disseminates a pamphlet, which Griggs prints in its entirety in chapter 22, calling for a change in the nation's racial policies.[22] Bluefield, however, does not believe this effort will be sufficient, telling Ellwood that the words of Charles Sumner and Harriet Beecher Stowe alone were not enough to bring about the end of slavery— "There had to be a John Brown and a Harper's [sic] Ferry" (161). Their ideological contest becomes physical in a dramatic scene in which Ellwood literally wrestles with Bluefield to prevent him from implementing his violent and suicidal course of action.

The Cuban campaign also plays a part in a plan Bluefield later concocts to defeat the most racially intolerant southerners at the polls. When his wife, who can pass for white (like Bluefield) but has been publicly exposed as being of African descent, literally loses her wits because of the South's insane policing of the color line, he takes on himself the task of solving the race problem in the United States, hoping that this will cure her. Assuming the identity of a white northerner, he meets with race-baiting southern politicians, encouraging them to urge the North to extend the harsh oppression of blacks operative in the South to the other side of the Mason-Dixon line. In speaking with the governor of the state, he claims that people in the North were impressed by southern gallantry "in the skirmish with Spain" (261) and thus that the moment is ripe to convert the North to the southern racial point of view. Although this stratagem succeeds in coaxing the governor and his confederates to overplay their hand by pursuing a path that ultimately results in their resounding defeat in a national election, the fate of African Americans remains unresolved at the end of the novel, with Ellwood leaving for Liberia to provide a refuge for U.S. blacks in case the nation does not grant them their citizenship rights.

Through the experiences of Martin, Ellwood, and Bluefield, *The Hindered Hand*, like *Imperium*, links U.S. expansion abroad and racial oppression at home. Beyond this, the combination of the wartime heroics of these characters and Ellwood's quick and unequivocal rejection of Hostility's genocidal proposal serves to remind readers of the long history of U.S. black patriotism that contrasts with white Southern disloyalty, to which Griggs alludes through the yellow fever plot. In the third edition, Ellwood tells Hostility that during the Civil War U.S. blacks "met the requirement of honor where-ever the test was applied—whether it was the test of the soldier on the field of battle or the slave guarding the women and children at home" (211), adding, "Let the Anglo-Saxon crush us if he will and if there is no God! But I say to you, the Negro can never be provoked to stoop to the perfidy which you suggest" (212). The scheme to infect reservoirs with yellow fever recalls and conflates acts planned and perpetrated by Luke Pryor Blackburn, a southern physician who had gained a reputation as an expert on yellow fever before the Civil War. In 1864, he went to Bermuda during an outbreak of the disease and collected soiled linens from victims, which he put into trunks and had shipped to Nova Scotia. He then hired a man to transport the linens to Washington, D.C., Norfolk, Virginia, and New Bern, North Carolina (all three of which were in northern hands). The plan, which was unsuccessfully implemented because the means by which the disease is transmitted from person to person was not understood, was to sell the linens at public auction and thereby infect the population, including Union soldiers, with the disease. Blackburn conceived a related but separate plot to have a small valise filled with expensive shirts soiled by Bermuda yellow fever patients brought to the White House and given to the president as a gift. During the trial following Lincoln's assassination, this plot came to light, and testimony revealed that Jefferson Davis knew about it and the other soiled linen scheme but did nothing to prevent them. The trial revealed yet another biological warfare plot concocted by Blackburn. This one involved introducing fatal levels of strychnine and other poisons into the Croton Distributing Reservoir at 42nd Street and Fifth Avenue in Manhattan, which supplied the nation's largest city with its water during the 1800s. After the war, Blackburn remained in Canada where he was tried and acquitted of violating that nation's neutrality act. Despite his treasonous actions and the crimes against humanity he sought to visit on U.S. citizens, he returned to the country in 1873 to treat victims of yellow fever without being arrested and six years later was elected governor of the state of Kentucky. He died in 1887 and is buried beneath a headstone praising him as a humanitarian.[23]

Susan Gillman and other critics have read *The Hindered Hand* in connection with Thomas Dixon's *The Leopard's Spots: A Romance of the White Man's Burden—1865–1900*, and there is ample reason for doing so.[24] In the chapter entitled "Two of a Kind," Ellwood compares Hostility's germ warfare plot with Dixon's efforts to slander U.S. blacks. In the first edition of the novel, Griggs depicts Ellwood discussing Dixon's book with A. Hostility (206–19), and in the third edition he expands his attack on Dixon, removing some of it from the narrative proper to a separate appendix entitled "A Hindering Hand: Supplementary to The Hindered Hand: A Review of the Anti-Negro Crusade of Mr. Thomas Dixon, Jr." (303–33). Hoping to win over Ellwood, Hostility draws his attention to a volume written by "a rather conspicuous Southern man who had set for himself the task of turning the entire Negro population out of America" (206).

In the first edition of the novel, Ellwood dismisses the book, attributing its influence to a series of recent events, including the death of Queen Victoria, the "rise in the present day of a poet of the whole English-speaking people" (i.e., Rudyard Kipling), and "the treacherous blowing up of Anglo-Saxon lads in the harbor of a Latin country and the war that followed," which brought about "a moment of Anglo-Saxon rapprochement" on both sides of the Atlantic that "was seized upon by this Southerner to assault the stranger within his gates" (207).[25] In the third edition, Griggs terms *The Leopard's Spots* a "book written for the express purpose of thoroughly discrediting the Negro race in America," which he regards as part of "a policy of misrepresentation [that is] the necessary concomitant of a policy of repression" (206).

In "A Hindering Hand," Griggs links white southern literature to repression and describes Harriet Beecher Stowe's *Uncle Tom's Cabin* and Dixon's *The Leopard's Spots* as acts of literary warfare, which is also the way he conceives his own book. Linking Dixon to war crimes and acts of high treason through A. Hostility, Griggs depicts Ellwood telling the Slavic agent in the third edition, "I pronounce you the true yoke of the fellow about whose book we have been talking, who, in the livery of the unifier of the human race, smites the bridges of sympathy which the ages have builded between man and man, who, inflamed racial egotist that he is, would burn humanity at the stake for the sake of a glare it would cast upon the pathway of the one race" (212). After soundly dismissing Hostility's suggestion that U.S. blacks use yellow fever to devastate the white South, Ellwood at the close of this pivotal scene utters a long prayer. In it he asks God to "watch with thine all seeing eye and nail with thine omnipotent hand the machinations of those who would poison human hearts and destroy the humane instincts that are the graces of our faulty world" (213), once more linking Dixon and Hostility. Moreover, he beseeches the Lord to "grant that the post of pilot of our planet" (213) will continue to be filled by the country of his birth. Alluding to the consequences of U.S. expansion, this latter passage reveals Ellwood's fears that the nation may abandon its ideals in pursuit of wealth and territory abroad as well as in its increasingly unjust treatment of African Americans at home.

The Hindered Hand addresses the empire abroad and the empire at home on several levels. Through its focus on African American soldiers who fought in the Battle of San Juan Hill, it participates in the ongoing response to Roosevelt's charges of cowardice and depicts the lack of recognition received by, the absence of opportunities available to, and the harsh treatment directed at blacks who served in the war against Spain. Moreover, the novel contrasts the long history of African American loyalty to the nation with white southern betrayal by linking A. Hostility's plot to infect the water supply implicitly with Confederate germ warfare schemes and explicitly with Thomas Dixon's early twentieth-century campaign to poison the minds of U.S. whites with race hatred through his divisive novels.

In *Imperium in Imperio* and *The Hindered Hand*, Sutton Griggs profoundly engages with not only the Spanish-Cuban-American War specifically and U.S. expansion generally but also the apotheosis of Jim Crow at home. In these novels, he compares the situation of blacks in the South to that of colonized people overseas and refers to, imagines, or engages in various types of war—imperial combat against Spain, racial conflict between the Imperium and the United States, biological warfare against the white people of the South, and literary strife between himself and Thomas Dixon.

PART TWO

African American Literature, the Philippine-American War, and Expansion in the Pacific

CHAPTER THREE

Black Burdens, Laguna Tales, and "Citizen Tom" Narratives

African American Writing and the Philippine-American War

Current renditions of U.S. history thoroughly expunge the Philippine-American War and related engagements in Cuba, Puerto Rico, and Guam to the extent that these warrant not even a paragraph in many high-school textbooks, and scarcely that in many college texts. Not only do most Americans know nothing about the conduct of the Philippine-American War; many do not even know that such a war took place.
—Matthew Frye Jacobson, *Barbarian Virtues*

Pile on the Black Man's Burden.
'Tis nearest at your door;
Why heed long bleeding Cuba,
Or dark Hawaii's shore? . . .

Pile on the Black Man's Burden
His wail with laughter drown
You've sealed the Red Man's problem,
And will take up the Brown.
—H. T. Johnson, "The Black Man's Burden"

Helen H. Jun has coined the term "black orientalism" to refer to representations of Chinese people in the black press in the second half of the 1800s and the early 1900s. Rather than categorizing it as either racist or antiracist, Jun contends that black orientalism, which draws on the discourses of U.S. orientalism and black racial uplift, must be seen as a "contradictory process of ne-

63

gotiation" of the citizenship status of blacks vis-à-vis other racialized groups in the United States (1049). On the one hand, African American journalists contrasted their people's religiosity and long-standing commitment to U.S. ideals with the putative heathenism, inscrutability, and untrustworthiness of the Chinese. As Jun states, "The formulaic narration of black military service, Christian morality, and nationalist identification that constructed blacks as American subjects would become a repetitive and frequent articulation in respect to discourses of Chinese exclusion" (1058–59). On the other hand, the black press condemned Chinese exclusion because of its implications for U.S. black citizenship. Jun explains that "black Americans felt threatened by the notion that federal legislation employing racially exclusionary language with respect to Chinese immigrants would be aimed at them" (1060). Just as they do in the black press's response to Chinese exclusion, citizenship considerations figure prominently in African American poetic and fictional texts that engage the U.S. takeover of the Philippines.

Writing at different historical moments and in a variety of genres, U.S. black authors responded to the annexation, pacification, and occupation of the Philippines in texts that express sentiments ranging from outright condemnation to unqualified approbation. African Americans reacted quickly and vehemently to Rudyard Kipling's widely disseminated and highly divisive poem "The White Man's Burden: The United States and the Philippine Islands" (1899), viewing ominously and condemning explicitly or implicitly the takeover of the archipelago. Readers at the time it was published noted the ambiguities of Kipling's poem and questioned whether it unequivocally endorses U.S. colonialism, and recent scholars have as well. African American writers, meanwhile, have consistently interpreted it as and objected to it for endorsing Anglo-Saxon racial hegemony abroad and at home.[1] Several journalists and editors, led by John Edward Bruce and Herbert Theodore Johnson, published parodies of the poem soon after it appeared, and send-ups kept appearing for many years. Eschewing parody in favor of religion and myth, Frances Harper and W. E. B. Du Bois also wrote poems that address "the white man's burden" and the controversies surrounding it. Whereas African American verse responses to Kipling's poem in some cases adopt a stance as unequivocally anti-imperial as Bishop Turner's, fictional texts about the subjugation of the archipelago by Sutton Griggs, Frank R. Steward, James McGirt, and F. Grant Gilmore do not, expressing mixed feelings about or unquestioning support for the Philippine-American War. Fiction depicting African American soldiers participating in the war in the Philippines often uses such military service to highlight black loyalty and patriotism, in some cases portraying Filipinos as bandits whose treachery toward U.S. rule starkly contrasts with black loyalty. A key theme in African American literature with a domestic setting, amalgamation figures significantly in Steward's, McGirt's, and Gilmore's narratives set wholly or partially in the Philippines. As discussed in the previous chapter, *Imperium in Imperio* and *The Hindered Hand* connect the Spanish-Cuban-American War and the empire at home. In his third novel, *Unfettered*, Griggs raises serious concerns about U.S. actions in Philippines and their domestic implications but then withdraws them. Drawing on the author's experiences as an army officer and military judge in the archipelago and featuring a narrator whose status as a white or black man is unspecified, Steward's formally experimental narratives published in the *Colored American Magazine* between September 1902 and October 1903 provide a unique perspective on the interlocking politics of the empire abroad and the empire at home and reveal considerable, if often subtly rendered, ambivalence about African American participation in the takeover of the Philippines and about the status of Filipinos and U.S. blacks as subject peoples. McGirt's short story "In Love as in War" (1907), which takes place entirely in the Philippines, and Gilmore's *The "Problem": A Military Novel* (1915), set partly in the archipelago, do not question the justice of the annexation and pacification of the islands but rather, similar to Cole and Johnson's *The Shoo-Fly Regiment*, use African American military participation in the Philippine-American War to underscore U.S. black manhood, patriotism, heroism, and professionalism and thereby participate in the ongoing campaign to rebut Theodore Roosevelt's published accusations of black cowardice in the Cuban campaign. Unlike much of the U.S. black poetry about the Spanish-Cuban-American War, Griggs's novels, and the African American verse responses to Kipling's "The White Man's Burden," McGirt's and Gilmore's narratives do not question or challenge Jim Crow practices or acknowledge the deteriorating state of relations between U.S. whites and blacks.

Black Men's and Black Women's Burdens: The African American Poetic Response to Kipling

To say that the simultaneous publication of Kipling's "The White Man's Burden: The United States and the Philippine Islands" in *McClure's Magazine* in the United States and the *London Times* in February 1899 created a sensation would be putting things mildly. Consisting of fifty-six three-beat lines divided into abcbdefe stanzas, each beginning with the line "Take up the white man's burden," the poem "circled the earth in a day, and by repetition became hackneyed in a week," in the words of a contemporary observer (qtd. in Harrison 389). Frederic Lawrence Knowles, author of *The Kipling Primer* (1899), stated that it "has probably been more widely read, discussed, and parodied than any other poem of the time" (187). In *Review of Reviews*, William T. Stead described it as "an international document of the first order of importance" (139); however, other Britons were less impressed, including Henry Austin, who dubbed it a "jingo jingle" (Knowles 187). In the United States, the poem reached a readership estimated at more than a million, triggering a voracious public appetite for information about the author that newspapers, journals, and book publishers were only too willing to satisfy (Murphy 23). The *New York Sun* claimed that the bout of pneumonia Kipling suffered in early 1899 generated more "personal anxiety and concern" among Americans than would have been occasioned by the illness of any "living man out of office," a sentiment reflected in a *New York Herald* cartoon entitled "Kipling's Burden" depicting the author seated at a desk surrounded by a sea of papers feverishly trying to "acknowledge the thousands of congratulations upon his recovery" ("Character Sketch" 319, 326). So numerous were the send-ups of Kipling's poem, addressing the plight of everyone from laborers to housewives to U.S. blacks, that one newspaper published a poem parodying all the parodies (Murphy 234).

To many proimperialists and anti-imperialists, the meaning of the phrase "the white man's burden" was clear. Roosevelt, a friend of Kipling, who had received a copy of the poem three months before its official publication and passed it on to his Republican ally Senator Henry Cabot Lodge, thought it made "good sense from the expansion standpoint," although he was skeptical about its literary merits (Brantlinger 172). Writing soon after the poem's appearance, Stead recognized it as a galvanizing document:

> It is a direct appeal to the United States to take up the policy of Expansion. It puts the matter on the highest and most unselfish grounds. The poet has idealized and transfigured Imperialism. He has shown its essence to be not lordship, but service. We can recall no nobler setting forth of the intrinsic *ministry* of empire. The whole presentation is steeped in the spirit of self-abnegation and self-sacrifice. It will be strange if these seven stanzas do not prove more than a match for all the millions and all the eloquence of anti-expansionists like Mr. Carnegie and Mr. Bryan. The poet has taken sure aim, and it is in the conscience of the American people that his bolt will lodge. (139)

Without using the word, Stead suggests that Kipling has created a compelling myth about Anglo-Saxon imperialism in the poem that opponents of expansion will find difficult to respond to effectively. Perhaps not coincidentally, the first installment of Joseph Conrad's *Heart of Darkness* appeared in *Blackwood's Magazine* in the same month that "The White Man's Burden" was published on both sides of the Atlantic. Marlow, the story's primary narrator, like Kipling, attributes a higher, altruistic purpose to Anglo-Saxon imperialism: "The conquest of the earth, which mostly means the taking it away from those who have a different complexion or slightly flatter noses than ourselves, is not a pretty thing when you look into it too much. What redeems it is the idea only. An idea at the back of it, not a sentimental pretence but an idea; and an unselfish belief in an idea—something you can set up, bow down before, and offer a sacrifice to" (196).[2] Although they failed to put forward a competing myth of comparable power, many white opponents of U.S. imperialism regarded Kipling's poem as a proexpansionist text to which they had to respond. Political cartoonists, prose writers, and verse parodists were quick to point out that if anyone bore the weight of empire it was nonwhites.[3] Among the many who lampooned Kipling from an anti-imperialist viewpoint was a young Edgar Rice Burroughs, of all people, who would later author the long series of books about Tarzan. His "The Black Man's Burden: A Parody" appeared in an Idaho newspaper in April 1899 (Blisard). Like their counterparts who promoted an overseas U.S. empire, those who took a stand against it were far from a cohesive unit. Consisting of, among others, southerners fearful of race mixture and the prospect of Filipinos gaining the franchise, Democrats and Republicans alike who objected to overseas expansion on constitutional grounds, and some surviving abolitionists concerned about the rights of Filipinos, this motley group concurred that the United States should not annex the Philippines but agreed on little else.[4]

In contrast to those who were certain of the meaning of the poem, a sizable number of U.S. whites, including prominent author and editor William Dean Howells, did not know how to interpret it, as Gretchen Murphy has noted. The combination of a clarion call to embrace colonialism, on the one hand, and an emphasis on the arduous nature of the imperial mission and the resultant ingratitude of subject peoples, on the other, proved baffling to many. Murphy pinpoints two ambiguities in the poem that troubled U.S. readers. The first concerned the goal of empire: was the purpose of the "white man's burden" to civilize—and in the process eventually democratize—nonwhite peoples or to establish the superiority of Anglo-Saxon civilization? The second had to do with the instability of the definition of whiteness itself (33). Instead of "supporting the linkage between whiteness and American empire," Murphy asserts that Kipling's poem "exacerbated anxieties about the meaning and importance of whiteness for a U.S. global mission" (26–27).

Unlike the U.S. whites who were uncertain how to respond to the poem, African Americans, taking issue primarily with its racial rather than expansionist ramifications, were not. As Patrick Brantlinger remarks, "Unless one wears a white blindfold while reading it, Kipling's 'The White Man's Burden' makes the question of the relationship between imperialism and racism inescapable" (173). Black newspapers and magazines published dozens of parodies in the weeks and months following the appearance of "The White Man's Burden." Some of these openly oppose U.S. expansion, reflecting the tilt against imperialism following the conclusion of the war with Spain. However, similar to Johnson's "The Color Sergeant" and in contrast to the vast majority of white responses, race either takes precedence over empire or becomes the entire focus in most of the African American send-ups of Kipling.

Whereas white poetic rebuttals to Kipling proved to be largely an ephemeral phenomenon, African American poets would signify on Kipling's poem and the concept of the "white man's burden" long after the question of U.S. expansion in the Philippines had been decided.[5] Without ignoring the political and moral considerations that dominate the parodies, Frances Harper and W. E. B. Du Bois turn to Christian doctrine and biblically inspired myth in responding to Kipling's poem. Seizing on the brief reference to divinity late in "The White Man's Burden," several of the African American parodists, including *Christian Recorder* editor Henry Theodore Johnson (the first two stanzas of whose "The Black Man's Burden" serve as the second epigraph to this chapter) assert that God will harshly judge white actions toward nonwhites. Largely eschewing formal parody and deemphasizing politics, Harper makes a plea for interracial Christian fellowship in "The Burdens of All," published in the expanded, 1900 version of *Poems* (in which "Maceo" and "Do Not Cheer, Men Are Dying" also appear). In the densely textured "Burden of Black Women," first published in 1907, Du Bois turns to the resonant, distinctly black Ethiopianist myth to counter Kipling's poem and white racial dominance at home and abroad.

Published in the *Colored American* newspaper on February 25, 1899, John Edward Bruce's "Why Talk of the White Man's Burden?" exhibits key traits found in several of the African American parodies. A noted and prolific journalist (often writing under the pseudonym Bruce Grit), a member of the American Negro Academy, the cofounder with Arturo Alfonso Schomburg of the Negro Society for Historical Research in 1911, and the author of two novels and several polemical tracts, Bruce late in life became a key figure in Marcus Garvey's Universal Negro Improvement Association. In his parody, Bruce uses meter, rhyme, and repetition in a manner that recalls "The White Man's Burden"; however, he repudiates the content of Kipling's poem by stressing the burdens that blacks have borne and by invoking the Bible. Each of its five stanzas raises one or more questions about the notion of "the white man's burden" and the assumption of white racial superiority intrinsic to it. The second asks,

> Why boast of the white man's power
> When the black man's load is heavier,
> And is increasing by the hour? (6–8)

And the third, invoking the beatitudes in Matthew's Gospel, enquires, "Know ye not that the children of meekness / Shall inherit the earth—at length? (11–12). In mocking Kipling's form throughout, decrying the white man's "brutal strength" (10), and identifying his speaker as one of the "victims" of the white man's "power and greed" (19), Bruce takes an implicitly anti-imperial stance; however, unlike much of Bruce's later writing, the poem lacks specific references to empire, making no mention of the Philippines and failing to specify whether "the black man" in the poem refers to U.S. blacks specifically, Africans and members of the African diaspora, or people of color everywhere.[6]

The titles of several of the other African American parodies, including Johnson's "The Black Man's Burden" (March 1899), Black Kansan J. Dallas Bowser's "Take Up the Black Man's Burden" (April 1899), the pseudonymous X-Ray's "Charity Begins at Home" (April 1899), Lulu Baxter Guy's "The Black Man's Burden" (1903), Daniel Webster Davis's "The Black Woman's Burden" (1904), and veteran African American journalist T. Thomas Fortune's "The Black Man's Burden" (1921) indicate the stress they place on domestic race relations. In contrast, Alice Smith-Travers's "The White Man's Burden," devoting nearly equal space to the empire at home and the empire abroad, refers to "burnings at the stake" (4) and "white caps riding in the night" (5) as "crimes" (9) outnumbering

> Those in the foreign Isle,
> Committed by heath[en] people
> "Half devil and half child." (10–12)

The poem asserts that U.S. annexation will not replace "the accursed rule of Spain" (14) with freedom but rather result in "a haughtier nation's reign" (16), one characterized by "the thirst for blood, and greed for gold" (19). A rare U.S. black parody of Kipling to mention Filipinos explicitly, Smith-Travers's "The White Man's Burden," which appeared in the *Indianapolis Freeman* in March 1899, uses domestic race relations to foretell the effects of U.S. rule on the Philippines.

Unlike the parodies of Kipling, Frances Harper's "The Burdens of All" aspires to be a kind of antidote to the divisiveness generated by his poem. Although written for U.S. blacks (and whites) generally, it almost reads as if Harper were addressing those African Americans who had published responses to Kipling, advising them not to fall into the trap of allowing his poem to determine the terms of the debate. Her use of meter, rhyme, and eight-line stanzas compares to Kipling's, but she does not signify on his language. Beyond the use of the colors "white," "black," and "brown" on three occasions to refer to Anglo-Saxons, people of African descent, and Filipinos respectively (implicit nods to racial strife at home and the situation in the Philippines) and the use of the words "burden" or "burdens" six times, the poem does not feature the repetition that characterizes "The White Man's Burden" and most of its parodies. Rather than mimicking Kipling's diction and themes, Harper echoes the phrasing and concerns of U.S. blacks who have attacked him in her references to "slavery" (18), "greed of gold" (23), "lust for power" (23), and "hate" (24). In the poem as a whole, however, she asserts that only by working cooperatively and following Christ's example can members of all races lift the burdens that weigh them down.

As if to say "enough already" to the war of words engendered by Kipling's poem, "The Burdens of All" begins,

> We may sigh o'er the heavy burdens
> Of the black, the brown and white;
> But if we all clasped hands together
> The burdens would be more light. (1–4)

The religious thrust of Harper's poem becomes clear in the next twelve lines, which assert that the solution to "life's saddest problems" (5) lies in the lessons of the "One who suffered / In Palestine long ago" (7–8), whose "precept" (9) to do unto others as you would have them do unto you will show people how "to be merciful and just" (16). She refers to Christ two times (7, 9) and to "God" two others (15, 20) in the first three stanzas, and to the "herald angel's refrain" in the final one, identifying "Peace on earth, good will to men" (31) as the "burden of their [sic] strain" (32). This shift to another meaning of the word "burden" reinforces the argument of the entire poem: people should stop bickering about the "burdens"—in the sense of troubles or heavy loads—that oppress them, Harper advises, and start heeding the "burden"—that is, the theme or the gist—of Christ's teachings revealed in the Gospels. To address and in the process extinguish the firestorm ignited by Kipling's poem, Harper, in a gesture that dates back to Phillis Wheatley and Olaudah Equiano in the eighteenth century, uses Christianity as a source of authority. She counsels people of all races, and U.S. blacks specifically, to turn to the New Testament for guidance in reducing their heavy burdens.

In responding to "The White Man's Burden," Du Bois, like Harper, does not resort to parody; rather, he seeks to oppose Kipling's myth of the imperial mission and Anglo-Saxon superiority with a powerful countermyth of particular resonance for U.S. blacks. In "The Burden of Black Women," published in four distinct versions, Du Bois depicts Africa (and the diaspora) as a woman who has long been suffering under the "burden of white men" but whose resurrection will awaken and transform the entire world.[7] Whereas Harper embraces the golden rule as a means to avoid and transcend interracial conflict, Du Bois invokes Ethiopianism, which entails a cyclical theory of race dominance that at times during its long history has lent itself to African American revenge fantasies.[8] The sixty-four-line, eight-stanza poem can be divided formally and thematically into three major sections, roughly corresponding to the thesis-antithesis-synthesis pattern critics have noted in some of Du Bois's other writings. The first two stanzas, a quatrain comprising two rhyming couplets and a sestet composed of a pair of rhyming triplets, depict Africa (and by extension the diaspora) as a long slumbering woman who has failed to heed the cries for her to awaken because "the Burden of white men bore her back, and the white world stifled her sighs" (10). Here Du Bois reverses Kipling's famous phrase; rather than shouldering the burden of empire, white men become the burden that the black woman must endure in three different ways: they "bore her back" in the sense of weighing down on her, in the sense of penetrating her, and in the sense of returning her to a state of somnolence. This line therefore not only refers to white oppression generally but also alludes to the sexual exploitation of black women in the United States during and subsequent to slavery and to the subjugation of Africa as a result of European colonialism.

In *The Art and Imagination of W. E. B. Du Bois* (1976), Arnold Rampersad describes "The Burden of Black Women" as being unique among the writer's texts for its "intense bitterness toward the white world" (106), an observation amplified by the biographer David Levering Lewis, who claims that in the poem, "Du Bois was carried away by his wrath against white racism into excoriation bordering on the homicidal" (16). These comments clearly relate to the poem's second major section, consisting of four stanzas ranging in length from nine to thirteen lines. The first decries white males—the "dirt" (12) and "scum" (13) of London and New York—as "spoilers of women" (14) and "conquerors of unarmed men" (15), "bearing the White Man's Burden / Of Liquor and Lust and Lies" (20–21). The second expresses a wish for their immediate death:

> I hate them, Christ!
> As I hate hell,
> If I were God
> I'd sound their knell
> This day! (28–32)

In keeping with one of the tenets of Ethiopianism, the third stanza attributes the current high position of whites to achievements stolen from other races and claims that those people currently subjugated will be the means of bringing the whites low once again:

> Who raised the fools to their glory
> But black men of Egypt and Ind?
> Ethiopia's sons of the evening,
> Chaldeans and Yellow Chinese?
> The Hebrew children of Morning
> And mongrels of Rome and Greece?
> Ah well!
> And they that raised the boasters:
> Shall drag them down again. (33–41)

Like its predecessor, the fourth stanza of the poem's middle section enumerates the past and current crimes of the white world that will contribute to its downfall, namely "their cheating of childhood / And drunken orgies of war" (46–47), and then draws on Old Testament and Christian imagery to imagine the means of the black world's awakening. The white world will be brought all the way down to the point at which

> some dim, darker Davad [David] a hoeing of his corn,
> And married maiden, Mother of God,
> Bid the Black Christ be born! (52–54)

Out of the ashes of centuries of exploitation, a miraculous virgin birth will produce a powerful leader personifying the black world's resurrection.

Moving beyond and reconciling the lamentation of the initial section and the bitterness of the second, the final ten lines, consisting of a sestet and a quatrain (and thus mirroring the opening of the poem), offer a glimpse of a harmonious new world free of exploitation, one in which

> the Humble and Simple and Strong
> Shall sing with the Sons of the Morning
> And Daughters of Evensong. (58–60)

In the phrase "the burden of manhood" (55) at the start of the poem's penultimate stanza, Du Bois plays, like Harper, on the double meaning of "burden," referring in this line to the meaning or gist of manhood, rather than its oppression or oppressiveness. Moreover, instead of focusing on the smothering weight of white manhood, as do the first two sections of the poem, the concern is with the newfound significance of manhood generally—"Be it yellow or black or white" (56)—in the era to come. Through its diction and form, the last stanza resembles the poem's opening quatrain. However, whereas the beginning forlornly addresses a "dark daughter" (1) and "wan spirit" (2) affiliated with a long slumbering "world" (4), the closing confidently calls on a "black mother" (61) and "wild spirit" (62) to "thicken the thunders of God's voice and lo! a world awakes!" (64).[9] Moving beyond the despair of the past and the anger of the present, "The Burden of Black Women" looks ahead to the hope of the future.

African Americans responded quickly and vehemently to Kipling's "The White Man's Burden" in a series of parodies that would continue to appear for over two decades. Although some of these verse responses explicitly condemn the takeover of the Philippines and U.S. overseas expansion, others focus on the poem's racism and its implications for U.S. blacks. Frances Harper and W. E. B. Du Bois respond to Kipling in nonparodic poems that draw heavily on religious imagery, the former urging people of all races to embrace Christ's teachings and the latter vividly imagining the resurgence of the black world and the decline of the white.

Interrogating U.S. Military Action in the Philippines: Griggs's *Unfettered* and Steward's Laguna Stories

As discussed in chapter 2, Sutton Griggs explicitly thematizes the prelude to the war with Spain in *Imperium in Imperio* and its aftermath in *The Hindered Hand*.

In an intervening novel, *Unfettered*, he directly links national electoral politics with expansion and compares the status of newly annexed Filipinos to that of U.S. blacks during and after slavery.[10] As in his other novels, Griggs intertwines a romantic plot with a political one. The title refers to Morlene Dalton's availability to marry the protagonist Dorlan Warthell and to the prospect of full emancipation for U.S. blacks. In addition to being highly intelligent, physically attractive individuals deeply concerned about their people's future, Dalton and Warthell have firmly held political beliefs. The former, who asserts her "interest in expansion is broadly humanitarian" (88) and, in a note to the latter, signs herself "THE ARDENT EXPANSIONIST" (121), welcomes the emergence of the United States as an imperialist power in the wake of the conflict with Spain, regarding "our territorial expansion" as "the march of destiny": "I am delighted to see our nation thus move forward, because we have such an elastic form of government, so responsive to the needs and sentiments of the people that bloody revolutions become unnecessary wherever our flag floats" (87). She imagines the United States stretching from Canada to Chile—"When our flag floats over the whole of the Western Hemisphere there will be nobody over here to fight us; we shall dare the European and Asiatic powers to go to war" (87)—and she looks forward to the day when the influence of the red, white, and blue will "extend to the entire earth" (88).

Her would-be husband views U.S. imperialism differently, however, at least initially. After years of ghostwriting highly influential speeches for a white politician, Warthell breaks with the Republican Party over its subjugation of the Philippines, echoing the misgivings of Griggs himself (who, as noted in the introduction, urged readers of the *Indianapolis World* not to support the Republican Party in the election of 1900 because of its Filipino policy). Anticipating Ensal Ellwood's prayer that the United States will continue to be "the pilot of our planet," Warthell fears "that enthusiasm over expansion may cause us to lose sight of fundamental tenets of our political faith" (88). In contrast to Dalton, whose expansionist reverie he characterizes as a "beautiful dream," Warthell expresses serious misgivings about the pacification of the Philippines: "Should our nation impose its will on the Filipinos, by the force of arms without the underlying purpose of ultimately granting them full political liberty, the weaker peoples the world over will lose their only remaining advocate in the white race, namely the people in the North" (89). Linking the empire at home and the empire abroad, he compares the oppression of blacks in the South to two instances of Anglo-Saxon imperial hegemony: the U.S. subjugation of the Philippines and British colonial rule in India (89). At a political gathering where he outlines his proposal for the formation of a new, anti-imperialist political party, Warthell is physically attacked and severely wounded and, as a result, cannot actively take part in the election of 1900.[11] Upon learning of the Republican victory in the contest, Warthell at first laments, "Has our government lent its sanction to the code of international morals that accords the strong the right to rule the weak? Alas! Alas!" (154). However, for reasons that Griggs does not elaborate, Warthell quickly reconciles himself to the Republican victory and comes to embrace Dalton's fervor for expansionism: "Instead of losing its position as the teacher of nations, our government was, he saw, to confirm its title to that proud position. So nobly, so thoroughly, was it to do its work of leading the Filipinos into all the blessings of higher civilization, that other nations in contact with weaker peoples might find here a guide for their nations to follow" (156). In these and other passages, *Unfettered* echoes the many references at the turn of the twentieth century to the contrast (and the struggle) between the stronger nations and the weaker nations, reflecting the widespread influence of racist science and social Darwinism.[12]

At one point in the novel, Griggs indulges in what can only be described as an imperialistic pun. Upon learning that Harry Dalton has died, thus removing what he believes to be the major obstacle to marital union between himself and Morlene, Warthell states as he goes to press his suit for her, "I have a little problem of desired expansion on my own hands, and I fear the government may have to wag along without me the best way it can for a while" (159).[13] However, to win her hand, he learns that he must do nothing short of solving the race question in the United States. Undeterred and conveniently bankrolled by a huge, newly discovered, African-derived legacy, Warthell composes a long treatise designed to do just that, which is appended as a sequel to the novel.[14] Like his main character, Griggs, who had been disappointed with the black community's reception of his first two works of fiction, felt that much was riding on "Dorlan's Plan." As he explains in *The Story of My Struggles*, "Naturally enough, I believed in myself, and as I have stated, I had the greatest faith in my race. But it seemed clear that one or the other of us was wrong. Either I was wrong in expecting support from the race, did not deserve it, or else the race was doing wrong in withholding support. I decided to make a supreme effort to decide that knotty problem. I decided to write another book and put forth all that was in me so that there could be no shadow of doubt where the fault was. It was thus that I wrote 'Unfettered'" (qtd. in Coleman 22). Despite his exertions on the narrative proper and the exhaustive, polemical plan accompanying it, Griggs's third novel was not embraced by African American readers as he hoped it would be.

Among the many things advocated in "Dorlan's Plan," most of which hinge on the establishment of a wealthy and powerful race organization that prefigures to some extent the National Association for the Advancement of Colored People, Warthell calls for educated blacks to go to "Puerto Rico, Cuba, Hawaii, the Philippines, and Africa" so as "to relieve th[e] congestion" of college-trained African Americans in the United States (257), echoing statements made by Wilberforce professor William Sanders Scarborough in the *Southern Workman* in 1900 (Gatewood, *Black*, 296–97). The plan concludes by advocating "the Americanization of the globe" (275), recalling not only Dalton's earlier enthusiasm for aggressive U.S. expansion but also the ideas put forward by the British journalist (and, as already noted, Kipling supporter) William T. Stead in *The Americanization of the World: The Trend of the Twentieth Century* (1901). Thus, in *Unfettered* Griggs raises legitimate concerns about the consequences of expansion both abroad and at home. Yet he ultimately chooses—without adequately explicating his reasons for doing so—to regard the new direction the nation has taken as providing desirable opportunities for African Americans and people in overseas locations that have recently come under U.S. control.

Nearly exact contemporaries, being born in 1872 and dying in the early 1930s, Griggs and Frank R. Steward were the sons of influential clergymen, but whereas the former's father was born into slavery, the latter's hailed from the free black settlement of Gouldtown in southern New Jersey. A graduate of Harvard College and its law school and a friend of Paul Laurence Dunbar, Steward, as noted in the introduction, served as a lieutenant in the Eighth Volunteer Infantry stationed in Cuba shortly after Spain's surrender, was appointed captain in the Forty-Ninth Infantry, a volunteer black regiment that saw considerable action in the Philippines, and worked as well as a military judge in San Pablo in the province of Laguna. Three short stories he published in the *Colored American Magazine* provide insight into not only the divided loyalties of some African Americans participating in the imperial enterprise but also the risks taken by U.S. blacks willing to examine publicly the morality of the empire abroad and contemplate its domestic implications. Appearing during Pauline Hopkins's tenure as an influential editor at the *Colored American Magazine*, these fictions directly engaging the subjugation of the islands may have contributed to her dismissal from the magazine. Hopkins reveals in a 1905 letter to *Boston Guardian* editor William Monroe Trotter (a classmate of Steward's at Harvard) that she was stripped of her editorial duties and eventually fired for her resistance to the demands of the magazine's new financial backers to de-emphasize literature, eliminate anything provocative, and stop running articles "ON THE FILIPINO" (243). The efforts to marginalize Hopkins at the magazine may also explain why Steward published only three of what he might have envi-sioned as a longer series of Laguna stories. Fighting abroad to bolster the cause of citizenship rights at home, Steward did not rebel against the U.S. coloniz-ing mission in the Philippines in the way that a handful of black troops who switched sides did, nor did he remain in the islands, as over a thousand Afri-can American soldiers chose to do when their regiments were ordered home in 1901 (Thompson 105). Nevertheless, brimming with political, moral, racial, ge-neric, and linguistic complexities, his fictions raise thorny questions about the U.S. presence in the archipelago while at the same time offering unique por-trayals of Philippine society, the U.S. military occupation, and men like himself who served as officers in the islands.

"Pepe's Anting-Anting: A Tale of Laguna" and "'Starlik': A Tale of Laguna" feature a racially unmarked protagonist and first-person narrator who serves as a captain in one of the volunteer regiments, similar to Steward himself. In "The Men Who Prey," which is not subtitled "A Tale of Laguna" (although that is its setting), a married, white U.S. Army captain lives with, impregnates, and then abandons a Filipina. In contrast to this final story, which condemns the pro-tagonist's actions, the first two stories do not make clear whether the narrator should be admired as a heroic, masculine, patriotic, cosmopolitan figure wield-ing authority over colonial subjects in need of guidance or criticized for his part in the sexual and colonial oppression suffered by those under his control. Taken as a whole, these fascinating stories identify the indigenous and impe-rial forces that had long oppressed Filipinos and continued to do so under U.S. rule. The first story, about a charm believed to make its wearer impervious to physical harm, appears to indicate the grip that centuries-old native supersti-tions have on much of the population. Hinging on the revelation that a Filipina rejected by the locals who turns to prostituting herself with U.S. soldiers in Manila is the daughter of a Spanish priest, the second story attests to three cen-turies of colonial depredations. Meanwhile, the third story shows that impe-rial sexual exploitation continues as a result of the U.S. occupation. This brief overview fails to do justice to the nuances of these fictions, particularly "Pepe's

Anting-Anting" and "'Starlik.'" In these "tales of Laguna," the narrator at times adopts the pose of an eyewitness expert, addressing the causes of Filipino resistance and offering suggestions for responding to it; however, several factors, including his linguistic deficiencies, naivete, and complicity with the ongoing exploitation of native women, undermine his authority and unsettle the assumptions undergirding the U.S. takeover of the archipelago. Utilizing a different narrative perspective and largely eschewing ambiguity, "The Men Who Prey" lacks the depth of the first two stories. Its depiction of the lax morality and hypocrisy of a white southern U.S. officer overtly connects the empire abroad and the empire at home in a manner that the other two do not.

Steward's stories employ what Reed Way Dasenbrock calls "strategic unintelligibility." In multicultural literature written in English, according to Dasenbrock, "not everything is likely to be wholly understood by every reader. The texts often mirror the misunderstandings and failures of intelligibility in the multicultural situations they depict" (12). Thus, as he goes on to explain in a statement of particular relevance to Steward's fictions, to render a literary text "unintelligible is not to make it unmeaningful: the use of opaque foreign words can be part of a deliberate artistic strategy" (15). As Seiwoong Oh, building on Dasenbrock, puts it, writers "often choose not to translate certain words or contexts so as to force readers outside their cultural boundaries to experience different cultures" (3). In his stories set in the Philippines, Steward bombards readers with words and phrases from a variety of languages—Spanish, English, Tagalog, and a pidgin or creole drawing on all of these—as well as with an array of cultural and religious beliefs, practices, and expectations. In some instances, he translates non-English words and glosses specific Filipino customs and rituals, but in many cases he does not, plunging the reader, by design, into a far from meaningless state of incomprehension. In "Pepe's Anting-Anting," the narrator refers to the "broken patois of Tagalog, Spanish and English" spoken by many of the locals in their dealings with U.S. soldiers as "a gibberish the Army of Occupation has brought about, a spoken tongue forever defying press or pen" (360). Unfamiliar with indigenous languages and armed with the rudimentary Spanish he learned at Harvard, which enables him to understand simple words and phrases and polite discourse but not the "Spanish idiom" spoken by the locals, he regards himself, at times, as being inadequate to the task of interpreter. Each of the first two stories, moreover, features at least one language lesson conducted mainly in Spanish in which a Filipina learns a bit of English and the narrator acquires a smattering of Tagalog. In these scenes the authoritative, foreign male and the obeisant, native woman typically conform to roles reflecting the dynamics of the occupation, even when he does the learning and she the teaching. The emphasis placed on efforts—successful and unsuccessful—to translate the words or mores of one language or culture into another perfectly suits these stories in which U.S. officers often misread Filipino intentions, actions, and loyalties.

"Pepe's Anting-Anting" contrasts a scientific cause for the death of an attractive, young Filipina with a pair of nonrational explanations, one of which the narrator himself appears to proffer as the accurate one. In doing so, the opening story presents the U.S. captain as a somewhat naive romantic rather than as a rational expert completely aloof from superstitious and devout Filipinos. The story begins with the narrator's description of the beauty of the teenaged Chata (whose looks, the "Despair of the West," cause him to "wince"), followed by a sexually charged language lesson. She utters a series of words in Tagalog and he, using his phrasebook, tells her the English equivalent—"man," "woman," "good," "evil." Then he boldly takes the lead with the word "sweetheart" (359). Her eagerness to learn not only English but "everything American" has earned her the scorn of the locals. Having observed not only this but also the bond between Chata and Pepe, who works as a clerk in the local U.S. Army headquarters, the narrator remains somewhat skeptical about the pretty girl's enthusiasm generally and the attention she has shown to him specifically. Unlike the local commanding officer, who expresses shock upon learning that the seemingly loyal Pepe has become part of the local band of insurgents, the narrator is not surprised, having been informed by the washerwoman Flora, whose *bata* (daughter) has been spying on the lovers, that Chata made an *anting-anting* for Pepe and that she sought to have it blessed by the Virgin Mary in the local church before he left to join the rebels. Shaped like a prayer book and filled with mysterious writing in an unspecified indigenous language, the amulet is explicitly related to the Catholic catechism (written in Spanish) followed by religious Filipinos and implicitly linked to the narrator's phrase book (written in English) with which he tries to make sense of the local argot.

Steward's initial Laguna story depicts efforts to interpret not only the significance of the *anting-anting* but also the demise of its maker Chata, who is buried with it one week after Pepe is killed along with other insurrectionists. The closing paragraphs offer more than one explanation for the girl's passing:

"Look see! Captain, look see!" I followed the hag's long finger, and saw about the dead girl's neck the silken string, and on her breast the little yellow book that looked to the bata like the catechism for the niñas in the school of the first teaching, but the corners were spattered red and I knew Pepe's Anting-Anting. Surely the affront to the Virgin was appeased!

When I looked up Flora had fallen to telling her beads, and praying and crossing herself.

The mourners thronged about the bier were groaning "probrecita! probrecita!" and lamenting that the dread paludissing had carried off another victim. But old Flora, the buyo-chewing hag of Calle Conception knew better.

So did I. (362)

Dismissing a scientific cause for the untimely death ("the dread paludissing," i.e., malaria), the sanctimonious Flora attributes it to Chata's sacrilegious act of bringing the indigenous, pagan charm into the church for Mary to bless (and thereby creating a threatening, hybrid object). At first glance, the narrator may appear to be agreeing with the laundress here; however, particularly in light of the attention the presumably Protestant U.S. captain has given to the relationship between Pepe and the girl, it is more likely that he rejects this reading of the situation by a strict Catholic. In doing so, however, he does not attribute the cause of death to malaria; rather, he seems to be hinting at a third interpretation—that Chata has died of a broken heart. In distancing himself from a rational interpretation and advancing a romantic one, the narrator unwittingly undermines the pose of a highly educated expert, free from the superstitions of the people over whom he rules, that he has attempted to construct for himself.

Through the second story's title, a "word in the native vernacular" (388), Steward underscores the theme of (mis)translation and (mis)understanding. Flora tells the narrator that Enriqueta, a Filipina who can speak English, has arrived in the vicinity, describing the young woman dismissively with the term "Starlik." Unable to offer a Spanish or English equivalent for this epithet, the washerwoman imitates the gestures, movements, and expressions of a snob, eliciting a laugh and a rather awkward English translation—"airish" (388)— from the U.S. captain. Learning that her father is a source of embarrassment for the beautiful young woman, the narrator assumes this man has joined the rebels, only to find out later that she, in the "lingo" of Flora, "Esta pickaninny de frailes!" In other words, as he goes on, in this instance, to translate and contextualize, "Enriqueta was the daughter of a hated friar! . . . It was an old story, which had come to me in painful iteration everywhere I travelled in the Philippines. This time it was Father Sebastian, the Augustinian curate of an interior town in Batangas, with the comely Conception . . . as the victim of the holy man's lust" (390). A denunciation of the continued presence of the "friars" in the country that takes up twenty-eight lines—roughly 15 percent of the story—follows.

Especially given the space accorded to it, the narrator's contentions that these priests, rather than the U.S. annexation and occupation, bear primary responsibility for Filipino discontent and that thus these men must be expelled from the islands appear to constitute the message of the story. However, certain things mitigate such a reading. The Laguna stories take some pains to demonstrate that, despite his self-acknowledged Harvard education, the narrator often fails to grasp fully all of the factors operative in any situation involving Filipinos. Moreover, rather than depicting the narrator—and U.S. soldiers generally—occupying the moral higher ground vis-a-vis the "hated" friars, "'Starlik'" suggests they may be equivalent. The narrator characterizes his questioning of the striking, half-Filipino, half-Spanish woman distrusted by the locals with the word "catechise" (389), diction that subtly links the smitten U.S. officer to the lustful priests he denounces, as does his resolve to "penetrate the mystery" connected with the young woman (390). In addition, it is likely he, as post *comandente*, who writes the "pass" allowing Enriqueta to travel to Manila where her knowledge of English proves useful as she services members of the Army of the Occupation.

In "The Men Who Prey," the protagonist, a white captain, and the narrator, whose race is not identified, are not identical, obviating the dramatic irony and narrative blind spots that make the first two stories so intriguing. Moreover, by not placing as much emphasis on language, (mis)comprehension plays less of a role in this story. Precisely because it identifies the race of the protagonist, as Gretchen Murphy points out (117), Steward's third Laguna tale clearly connects the empire abroad and the empire at home by revealing that the pattern of colonial sexual exploitation resulting in mixed-race offspring does not end with the departure of the Spaniards but flourishes during the U.S. occupation. If, as Murphy asserts, the title character of "'Starlik'" represents "a new version of the tragic mulatta" (109), Jacinta in the third story must be read in connection with this staple of U.S. fiction as well. A pretty, young laundress who enters into a long-term sexual liaison with Captain Duncan Lane, she finds herself abandoned in the late stages of pregnancy by her white lover when his tour of duty in the Philippines ends. Adding further insult and irony, we are informed that, upon his arrival in San Francisco, he will be met by his family, including a young daughter he has not yet seen whom his wife, at his suggestion, has christened Jacinta.

In contrast to the ambivalent, nuanced "Pepe's Anting-Anting" and "'Starlik,'" which present the narrator-protagonist as somewhat naive and unwittingly complicit, Steward's third story openly denounces the main character, a white U.S. captain, resorting to sarcasm at times to do so. Referring to him as "the fondest of fathers and most devoted of husbands" (722–23), the narrator depicts Lane availing himself of the "charms" of Jacinta immediately after writing "an epistle brimming with love and tenderness and pride" to his white wife back in Texas (723). Describing how Jacinta faints and a midwife is summoned to attend to her shortly after Lane departs, the tale's conclusion begins with the following sarcastic passage: "What boots it that a Filipino leaning against a post at the Anda wharf, swoons and falls in a heap just as the launch with the officers of the —— Infantry pulls off for the transport? May days are fiercely hot in the tropics; even gugus are known to succumb sometimes" (723).[15] Murphy refers to the narrator's "callous disregard of suffering" in the story's closing paragraphs, which she links to the white protagonist's heartlessness (116). Although I would not go so far as to connect the narrator with Lane, the ending of the story does reveal the former to be more concerned about exposing the sexual exploitation and hypocrisy of the latter than in sympathizing with the plight of his Filipino victim.

Whereas the texts examined in this book that feature African American soldiers typically refrain from openly questioning U.S. expansion, those that lack black fighting men tend to be the ones that criticize or denounce the empire abroad. Steward's final story can be seen as conforming to this pattern. He does not identify the race of the narrator-protagonist of the first two stories—who may also be the narrator of "The Men Who Prey"—but, given the links between this character and the author (both are Harvard-educated captains in the Army of Occupation), readers of the *Colored American Magazine* may have assumed this character is black. In contrast to the first two Laguna stories, which subtly raise questions about the U.S. military presence in the Philippines, "The Men Who Prey," featuring a white U.S. Army captain who sexually exploits and abandons a pregnant Filipina without giving the matter a second thought, adopts an explicitly condemnatory stance.

The Role of the Philippines in McGirt's and Gilmore's "Citizen Tom" Narratives

As noted in the preceding chapter, Stephen Knadler asserts that in the wake of the war against Spain, Washington and other black leaders "drew on a long history of romantic racist imagery," from Stowe's *Uncle Tom's Cabin* to Page's plantation fiction, "to portray African Americans as patriotic 'Citizen Toms.'" As flag-waving rituals reached a peak in part as a response to the increasing number of immigrants, the figure of the loyal and obedient "Citizen Tom," Knadler argues, made U.S. black participation in the era's "sentimental patriotism" possible (*Remapping* 144). Given their support for expansion abroad and their refusal to challenge assaults on African American citizenship rights at home, James McGirt's short story "In Love as in War" and F. Grant Gilmore's *The "Problem": A Military Novel* might well be dubbed "Citizen Tom" narratives. In contrast to the explicit or implicit condemnation of U.S. imperialism in the vast majority of the African American verse responses to Kipling's poem, the reservations expressed about the U.S. takeover of the Philippines in Griggs's *Unfettered*, the highly nuanced ambivalence about the occupation of the islands in Steward's "Pepe's Anting-Anting" and "'Starlik'" and the more explicit denunciation in "The Men Who Prey," these texts question neither the annexation of the islands nor the methods employed by the U.S. military in the Philippine-American War and its aftermath.

The furor generated by the *Atlanta Constitution*'s account of Bishop Turner's repetition of his "dirty rag" comment in a domestic rather than an imperial context may be relevant here. In a February 16, 1906, article, the newspaper reported that Turner, speaking to a black audience in Macon, declared in relation to white mob violence, "I used to love what I thought was the grand old flag and sing with ecstasy about the Stars and Stripes, but to the negro in this country the American flag is a dirty and contemptible rag. Not a star in it can a colored man claim, for it is no longer the symbol of our manhood, rights and liberty," to which he was quoted as adding, "without multiplying words, I wish to say that hell is an improvement upon the United States when the negro is involved" ("He Prefers"). Charges of treason were leveled against Turner; he sent a letter to the editor of the *Constitution* clarifying and contextualizing his statement; and a concerned President Roosevelt wrote to Booker T. Washington about the matter. Responding to a letter from the "Wizard of Tuskegee," who told Roosevelt the bishop must have been misquoted, Turner expressed gratitude for Washington's "voluntary explanation to the President, U.S.A.," defiantly adding that if arrested, he would "be able to prove forty times more treason perpetrated against my race under the shadow of the United States flag" than they could "establish against me" ("The American Flag" 198).[16] The controversy suggests that doubts about U.S. black loyalty following the official conclusion of the Philippine war in 1902—and particularly in the wake of the 1906 Brownsville incident, which resulted in the dismissal of over a hundred black soldiers, many of whom had served abroad—may account in part for the existence of these "Citizen Tom" narratives.

Setting their stories in the archipelago because the existence of an overseas empire makes it possible for them to do so, McGirt and Gilmore use locations abroad as fictive spaces where they can imagine U.S. black males achieving not merely equality with but temporary superiority over privileged southern white men in a manner impossible at home. Each makes the mythic figure of the black sergeant who saved the day in Cuba the protagonist of a story in which he competes with a white officer for the affections of a beautiful nonwhite woman. In the process, these "Citizen Tom" narratives adopt a compromised political position vis-à-vis the empire at home. In the words of Jennifer C. James in *A Freedom Bought with Blood*, although they utilize "the Pacific and the Caribbean, the imperial 'elsewhere,'" as places "for imagining black masculinity apart from the stereotypes dominating the national consciousness," such fictions also demonstrate that "the need to imagine the military and imperialism as creating zones of egalitarianism" prevented some U.S. blacks "from connecting what African Americans were experiencing domestically to the violence people of color abroad were being subjected to at the hands of U.S. troops" (163). I would add that, particularly in the case of Gilmore, the unwillingness to address, much less openly challenge, Jim Crow practices at home and abroad for fear of diluting their portrayal of African American patriotism, discipline, and obedience has notable generic and narrative implications. Similar to fiction set in the United States, these texts thematize miscegenation and, in the case of *The "Problem*," the threat of incest. Whereas McGirt draws on the imperialist adventure tale to produce a fantasy in which the hero wins a wealthy Filipina princess, Gilmore turns to the conventions of domestic sentimentalism, writing what he, in the preface, categorizes as a "romantic novel" in which the overriding mystery concerns the ancestry of the central, U.S.-born female figure.

As he does in his poems that refer to the war with Spain, in his short story set in the Philippines McGirt approves of U.S. expansion and uses military service abroad to highlight black manhood and patriotism. Foregrounding the narrative in African American loyalty to the nation, the narrator claims that "In Love as in War" was inspired by a statement by a U.S. Army general, which emphasized "one thing as characteristic of the Negro, and that was his obedience to his superior officers" (63)—almost certainly a reference to the passage in Major-General Joseph Wheeler's introduction to Herschel V. Cashin's et al. *Under Fire with the Tenth U.S. Cavalry*, which invokes Thomas Nelson Page's "Marse Chan." The narrator states that the Filipinos greet his company, "which led the famous charge up San Juan Hill and won the day" (64), as celebrities, not enemies. They become "the talk of the natives in all the surrounding villages" and the subject of numerous accounts in "native papers" (64); moreover, he asserts they have been sent to the archipelago shortly after the Cuban victory in order to "quiet some trouble with the natives" (64), language that reflects the U.S. government's attempts to downplay the Philippine-American War as a limited military action to quell an "insurrection" led by a group of "rebels" rather than a large-scale land campaign.

The imperial setting, moreover, enables the author to incorporate a frankly sexual dimension unimaginable in a U.S. domestic context into the story. McGirt depicts the women of the Philippines as eager to gaze on U.S. black soldiers and as being sexually available to them: "The Filipinos are a nation who naturally admire heroism and dare-deviltry in war, so when it was known on the island that this famous company had landed on its shores, the Filipino women, both high and low, began to flock around the camp, that they might see and know these men" (65). As the soldiers parade on "Review Day," well-dressed "ladies" with opera glasses accompanied by servants as well as several women "of the ordinary class" gather to watch the drill. The protagonist of the story, Sergeant Roberts, attracts the most attention because of his appearance and his reputation for bravery. Described as "a tall, dark, brown skin man, about six feet in height" (65), the sergeant becomes the center of attention not only for his physical presence but also his fame gained in ignoring orders to retreat and leading his company in the "dash" up San Juan Hill (67). Attractive to the members of the opposite sex in this imperial location because rather than in spite of his color, Roberts causes a near stampede among the native women who stumble over the white commissioned officers in pursuit of "the privilege of honoring this war demon, 'Sarge,' if only to kiss his hand" (66). Because doing so would reinforce stereotypes about the voracious sexual appetites and lax morals among African American men and women, McGirt does not portray either black or white U.S. women fawning over Roberts in such a manner. However, the existence of an overseas colony makes it possible for him to present Filipino women in a way that heightens African American virility without impugning the chastity of U.S. black women or threatening to violate the taboo of sexual union between African American men and white women.

McGirt takes the fantasy even further by portraying a contest between Roberts and Lieutenant Vaughn, "a graduate of West Point and a scion of one of New Orleans' most blue-blooded families" (68). The men vie for the favor of "Princess Quinaldo, acknowledged as the Queen of the Island, both by right of beauty and wealth" (67), who "was closely related to one of the present rulers on the throne to-day and who had inherited more than a million in her own right, to say nothing of lands and cattle" (68). McGirt does not identify the specific island or ruler in question, nor does he explain the suggestively named Quinaldo's royal title; rather, he simply presents her as the most desirable prize the Philippines has to offer: a rich, propertied, pedigreed, seductive, exotic, and highly available beauty just waiting to be taken. After the parade, as the elite women speak with the white officers and "the middle class native women" mingle with the black soldiers (68), Quinaldo asks Vaughn to introduce her to "Sarge," and during the ensuing interview she slips Roberts an invitation to a reception. In response to his letter of regret, he receives a perfumed love note appointing a time for them to meet. Alone with her for the first time, "Sarge" further enraptures the "infatuated, love stricken princess" (70) through his eloquent recounting of his "hair-breadth escapes" (71) in the West and Cuba, to which she, in another echo of *Othello*, replies, "Brave! wonderfully brave!" (71). When a jealous Vaughn interrupts them, asserting his superior rank and "blood" vis-à-vis Roberts, claiming that Quinaldo's behavior with "Sarge" has been insulting to him "and to all Americans of the company" (73) and demanding that she choose between them, her decision is a foregone conclusion. The only suspense concerns whether the sergeant will face disciplinary proceedings for insisting that his superior officer stop making such statements.

As if to mitigate the black sergeant's hypersexualized portrayal earlier, McGirt depicts the protagonist as a model of restraint, obedience, and decorum at the story's conclusion. He not only requests that his captain take his weapons from him and place him under guard to prevent any further trouble with the lieutenant but, in contrast to Vaughn who dismisses his defeat with the transparent falsehood that he never entertained serious feelings for the princess because of the taint of miscegenation, Robert secures "sanction from the priest for their union in wedlock at a very early date" (75). The final lines offer a portrait of marital bliss between an interracial couple in an imperial setting that nonetheless evokes U.S. domesticity. Given that they are described as "living happily, man and wife" three weeks later (76), they likely make their home in the Philippines; however, the reference to a framed commendation for bravery in their "parlor" (76) suggests a U.S.-style domicile—rather than an opulent palace (or a more humble native dwelling)—and, by extension, conventional, stateside morality and values. A significant number of black soldiers chose to remain in the Philippines and, as noted in chapter 2, proposals to ship large numbers of U.S. blacks to the archipelago were advanced by racist southern whites and by prominent African American figures, including journalist T. Thomas Fortune and educator William Saunders Scarborough. In sum, McGirt's story offers African American men a threefold fantasy. First, appropriating the mythic figure of the heroic black sergeant, it portrays the black fighting man as irresistible to the exotic women of the Philippines. Second, following the outlines of the colonial adventure tale (with its frequent depiction of a man from the West securing foreign spoils because of his superior qualities), it vividly portrays the opportunities said to be available to U.S. blacks in the nation's newly acquired overseas possessions. Third, it suggests that all of this—that is, virility, wealth, personal fulfillment—is available in a location where, on the one hand, white privilege does not always triumph and where, on the other, U.S. values to which many African Americans subscribe hold sway.

Like McGirt, Gilmore expresses no reservations about U.S. expansion abroad or Jim Crow practices at home and portrays a black sergeant as part of a love triangle involving a southern white officer and a nonwhite woman.[17] Whereas McGirt locates "In Love as in War" entirely in the Philippines, enabling him to produce a fantasy about sexual and economic opportunities available to black men in the empire overseas, Gilmore sets a few early scenes in Cuba and the Philippines and the rest in the United States, structuring his text, as earlier writers do, around a contrast between African American loyalty, bravery, and restraint, on the one hand, and southern white betrayal and licentiousness, on the other. Using the war against Spain in the Caribbean as the means to highlight African American valor, he makes the heroic black sergeant and the intrepid white colonel equally mythic figures; meanwhile, by depicting Filipino soldiers as a band of outlaws rather than an opposing army, he associates the islands with disloyalty to the United States and thus the antithesis of the fidelity epitomized by black soldiers whose service to the nation he makes the subject of a separate chapter unrelated to the novel's plotline. Although he appears to want to signal that the black sergeant's exposure of his white southern rival's treason ushers in a sea change in relations between the races, Gilmore's refusal to confront domestic racial injustice in the years following the wars in Cuba and the Philippines results in a highly problematic conclusion.

Describing the Cuban campaign as a "war for the elimination of despotism and tyranny" (17), Gilmore recounts the Battle of San Juan Hill twice in *The "Problem"* to establish the courage and competence of the African American protagonist, Sergeant Henderson. In the process, he produces, in the words of James Robert Payne, "one of the fullest presentations in American literature of the motif of the heroic Black sergeant, thereby reinforcing an Afro-American supplement to the mainstream American myth of the Rough Riders" (29). To do so, he creates the white Colonel Roswell, who leads a band of "roughriders" (17). Without question, the depiction of this character entails what Jennifer James terms a "diminishment" (161) of the historical person Theodore Roosevelt, as Roswell remains a soldier throughout the story and at one point weeps over Henderson's legal troubles. However, unlike Roosevelt himself, who sought to minimize the contributions of black soldiers in his written accounts of the famous battle, Gilmore seeks not to emasculate the storied figure of the white colonel but rather to depict Henderson as his equal in potency. Brimming with patriotism and, especially in the case of Roswell, impetuosity, each man leads an attack on Spanish forces without receiving orders to do so. In the narrator's version, as the outnumbered roughriders are "being cut down and their fearless leader, with his remaining comrades [stands] in danger of complete annihilation," Henderson "dashe[s] forth followed by his true heroic comrades," shouts out, "Hold your own, Colonel; we're coming," and turns certain defeat into stunning victory (20). Shortly thereafter, General Funston, a character based very loosely on the historical person of the same name, who in the novel serves as the commander of U.S. forces in Cuba and the Philippines, offers an additional account of the battle that reinforces Henderson's bravery and his equivalence to Roswell (as well as serving to awaken a desire for life in the narrative's female protagonist): "I saw the Colonel, sabre in hand, fighting like mad. Around him, on every side, were Spaniards; his men dropping here and there. When out from the smoke and muskets I saw Henderson, sword in hand, cutting to the right and to the left. . . . I saw the color bearer shot down, and I heard the groans of the wounded; when over the prostrate forms of his own brave men Henderson plunged, and I heard his voice, clear and distinct, shouting 'Charge!' and mid the shots of enemies' rifles he reached the Colonel's side, followed by his brave comrades. They gained the hill and saved the day" (22). Brandishing phallic weapons—but not the revolver that figures so prominently in Roosevelt's disputed account—as many of the men they lead fall around them, Roswell and Henderson unite to fight side by side and secure the U.S. triumph.

If, as Amy Kaplan argues, Roosevelt in the *Scribner's* article sought to mitigate the image of white and black U.S. troops fighting side by side that challenged Anglo-Saxon superiority, Gilmore in this passage reintegrates the battlefield. He makes the black sergeant an equal partner of the white colonel on San Juan Hill yet offers no challenge to the racial hierarchy away from the scene of battle. Seriously wounded in rescuing Roswell, Henderson is nursed back to health by Freda Waters, a fair-skinned beauty of unknown parentage who has come to the Caribbean with the Red Cross. Accompanied and closely monitored by her would-be husband, army surgeon Fairfax, in whose wealthy white Virginia family she has grown to maturity, the previously phlegmatic Freda begins to develop feelings for Henderson during the sergeant's recuperation. After observing the love growing between this "Desdemona" and "Othello" (25), the jealous Fairfax betrays his Hippocratic oath and his country by poisoning his fellow U.S. soldier; however, Henderson's "indomitable, physical and mental construction" (27) enables him to survive. Attesting to his restraint and Washingtonian sense of his place, Henderson makes no attempt either while abroad or at home to act on the strong emotions the apparently white Freda stirs in him. He repeatedly asserts that he has committed himself to his country, going so far as to state late in the narrative, "I will marry my first love, the only love I ever knew, 'To fight for the glory of the Stars and Stripes'" (78).

Whereas the scenes set in Cuba stress African American bravery and patriotism, those set in the Philippines highlight the opposite: cowardice and treason. Mischaracterizing the Filipino people and minimizing the scope, ferocity, and devastation of the Philippine-American War, Gilmore describes the archipelago as a land of "barbarism," "idolatry," and illiteracy, reduces Emilio Aquinaldo to the status of a "bandit chieftain" (29–30), and asserts that the role of the U.S. military in the islands primarily entails the rooting out of "cowardly assassins" responsible for "numerous depredations against life and property" (58). All of this has the effect of rendering Filipinos as, at best, uncivilized nonwhites requiring strict discipline and, at worst, willfully disloyal subjects of the new U.S. empire meriting severe punishment—a portrayal very much in keeping with the "new-caught sullen peoples / Half-devil and half-child" of Kipling's "The White Man's Burden" (7–8). When the new conflict brings the soldier Henderson, the nurse Freda, and the physician Fairfax to the islands, Fairfax, determined to eliminate his rival once and for all, flaunts the oath he "had sworn to be true to his flag and country" (59) by enlisting the help of Pinto, the Filipino guerrilla leader, in a plot to ambush Henderson: "In the gleam of moonlight these two arch conspirators bonded themselves for the death of an innocent hero, whose whole thought was to do his duty for the glory of his country" (61). The language of this passage, coupled with the fact that Fairfax disguises himself in the attack as a Filipino (likely darkening his face in the process), not only underscores the magnitude of the southerner's betrayal of his country but suggests that he commits what amounts to a symbolic act of amalgamation. Henderson's physical prowess and professional competence ensuring his survival, he divests Fairfax of his engraved sword, an obvious symbol of his manhood, acquiring thereby proof of the surgeon's treason; however, for Freda's sake he does not divulge the identity of his would-be assassin to Funston.

To ensure that readers do not miss the emphasis he wishes to place on African American patriotism and loyalty—the polar opposite of white southern betrayal—Gilmore interrupts the plot with a brief history of U.S. black military service. Chapter 6 includes references to Crispus Attucks, who struck "the first blow for freedom" in the Revolutionary War (63); black fighting men, who "were conspicuous in the battles of New Orleans and Lake Erie" in the War of 1812 (63); "William Carney of the 54th Massachusetts, [who] though wounded in the head, shoulder, and in both legs, carried the national flag of his regiment," refusing to allow it to touch the ground (64); the "negro soldier who hauled down the Confederate flag" (64) at the fall of Richmond; and, through a long poem entitled "The Troopers of the Ninth U. S. Cavalry" attributed to J. S. Slater that is quoted in full (65–70), the actions of the Buffalo Soldiers against Native Americans in the western United States. Whereas James reads the chapter as "a particularly messy narrative moment" of "invasive discourse" that amounts to a "military occupation" of the narrative (152), Payne argues that it is "keyed to the novelist's essential themes and concerns including the central drama of the Fairfax-Henderson rivalry," a conflict that "recapitulates in fictional form the American tradition of Black soldiers versus traitorous Southerners, as when black troops captured the Confederate capital and hauled down the rebel flag" (30). Like the authors of several of the African American poems about the Spanish-Cuban-American War discussed in chapter 1, Gilmore situates the U.S. black soldiers who fought in Cuba and the Philippines at one end of a continuum of loyal African American military service. Having fought native peoples in the U.S. West, distinguished himself in Cuba, volunteered for dangerous scouting missions in the campaign against "bandits" in the Philippines, and respected the color line at home and abroad, Henderson represents the latest generation of African American soldiers who have bravely and obediently risked their lives for their country.

A summons from Amanda Williams, an African American woman near death who was her nursemaid, enables Freda to escape temporarily from Fairfax whom she has consented to marry out of a sense of duty. At Williams's cottage she is visited by Funston who has learned of not only Fairfax's treason but also Mrs. Fairfax's withholding of a legacy of $10,000 that her deceased husband, Colonel Fairfax, intended for Freda. Coincidentally, Henderson has also journeyed to the cottage to tell Freda of the attack on him in the Philippines. He stays on to protect her from Fairfax but once again refuses to enter into a relationship with her because it would transgress the color line. When Fairfax arrives in order to bring Freda home and to arrest Henderson on an old charge of trespassing, the sergeant turns the tables by accusing the surgeon of treason, producing the engraved sword and Pinto's confession about the conspiracy. Confidently asserting his physical and moral superiority, he offers Fairfax the choice between immediate arrest or a duel the next morning, stating,

> I have no fear as to the result, for one so despicable, who will sell the birthright of his country to a hostile tribe, cannot hope for success in an equal conflict. If you fail to meet me I will haunt you to the four ends of the earth that you may be brought before proper authorities, court-martialed, and shot down like a dog that you are. You need not restrain him, officers, he's before his master now. (81)

This key passage reverses the imagery used in white writing to consign African American soldiers to abject subservience. Not only does it position a loyal black army regular as the "master" vis-à-vis a disloyal white officer but, in opposition to the texts by Richard Harding Davis and Thomas Nelson Page that associate blacks with faithful watchdogs, it relegates Fairfax to the status of a whipped cur.[18] Moreover, very much in keeping with the portrayal of Filipinos earlier in the novel, Henderson here links the islanders to the Native Americans against whom he likewise fought in service to his country. Sometime later, when Fairfax, about to be taken away on treason charges, appeals for mercy to the man he has remorselessly plotted to destroy, Henderson utters the words "may God in His infinite grace forgive him as I forgive" (90), rips up the confession, and breaks the incriminating sword in two. By depicting the black sergeant absolving the southern officer of his transgressions in a Christ-like manner, Gilmore adds an openly religious dimension to his hagiographic portrayal of Henderson.

Returning to the days of Reconstruction, the starting point of story, the final chapters significantly expand the novel's depiction of southern betrayal and lawlessness—associated twice in the novel with the words "the sins of the fathers visited upon the children unto the third and fourth generation" (52–53). Learning of the imminent marriage, Amanda breaks her silence about Freda's parentage to prevent the "greater wrong" of incest (83). As the narrator explains in the conclusion, Colonel Fairfax, grossly abusing his role as benefactor to the family of his recently deceased friend and business associate Hezekiah Williams, repeatedly raped Williams's daughter Amanda, resulting in the birth of a light-skinned baby girl. Taking Freda from her mother when the child had reached the age of five, the colonel brought the girl into his own home, declaring her to be an orphan. In doing so, he recreated the plantation dynamic by placing his illegitimate African-descent daughter in the same home with his legitimate white son. Despite the privileges she may enjoy, Freda's position in the Fairfax home recapitulates that of a slave; (secretly) black and illegitimate, unable to leave, chosen as a "playmate" (7) for Fairfax whom she must marry (and thus have sexual relations with), Freda leads a zombie-like existence in the Fairfax household while retaining happy memories of her time with her (unrecognized) mother, Amanda. The elder Fairfax's military title and Virginia home—he is identified on the first page as being "of Richmond, Va." (5)—associate him with another traitorous action, the South's attempt to break up the union in the Civil War. Thus, over the course of the novel, Gilmore opposes a pattern of white southern betrayal that spans generations with U.S. black military service running from the eighteenth to the twentieth century, as well as contrasting the wantonness of the former with the restraint of the latter, so as to underscore African American patriotism, discipline, and loyalty.

Reflective of the "generic tension" between realism and romanticism James sees as operative throughout the novel (152), the abrupt, awkward, gap-filled ending of the story is designed to reinforce the novel's portrait of U.S. blacks as loyal citizens willing to die for their country and posing no threat to white dominance in Jim Crow U.S. society. The closing pages of The "Problem" diverge from the conclusions of the vast majority of the nineteenth- and early twentieth-century narratives culminating in the revelation of hidden black ancestry. Rather than being reduced to a tragic mulatta, Freda embraces the news that she is Amanda's child, which enables her to pursue her heart's desire for the first time. Ending with a total of three impending marriages, Gilmore's novel also differs from turn-of-the-twentieth-century African American historical romances, whose open-ended conclusions, as Carla Peterson has noted in "Commemorative Ceremonies and Invented Traditions: History, Memory, and Modernity in the 'New Negro' Novel of the Nadir," indicate their skepticism about resolution. In keeping with the narrative's refusal to breach the barriers that structure early twentieth-century U.S. society, each of these unions brings together people of the same race and caste—the upper-class white characters Funston and Mrs. Fairfax; the "dark lovers" (79) Pete, Funston's faithful, dialect-speaking black servant, and Quito, the widow of a Cuban soldier; and the heroic black sergeant Henderson and the newly revealed mixed-race woman, Freda.

Gilmore must tack on this brief, happy ending because taking the story into the present would force him to acknowledge, first, the ongoing violence toward and dispossession of African Americans on the part of whites North and South, which would underscore the huge disparity between the Jim Crow–era United States and "the place where there is no race, no creed, no color" that he looks forward to in his preface, and, second, just how limited the opportunities empire has provided for black soldiers have proven to be. Through the breaking of the engraved Fairfax sword, the symbol of generations of murder, robbery, and sexual exploitation perpetrated on African Americans, Gilmore wishes to posit that the legacy of slavery has finally come to an end; meanwhile, by means of Henderson's actions in Cuba and the Philippines, he seeks to demonstrate that U.S. black military loyalty dating back to before the Revolutionary War has remained constant if not intensified in the era of U.S. overseas expansion. However, in 1915, the year he published the book, the opposite was closer to the truth. As practices such as lynching, disenfranchisement, peonage, and concubinage continued unchecked, enthusiasm for expansion, or more precisely U.S. imperial war—the means, the novel contends, for African American men to establish their bravery and loyalty and thereby obtain recognition—waned after 1902, the declared end of the Philippine-American War. With many fewer Filipinos—and no more Native Americans and Spaniards—left to face in battle, U.S. black troops were no longer needed to fight expansionist wars. Just as many African American soldiers faced harassment and violence en route to and from Cuba, when the black regulars returned from the Philippines and were stationed on U.S. soil they were greeted with hostility by white communities. The result was a series of incidents, the most prominent in Brownsville, Texas, but there were others in Kansas and Oklahoma, which led to all of the black regiments being shipped to the archipelago by the end of 1907 to get them out of the United States as a consequence of what the *New York Times* termed the "recent outbreak of lawlessness among them" ("All Negro"). Far from serving as a site where African American troops could demonstrate their discipline, patriotism, and bravery, the Philippines had thus become an imperial outpost to which the government could exile U.S. black fighting men.

By making the mythic figure of the black sergeant who saved the day on San Juan Hill the focus of their fictions, McGirt and Gilmore join the chorus of U.S. black writers, including Johnson and Griggs, refuting Roosevelt's accusation of African American military cowardice. However, "In Love as in War" and especially *The "Problem"* illustrate the compromised political position adopted by "Citizen Tom" narratives. Their refusal to challenge openly or even to question Jim Crow practices at home and abroad for fear of diluting their portrayal of African American discipline, obedience, and patriotism has genre implications as well. Setting his story entirely in the Philippines, McGirt creates a fantasy about the sexual and economic possibilities for loyal U.S. black soldiers in the new U.S. overseas empire. Gilmore produces the most elaborate African American retort to Roosevelt's accusations of black cowardice in the Cuban campaign. However, his refusal to acknowledge the realities of the empire at home robs it and his related desire to contrast African American fidelity with white southern betrayal of their potency.

Between 1899 and 1915, African Americans responded to the annexation, pacification, and occupation of the Philippines in poems, short stories, and novels reflecting a wide range of positions on overseas expansion and domestic race relations. Some of the verse parodies of "The White Man's Burden," which began appearing in early 1899, adopt an explicitly anti-imperial stance while also condemning the race chauvinism expressed in Kipling's poem, and Du Bois draws upon biblical imagery and Ethiopianism in his bluntly anticolonial nonparodic poetic retort to Kipling, "The Burden of Black Women." In his novel *Unfettered*, Griggs expresses serious reservations about the takeover of the Philippines and then inexplicably withdraws them. Steward's first two Laguna stories raise subtle questions about the military occupation of the archipelago and his final Laguna story, "The Men Who Prey," openly condemns the role of white U.S. soldiers in the exploitation of Filipino women. McGirt's and Gilmore's fictions set wholly or partly in the Philippines use the heroic black sergeant of San Juan Hill to emphasize African American bravery and loyalty. The combination of their staunch support for U.S. expansion and refusal to question Jim Crow or acknowledge the deterioration of U.S. race relations renders the happy endings of these "Citizen Tom" narratives problematic.

·

Annexation in the Pacific and Asian Conspiracy in Central America in James Weldon Johnson's Unproduced Operettas

I read the autobiography you sent me and was much impressed with it. Ugh! There is not any more puzzling a problem in this country than the problem of color. It is not as urgent, or as menacing, as other problems, but it seems the more utterly insoluble. The trouble is that the conflict in many of its phases is not between right and wrong but between two rights.
—Theodore Roosevelt (to Brander Matthews) on *The Autobiography of an Ex-Colored Man*

[T]he fear that lies closest to [the heart of the Latin American] is not that southern republics will lose their independence to the United States, but that they will fall under the bane of American prejudice, a process which he has without a doubt, observed going on slowly but surely in Cuba, Puerto Rico and Panama.
—James Weldon Johnson, "Why Latin-America Dislikes the United States"

In *Afro-Orientalism*, Bill V. Mullen contends that U.S. black engagement with Asia began with a series of articles W. E. B. Du Bois published in the *Crisis*; however, as established in chapter 3 and confirmed in the ensuing discussions of James Weldon Johnson's libretti for operettas dating from 1899, it occurred earlier in the context of and in response to the U.S. policy of overseas expansion at the turn of the twentieth century. Since the early 1990s, considerable critical attention has been devoted to the relationship between U.S. cultural productions and imperialism. More recently, scholars have begun to address the transnational and hemispheric implications of U.S. black literary texts. Given these trends, it is not surprising that Johnson, a major literary figure as well as a prominent race activist, who worked for six years as a U.S. diplomat in Latin America and whose literary and nonliterary texts explicitly and implicitly address expansion and its connection to race relations at home, has been one of the few African American writers whose views on and links to U.S. imperialism have been the subject of scholarly scrutiny. At roughly the same time that critics have begun to pursue this line of inquiry in connection with Johnson, a new book has directed long overdue attention to his theatrical work. Focusing on *The Shoo-Fly Regiment* and *The Red Moon*, two pioneering Broadway shows written and produced by Cole and Johnson (one of two names—the other being Cole and Johnson Brothers—used for the partnership comprising James Weldon Johnson, his brother J. Rosamond Johnson, and Bob Cole), Paula Marie Seniors's *Beyond "Lift Every Voice and Sing": The Culture of Uplift, Identity, and Politics in Black Musical Theater* (2009) contextualizes and argues for the significance of the team's productions, particularly their pathbreaking depictions of African American college students and soldiers.

In "The Ever Expanding South: James Weldon Johnson and the Rhetoric of the Global Color Line" (2009), Amanda M. Page accurately states that the influence of Latin Americans within and outside of the United States on Johnson "ultimately reveals the interconnectedness of domestic and international struggles for equal rights and the limitations of applying a binary framework (whether black/white or North/South) to a much more complex reality" (41). It should be noted, however, that Page's list of binaries does not include proimperialism/anti-imperialism, an opposition dominating her own and other scholars' recent treatments of Johnson. Let me be clear: it is not that we should avoid addressing imperialism in connection with African American writers—on the contrary, one of the arguments of this book is that there has been far too little attention to the subject. It's that simply classifying authors or their writings as either proimperialist or anti-imperialist fails to account sufficiently for the complexities of the text, the writer, and the era. Even though he wrote or cowrote several texts set abroad that concern U.S. imperialism, recent readings of Johnson by Page, Harilaos Stecopoulos, and Brian Russell Roberts have focused on his lone novel *The Autobiography of an Ex-Colored Man*, originally published in 1912 (although portions of it were written in New York prior to 1906) and on Johnson's consular service in Venezuela and Nicaragua. As Page and Stecopoulos point out (and I note in chapter 1), Johnson's supranational perspective can be seen in the brief but significant role that the Cuban Revolution plays in *Ex-Colored Man*. Although the protagonist leaves Florida permanently shortly after he becomes a cigar factory *lector*, someone who reads newspapers and novels to his co-workers and settles arguments among them, his facility with Spanish and languages generally and his experience with another culture serve him well when he travels to Europe.[1] Such knowledge also helps him get a job in the South American department of a major New York firm after he chooses to sell his birthright for "a mess of pottage" and pass for white following a harrowing episode in which he witnesses the lynching of black man. Looking beyond the frame of the nation in the novel's fifth chapter, Johnson depicts non-Anglo culture thriving in and branching northward from Florida to counteract Western imperialism and U.S. race prejudice.

In conjunction with their focus on *Ex-Colored Man*, an overriding concern of the recent articles about Johnson has been the consistency or inconsistency of his views on U.S. expansion. Page and Stecopoulos posit a shift or evolution in Johnson's position toward the empire abroad. The former traces the writer's trajectory from what she sees as "a hesitant embrace" to an "outright denunciation of imperialism" (26–27). Page faults Johnson's novel for "sidestepping questions of American imperialism" after the defeat of Spain in 1898, "oversimplifying the racial dynamics of the [Cuban] revolution," "construct[ing] the United States as a cradle for Cuban liberty" (29–30), and failing to evince the "more openly critical view of the connection between United States foreign policy and its accompanying racism" that characterizes his nonfictional writings appearing after *Ex-Colored Man* (36), particularly those reflecting his "dedication to the liberation of Haiti" (26) during the long U.S. occupation of the black republic, which began in 1915. "By the time of the novel's publication," she states, "the U.S. had a well established presence in Cuba and Latin America. This marked lacuna in Johnson's presentation of the aftereffects of the Cuban Revolution illustrates the contradictions in his feelings about U.S. imperialism in the region. Though he wants to celebrate what he viewed as Cuba's superior race relations [compared to the United States], Johnson remained greatly invested in the idea of the U.S. as a powerful, continental nation" (30–31). Meanwhile, in "Up from Empire: James Weldon Johnson, Latin America, and the Jim Crow South" (2007), Stecopoulos, describing Johnson as conflicted over U.S. imperialism, characterizes him as a "talented and opportunistic" African American, who "endorsed U.S. imperialism and defended U.S. interests in Nicaragua" (37) while serving as consul there. He sees Johnson critiquing his own actions in *Ex-Colored Man*, flagellating himself, as it were, with a metaphorical big stick.[2] In contrast to these readings, Roberts in "Passing into Diplomacy: U.S. Consul James Weldon Johnson and *The Autobiography of an Ex-Colored Man*" (2010) defends the writer by asserting that in responding to imperialism Johnson in his novel employs a "strategic indirection" (291) characteristic of other U.S. black diplomat writers that has been unfairly branded as hypocrisy by some observers and has not received the critical attention it deserves. As a result of limiting themselves primarily to the novel and Johnson's consular service and striving to classify him as either pro- or anti-imperialist, these scholars have failed to acknowledge that Johnson's position on expansion in individual literary productions depends on several factors, including the generic and literary traditions with which the text engages, where it falls within Johnson's career as a writer, and the historical moment of its composition. By expanding the analysis of Johnson to encompass his texts in other genres set in the Caribbean, Latin America, and the Pacific in the pages devoted to him that follow, I complicate recent assertions about the author's response to empire. After providing biographical information on Johnson, this chapter draws on archival material that has not received significant attention from scholars to establish Johnson's views on war and to survey his dramatic texts that address imperialism, specifically his work as a librettist and lyricist for the various incarnations of *Toloso* (including *The Fakir* and *The Czar of Czam*), about the U.S. annexation of a Pacific island kingdom, as well as for *El Presidente, or the Yellow Peril*, which takes place in Nicaragua and addresses Japan's rise to world prominence as a result of its defeat of Russia in 1904.[3]

Jacksonville and Beyond

Critics have long noted that Johnson's Caribbean ancestry, Florida upbringing, and command of Spanish gave him what we would now call a transnational perspective on the status of African Americans within the post-Reconstruction United States.[4] He was born in Jacksonville in 1871 shortly after his parents moved there from the Bahamas. His maternal grandparents were Haitians who settled in Nassau, where his mother married his Virginia-born father, who had relocated there to work in the Royal Victoria Hotel. Johnson, who rhapsodizes the beauties of his native state in his early poem "Ode to Florida," termed Jacksonville "the most liberal town in the South" in an 1895 newspaper article (qtd. in Levy 8) and a place that long after the end of Reconstruction was "known far and wide as a good town for Negroes" (*Along* 45).[5] In his autobiography, *Along This Way*, he refers to it as "a cigar manufacturing center" with "a Cuban population of several thousand" (60) and also describes his fluency in Spanish achieved through years of conversing with Ricardo Rodriguez Ponce, a Cuban boy who lived in Jacksonville with the Johnson family and later accompanied Johnson to Atlanta University. Moreover, he claims that he had no experience of "racial prejudice as a concrete fact" (65) before he took the train to college in 1887 and credits his facility with another language, as well as his knowledge of a foreign culture, with enabling him to avoid having to ride in the Jim Crow car on the journey to Atlanta because the conductor suspended his efforts to enforce the color bar when he heard Johnson speaking Spanish to Ricardo. Johnson closes his description of the episode with the observation that "in such situations any kind of a Negro will do; provided he is not one who is an American citizen" (65). This passage indicates that at a young age Johnson learned that foreigners—even foreigners of color—typically received better treatment in the South than U.S. blacks, who were "American citizens" without the rights of citizenship. A decade and a half later, Johnson had another experience on a train from Jacksonville he recounts in *Along This Way*. On this trip to New York, Johnson engaged a Pullman berth, which technically should have prevented him from being subject to the Jim Crow laws of southern states, although he was not, as he notes, "exempt from violence" from white passengers, crew members, or mobs (87). Warily entering a smoking car in which there are five white men engaged in conversation, Johnson is greeted with silence. The tension is broken when a young man, who had served as an officer in the war with Spain, points out Johnson's "genuine Panama hat" to his father, a railroad official and the dominant figure in the group. Johnson passes the hat around, and when the young officer sees that it was made in Havana, he asks Johnson, in Spanish, whether he can speak the language, to which Johnson replies, "Si, señor," leading to an exchange in that tongue. Johnson does not participate extensively in the ensuing conversation, except to express his opinion about the situation in Cuba. Nevertheless, in a passage that echoes—and signifies on— Theodore Roosevelt's recollection of what the Rough Riders had to say about the (colored) Ninth and Tenth cavalries, namely, that "they can drink out of our canteens," Johnson slakes his thirst along with the others when the railroad man passes around his whiskey bottle:

The whole party spent the time in the smoking compartment, talking, joking, laughing. The railroad official went into his bag and brought out his private flask of whisky, from which each of us, including the preacher, took several samples, all drinking out of the same glass. Before we reached Savannah a bond of mellow friendship had been established. My newly made friends got off in Savannah, and I went to bed repeating to myself: In such situations any kind of a Negro will do; provided he is not one who is an American citizen. (89)

Johnson repeats the sentence he used in commenting on the earlier train episode to underscore the cruel joke that was African American citizenship in the era of Jim Crow. Despite their long-standing presence in the nation and their significant contributions to it, despite the Fourteenth and Fifteenth amendments to the Constitution, and despite their military service to the nation (most recently in the Caribbean and the Philippines), U.S. blacks were denied the rights that white citizens took for granted. Moreover, by custom and by law they were subjected to a caste system from which noncitizens, even noncitizens of color, were often exempt.

At the 1893 Chicago World's Fair, Johnson met Paul Laurence Dunbar, who had published his first book of poetry the previous year, and he likely heard Frederick Douglass speak.[6] After completing his undergraduate degree in 1894, Johnson returned to Jacksonville where he served as principal of the grammar school he had attended, which he expanded to include a high school. During the 1890s, the multitalented Johnson founded a newspaper, became the first black person admitted to the Florida bar, and began collaborating with his brother J. Rosamond Johnson, who had returned to Jacksonville after studying at the New England Conservatory of Music in Boston. Nearly lynched by soldiers for meeting in public with a woman who appeared to be white in the aftermath of the fire that destroyed much of Jacksonville in 1901, Johnson, though profoundly shaken by the incident, actively combated white intolerance throughout his career—unlike the main character of his novel, who abandons his people after witnessing a white mob's brutal murder of a black man. He became politically active while studying at Atlanta University, writing articles denouncing lynching, a practice he would vigorously campaign against during the last three decades of his life. An admirer of Booker T. Washington, Johnson also enjoyed a long friendship with W. E. B. Du Bois, whom he met in 1904. In the early years of the twentieth century, he formed a partnership with his brother and Bob Cole that enjoyed considerable success in musical theater in New York. Having accepted a consular post in Puerto Cabello, Venezuela, Johnson did not travel with *The Shoo-Fly Regiment*, which toured extensively between 1906 and 1908 and had a run on Broadway.[7] He received the diplomatic appointment through the influence of Washington and in return for the services he rendered Theodore Roosevelt and the Republican Party in the 1904 election, most notably the composition of a campaign song in support of the President.[8] In 1908 he was transferred to Corinto, Nicaragua, where four years later he played a role in supporting U.S. interests during a revolution. Up against "politics and race prejudice" as a result of the Democratic victory in the 1912 election, which resulted in William Jennings Bryan taking over as secretary of state, and thus with no chance to advance in the diplomatic corps, Johnson retired (*Along* 293).

After returning from Central America, he delivered an address in New York City entitled "Why Latin-America Dislikes the United States" (1913), which states that the true cause of pan-American resentment toward the United States is "our national and local Negro problem" (196). Noting that newspapers throughout the hemisphere highlight the acts of racial discrimination and antiblack violence that occur in the United States, Johnson contends, in a passage that serves as the second epigraph to this chapter, that Latin Americans fear the influence of U.S. race prejudice more than they do the prospect of their nations being swallowed up by the colossus of the North. In providing this explanation for anti-Americanism, he challenges the belief of U.S. whites that they can deny citizenship rights to and perpetrate atrocities on African Americans with impunity. In the last twenty-five years of his life, Johnson wrote editorials for the *New York Age*, worked for and led the National Association for the Advancement of Colored People (NAACP), taught at Fisk University and New York University, and wrote and edited collections of poetry and books about African American spirituals and black history.

Johnson on War

Like so many turn-of-the-twentieth-century African American texts that engage U.S. imperialism, several of Johnson's writings grapple with war, even though he was opposed to it. He declares his antiwar sentiments in his unpublished prose piece "The War Catechism," written while he lived in Jacksonville, and in his poem "And the Greatest of These Is War," published in *Fifty Years and Other Poems* (1917). In the former, Johnson attributes the existence and perpetuation of war to a combination of, on the one hand, the "Ignorance" of the people who suffer and die in the fighting and, on the other hand, the "Ambition, Vanity, Greed," and manipulative tactics of those in power. In this text composed during the Spanish-Cuban-American War, he casts a cynical eye on the manner in which the most potent of patriotic symbols—the flag—can be used to motivate people to engage in warfare, asserting that patriotism generally and flags in particular have the power to coerce people into committing shameful, self-demeaning acts resulting in tremendous destruction and misery. It is precisely such self-inflicted debasement and suffering that a mature Johnson emphasizes in "And the Greatest of These Is War," published during the First World War. This allegorical poem, reminiscent of Milton's portrayal of Pandemonium in *Paradise Lost*, depicts Famine, Pestilence, and War boasting to Satan of the misery they have wrought on humankind. When it is his turn to speak, War argues that he surpasses Famine and Pestilence because, rather than, as they do, rousing in "Man's breast / The God-like attributes of sympathy, of brotherhood and love" (32–33), he stirs "in Man the demon and the brute" (35), instilling "black hatred in his heart and red revenge" (36) and thereby leads "Man hellward" (45). Concurring, the prince of demons crowns War "chief" among the "scourges of humanity" (47).

Although staunchly antiwar, Johnson writes about U.S. black military service in "The Colored Sergeant" and *The Shoo-Fly Regiment* and armed conflict generally in *The Autobiography of an Ex-Colored Man*, *Toloso*, and *El Presidente; or, The Yellow Peril*. Similar to other African American writers and public intellectuals in the late 1800s and early 1900s for whom race frequently trumped empire, the participation or lack of participation of U.S. blacks in war in part determines Johnson's position on U.S. imperialism. Specifically, because he does not wish to demean or diminish the efforts and actions of African American soldiers, he refrains from openly questioning the U.S. war effort in Cuba in "The Color Sergeant" and U.S. suppression of the Philippines in *The Shoo-Fly Regiment*. In contrast, in *Toloso* and *El Presidente; or, The Yellow Peril*, texts that do not feature or refer to African American soldiers, Johnson directly addresses and implicitly or explicitly critiques imperialism.

The Shoo-Fly Regiment *and Johnson's Libretti and Lyrics for Unproduced Operettas*

In the absence of an extant script, Paula Seniors has done an admirable job of not only reconstructing the plot of *The Shoo-Fly Regiment* (1906–8) from promotional materials, contemporary reviews and articles, and miscellaneous notes scattered among various libraries but also of placing the show in its theatrical, historical, political, and cultural context. Her research has established that the main storyline concerns Tuskegee graduate Edward (Ned) Jackson, who, unable to marry Rose Maxwell, daughter of the principal of Lincolnville Institute, volunteers to fight in the Philippines. After Ned leads the successful charge to capture Allen Hill and receives commendation for his bravery, Professor Maxwell drops his opposition to the marriage (41–42).[9] Seniors regards Cole and Johnson as innovators who "used the very tools of hegemony to create a distinctly black theater informed by black politics, history, and culture" (4). Noting the predominance of minstrel stereotypes in nineteenth- and early twentieth-century U.S. musical theater, she argues convincingly that *The Shoo-Fly Regiment* broke new ground through its portrayal of a serious, romantic relationship between two educated, morally unimpeachable African Americans. Moreover, Seniors asserts that, despite Cole and Johnson's public support for Roosevelt, the team implicitly critiques his racial politics by providing a compelling counternarrative to his accusations of black cowardice in his published account of the Battle of San Juan Hill through the depiction of heroic, masculine U.S. black officers and enlisted men.

Because an entire book on the order of Seniors's *Beyond "Lift Every Voice and Sing"* could be written about *Toloso* and *El Presidente; or, The Yellow Peril*, I aim in the sections that follow to do no more than to indicate when and under what circumstances the unproduced operettas were written, summarize these texts, and suggest possible ways we might read them, particularly in connection with U.S. expansion. Unlike *The Shoo-Fly Regiment*, libretti exist for these operettas; however, because these shows were never produced, there are, of course, no reviews or promotional materials. Lacking U.S. black characters and placing a premium on satirical humor, these archival texts, unlike "The Color Sergeant" and *The Shoo-Fly Regiment*, do not stress African American heroism, patriotism, professionalism, and accomplishment. Rather, in contrast to Johnson's poem, which tacitly approves of the war in Cuba while explicitly condemning U.S. race prejudice, and *The Shoo-Fly Regiment*, which did not, similar to the African American fictional texts about the Philippine-American War discussed in chapter 3, explicitly tackle the justice or injustice of the pacification of the Philippines, the unproduced shows openly address U.S. imperialism. In particular, *The Czar of Czam*, the final version of *Toloso*, satirically depicts the annexation of a Pacific island nation as a cynical, hypocritical, and ridiculous landgrab destined to destroy the native culture. Additionally, these texts trade in and, particularly in the case of *El Presidente*, highlight stereotypes that turn-of-the-twentieth-century U.S. whites held about Pacific islanders, Latin Americans, and East Asians.

U.S. Expansion in the Pacific in Toloso

Looking back on *Toloso* in the 1930s, Johnson saw the operetta as a somewhat controversial attempt to send up U.S. imperialism. His statements about it in a speech at a testimonial dinner given to him by the NAACP in New York in May 1931 and in *Along This Way* two years later indicate that he composed the libretto and the song lyrics and that his brother composed the music for the original version in Jacksonville, likely in early 1899, a date that roughly coincides with the annexation of the Philippines. Johnson recalls that at the time they wrote the comic opera, the war with Spain was ongoing and that the year before Hawaii had been annexed (the exact date was July 6, 1898). He adds that he and his brother brought a completed version of *Toloso* to New York with them in the first half of 1899 (*Along* 149; "NAACP" 125), which corresponds with the 1899 date affixed to the first two versions of the operetta in the Johnson Papers at the Beinecke Library. At the NAACP dinner, he told the audience, "I don't believe that egotism is my chief fault, but I have looked over that opera since those days after our seven years of experience on Broadway and found it far from being bad" (125). Thus, even after thirty years, he continued to think highly of it.

In his recollections, Johnson associates *Toloso* with the tongue-in-cheek writing of the humorist George Ade, who, Johnson noted in his speech, "several years later, used the same theme [i.e., a satire of U.S. expansion] successfully" (125). In 1899, Ade published a series of sixteen newspaper columns, collectively known as the Stories of Benevolent Assimilation, mocking U.S. efforts to Americanize Filipinos, in his long-running Fables in Slang column in the Chicago *Record*. Three years later he wrote the popular satirical musical to which Johnson refers, *The Sultan of Sulu*. Although the first two versions of *Toloso* could not have been influenced by Ade's Benevolent Assimilation columns, which were published from July 8 to October 18, 1899 (Gianakos 2), the later and more explicitly anti-imperialist versions could have been.[10] In *Along This Way*, Johnson explains the genesis and basic plot of *Toloso* as follows: "We decided to write a comic opera satirizing the new American imperialism. The setting was an island kingdom in the Pacific. The story was concerned with Tolsa, the beautiful princess; her prime minister, a crafty old politician; the entrance of an American man-of-war; the handsome, heroic American lieutenant; and finally annexation. Old stuff now, but not so then. In fact, nothing of the sort had yet been produced on the American stage" (149). He speculates that the show was never produced because "managers were a bit afraid of it; the Spanish-American War had just closed, and they may have thought that audiences would consider a burlesque of American imperialism as unpatriotic" (151). Some of the numbers from *Toloso* did later appear in Broadway musicals, and the opera launched the brothers' careers in show business by providing them with the opportunity to meet the major players in music and theater in New York. One of these was the already established Bob Cole, with whom Johnson and his brother would join to form a long-running team and write two additional versions of the operetta.

The Johnson Papers at Yale contain four versions of *Toloso*. The first version, a handwritten notebook, is simply entitled *The Royal Document*, the king's daughter having not yet been named (three acts, "libretto by James W. Johnson. Music by Rosamond Johnson").[11] The closely related second version, a typescript with the title *Tolosa; or, The Royal Document* (three acts, "book of words by J. W. Johnson. Music by Rosamond Johnson") likewise bears the date 1899.[12] Bob Cole became involved in the project in connection with the next version, *The Fakir* (undated, three acts "written with Bob Cole, based on his [Johnson's] early unproduced opera 'Tolosa.' Libretto—J. W. Johnson and Bob Cole. Lyrics— J. W. Johnson. Music—J. Rosamond Johnson"), and he apparently played an even more significant role in the final incarnation, *The Czar of Czam* (1902–5, two acts "by Cole and Johnson Bros. Book by Bob Cole. Lyrics by J. W. Johnson, and music by Rosamond Johnson").[13]

All four versions take place on a Pacific island kingdom (known as Pototos or Patotos in versions 1, 2, and 3, and Czam in the fourth), whose people have had little contact with the outside world. A conniving U.S. adventurer (referred to variously as Dr. Samuel Skinner, Lordy Aspy Racion, Lord High Treasurer, and Mr. Hocus Pocus, a medicine fakir) appears and, using the standard tricks of con men and mountebanks, endears himself to the king (known, over the four versions, as Bartolos, Malatos, Tomotos, and Tomatós XIII). Skinner succeeds in getting himself appointed as the monarch's most trusted advisor with ready access to the royal treasury; however, desiring to become ruler himself, he secures from the king a statement of permission—the royal document—

to marry his daughter Tolosa, who detests Skinner and is already betrothed to a native prince. A U.S. man-of-war, the uss *Galore*, coincidentally arrives on the scene at this time. Its commanding officer (named Clarke in versions 1 and 2, Graball in the third, and Robert Hall in the fourth) thwarts the swindler's plan by tricking him into marrying his—Skinner's own—estranged wife (who happens to be aboard the *Galore*) instead of Tolosa and, in the latter two versions, takes possession of the island kingdom for the United States without having to fire a shot. Despite Johnson's use of the word in describing the operetta in *Along*, there is no explicit mention of annexation in the first two versions. In contrast, the word pervades *The Fakir*; not only does the captain's name, Graball (i.e., "grab all"), refer to it but so does the description of him in the cast of characters—"Captain Graball, Annexation Agent and Captain U.S.S. Galore." However, in the libretto for *The Fakir* the position on annexation is not as blatantly condemnatory as it is in *The Czar of Czam*. The third version's islanders acknowledge that they have no choice but to bow to the ship's superior firepower, but they choose to look at the prospect of becoming a U.S. possession positively. In contrast, in *The Czar of Czam*, the natives openly and vocally resist, and the anti-imperialist satire reaches a crescendo. Explaining to the king that he has no choice in the matter, the captain predicts that annexation will bring "civilization" replete with poor houses and jails. Moreover, one new character, a missionary named T. M. Goode, destroys native idols, curses when he thinks he's alone, and introduces Revolutionary Rye (i.e., a brand of alcohol) to the islanders, while another new character, Madame Smithe, a dressmaker, tries to cajole native women into wearing U.S. clothes, including lingerie and hoop skirts.

The corrections and marginal comments—both in pencil and in ink—that appear on the typescripts for the third and fourth versions make particularly intriguing reading. The notes on the former—there are two typescripts with notes of *The Fakir*—look ahead explicitly to *The Czar of Czam* and suggest the introduction of new characters—some of whom do and some of whom do not appear in *The Czar of Czam*. The comments on the final version, including a key one signed by Johnson's brother—"Make Capt. character much lighter—cut out all stuff concerning Annexation—Rosamond"—and another note referring to Revolutionary Rye—"? too strong for U.S.A.?"—raise the question of whether the anti-imperial satire has gone too far, particularly in connection with the U.S. captain. From *The Royal Document* and *Tolosa* to *The Fakir* to *The Czar of Czam*, this character changes from being a conventional hero who saves the princess from Skinner's plot to a person and representative of a government that differs in no appreciable way from Skinner himself. Moreover, whereas he gallantly refrains from making any advances toward Tolosa, despite ample opportunities, in the first two versions, in the last one he leeringly states, "All of the information I have gathered is favorable to your case. The physical condition of your male population is much in your favor for annexation and the beauty of your female population is more so, eh boys?" Here the U.S. captain directly associates acquiring the island with taking possession of comely native women.

Given the lack of overt references to annexation before he comes on board and Rosamond's serious reservations about the brazenness of the captain's actions in *The Czar of Czam*, it would appear at first glance that the shift toward an explicit critique of U.S. imperialism in *Toloso* is attributable largely to Bob Cole's increasing involvement in the project. However, several factors complicate this reading. First, writing without Bob Cole, the Johnson brothers address imperialism in the first two versions of *Toloso* and in *El Presidente; or, The Yellow Peril*, even if they do not openly condemn the United States in the way that Cole and Johnson do in *The Fakir* and *The Czar of Czam*. Second, as the author of the 1899 libretti that inspired the third and fourth versions, the colibrettist of *The Fakir*, and the lyricist for all of the versions, Johnson played an indispensable role in the project from start to finish. Third, in his address to the NAACP, Johnson fondly recalls the early versions written with his brother *and* "The Czar of Zam [*sic*]" (125), suggesting that he was not troubled by the pointed nature of the satire of U.S. expansion in the final version. Fourth, Seniors's description of *The Shoo-Fly Regiment* and James Weldon Johnson's lyrics for it in the Johnson Papers at Yale indicate that this Cole and Johnson show, similar to the first two versions of *Toloso*, refrains from explicitly interrogating the empire abroad in the way that *The Czar of Czam* does.[14] Thus, this production, in which Cole played an integral role, does not openly condemn expansion. Fifth, and perhaps most important, as discussed in the preceding chapters of this book, things were very different in the first few years of the new century as opposed to early 1899. U.S. black soldiers returning from Cuba had been subjected to scorn and violence and had seen their courage in battle publicly questioned. In addition, the Philippine war proved to be long, cruel, and bloody. Thus, the movement toward a blatantly anti-imperial satire in *The Fakir* and especially *The Czar of Czam*, texts which do not feature African American fighting men, may have reflected a shift in James Weldon Johnson's thinking on the subject comparable to the increasingly antiexpansionist stance adopted by many U.S. blacks during those years.

Nailing the Big Stick to the Wall

In addition to satirizing U.S. imperialism, *El Presidente; or, The Yellow Peril* (undated, three acts, "words and verses by James W. Johnson. Music by J. Rosamond Johnson"), as its name suggests, exploits but also draws attention to U.S. prejudices about non-Anglo-Saxons, namely Latin Americans and Asians.[15] Given its references to big stick diplomacy, the U.S. construction of the Panama Canal, and the purported attempt by Nicaraguan president José Santos Zelaya to interest Japan in building a competing canal in his country, as well as the use the libretto makes of white fears of a "yellow peril" (a phrase popularized by Jack London, among others, in the early 1900s), it could not have been written before 1909 and was likely composed after 1912 when Johnson played a role in supporting his country's interests as consul in Corinto during a revolution against a president backed by the United States. The absence of any reference to Bob Cole in the text suggests, moreover, that the Johnson brothers worked on it sometime after their partner's death in 1911, likely in 1914 when James Weldon Johnson tried, briefly, to write once more for the New York stage (*Along* 303).

In the operetta, a pair of Japanese commissioners, at once comically absurd and sinisterly crafty, conspire with the corrupt, mendacious Nicaraguan dictator Guzman to build a canal through that country before the United States finishes the Panama Canal.[16] In a plot twist that exploits U.S. xenophobia and nativism, the plan is for part of the Japanese fleet to divert the U.S. Navy by passing through the new canal while the Asian nation's remaining ships attack the West Coast of the United States and Japanese already in the country support the war effort. Fears of a "yellow peril"—hordes of Asians challenging the supremacy of whites—arose in the mid-nineteenth century and were renewed in the early 1900s by London and others following Japan's defeat of Russia in 1904. London served as a reporter in Korea during the Russo-Japanese War and was alarmed by Japanese military efficiency. In 1904 he published an essay entitled "The Yellow Peril" in the *San Francisco Examiner*, raising the specter of the technologically savvy Japanese leading the industrious but hitherto ineptly governed Chinese in a huge Asian bloc outnumbering and capable of challenging the white race. In 1906 or 1907 and thus only a year or so after Sutton Griggs published *The Hindered Hand* with its Slavic plot to wipe out southern whites by infecting the water supply with yellow fever germs, London wrote a futuristic short story called "The Unparalleled Invasion," in which the West uses germ warfare to prevent being overrun by Asians.[17]

Whereas Japan's defeat of Russia in 1904 engendered fears of a yellow peril in white writers such as London, it offered rays of hope to some U.S. black public intellectuals. In "The Color Line Belts the World" (1906), W. E. B. Du Bois declares, "For the first time in a thousand years a great white nation has measured arms with a colored nation and has been found wanting. The Russo-Japanese War has marked an epoch. The magic of the word 'white' is already broken, and the Color Line in civilization has been crossed in modern times as it was in the great past. The awakening of the yellow races is certain. That the awakening of the brown and the black will follow in time, no unprejudiced student of history can doubt" (34). A year later, in *The One Great Question*, Griggs describes the emperor of Japan as "the potential leader of the colored world" (54). Du Bois's passage asserts that Japan's victory signals the rise of Asians and Africans; meanwhile, Griggs's suggests that nonwhite peoples across the globe may come to look to the Japanese ruler for guidance and inspiration.

Referring to Roosevelt's diplomatic policy toward Latin America that in 1905 became codified as his corollary to the Monroe Doctrine, *El Presidente* frequently uses the phrase "the Big Stick," most notably at the end of act 1 when Guzman and his chief aide Plumas, the Japanese commissioners Uchi and Kogi, and concessioners from England, France, and Germany all join together to sing "We Will Nail the Big Stick to the Wall." In this number and elsewhere in the show, "the Big Stick" serves as a synonym for the United States. Although the text breaks off before the various plot threads have been tied up, it seems likely that a (white) U.S. engineer overseeing the building of a railway line, Henry Thurston, who finds out about the conspiracy, will be able to put a stop to it. All indications are that the United States will prevail in another contest, that between Marion Breeze, daughter of the U.S. consul, and Paquita, Plumas's daughter, for Thurston's affections.

Although *El Presidente; or, The Yellow Peril* pokes fun at U.S. foreign policy in Latin America, its use of degrading stereotypes of Latin Americans and Asians can be seen as having the effect of casting characters from the United States and the nation's policies in the region in a favorable light. Thus, the text appears to support Roosevelt's and his successor William Taft's approach to and actions in the Caribbean and Central and South America, as well as illustrating the moral and intellectual superiority of Anglo-Saxons over Latin

Americans and Asians. Yet sufficient evidence exists to advance an alternative interpretation. Caricatures were indeed the stock and trade of musical theater in the early 1900s, as indicated by the frequent use of ethnic stereotypes, such as those of natives in *Toloso* and Ade's *The Sultan of Sulu*, and by the persistence of minstrel characters on the U.S. stage. However, the ubiquity and intensity of the caricatures in *El Presidente; or, The Yellow Peril*, with the Nicaraguan leader and the Japanese commissioners made to appear so thoroughly corrupt and unscrupulous that the stereotyping seems to become the very focus of the text, suggest that Johnson may have had some deeper purpose in the operetta. Although the libretto appears to approve of U.S. efforts to police Latin Americans deemed incapable of disciplined self-government and to reinforce racist fears of Asians hordes overrunning the white race, it can also be read as an exposé, a nailing to the wall so to speak, of race chauvinism. Supported by scientific racism and ideas about survival of the fittest, U.S. white racial beliefs not only engendered ridiculous fantasies about threats from people abroad comparable to those depicted in the comic opera but also justified black disenfranchisement, legalized segregation, and lynching at home.

In his reflections about *Toloso*, Johnson does not connect the project with ringing denunciations of imperialism by figures such as Du Bois and Mark Twain but rather Ade's farcical *The Sultan of Sulu*, suggesting the importance he placed on the generic traditions and conventions of the operetta. As Seniors argues compellingly in *Beyond "Lift Every Voice and Sing"* in connection with *The Shoo-Fly Regiment*, the comic opera form did not prevent writers from breaking barriers and making political statements. It did, however, determine how such barriers could be breached and how political issues could be engaged. The absurdity, exaggeration, and lightheartedness of this popular form of entertainment precluded fiery polemic but also made it possible to broach controversial subjects and poke fun at the powerful in a cavalier manner. In *The Czar of Czam*, for example, when, in an attempt to establish that he possesses the one-thousand-year ancestry requisite for marrying the princess, Skinner/ Hocus Pocus mentions George Washington, the king naively asks, "He had a son named Booker, didn't he?" Skinner replies, "Booker? No,—he was connected with the Roosevelt side of the family!" Using the humor characteristic of the genre, Johnson here refers to Roosevelt's decision, shortly after assuming office, to dine at the White House with the most prominent U.S. black leader, which endeared the president to many African Americans and angered southern whites.[18] Appealing to a large and diverse audience, the comic opera genre offered possibilities for the Johnson brothers, with and without Bob Cole, to burlesque U.S. imperialism and in the process raise questions about the racial beliefs held by U.S. whites. James Weldon Johnson's work in musical theater indicates that references and responses to imperialism were integral to the cultural productions of the period. Along with chapter 3, this chapter demonstrates that before Du Bois's articles about Asia appeared in the *Crisis* in the 1910s, before his 1928 novel *Dark Princess* was published, and long before the Afro-Asian Conference held in Bandung in 1955, which is the subject of Richard Wright's *The Color Curtain*, African American writers engaged with the Pacific rim, specifically the annexation of Hawaii, the military takeover of the Philippines, and the rise of Japan.

Pauline Hopkins, the *Colored American Magazine*, and the Critique of Empire Abroad and at Home in "Talma Gordon"

Never until we welcome the Negro, the foreigner, all races as equals, and wedded together in a common nationality, will we deserve prosperity and peace.—Pauline Hopkins, "Club Life among Colored Women"

This country was born with a devotion to the pursuit of profit, and rarely has there been an enterprise as lucrative as the slave trade. No amount of lip service paid by Washington and Jefferson regarding the offensiveness of the "peculiar institution" could mask the fact that half the country relied on slave labor for its existence, and entrepreneurs and seaman from the other half provided it. If the South called for slaves it was largely the New York and New England captains and their ships and crews that delivered them.—Ron Soodalter, *The Hanging of Captain Gordon*

Although some critics, beginning with Gwendolyn Brooks in 1978, have cast Pauline Hopkins (1859–1930) as a conservative, Booker T. Washington regarded her very differently. Alarmed by what he deemed the radical nature of her own writings and those of others that she published in the *Colored American Magazine*, the most powerful African American leader of the late nineteenth and early twentieth century actively took steps to silence her. Hopkins's April 16, 1905, letter to *Boston Guardian* editor and Washington antagonist William Monroe Trotter suggests that she lost her position at the magazine in part because of her commitment to linking discrimination at home with imperialism abroad. For researchers who have long sought to know the real story behind her departure from the magazine and to learn specific details about her personal life, this letter, published for the first time in *Daughter of the Revolution: The Major Nonfiction Works of Pauline E. Hopkins* (2007), edited by Ira Dworkin, makes riveting reading. In the *Voice of the Negro*, Du Bois had charged Washington with paying off editors to get articles favorable to his policies published and to suppress criticism. Concerned that the Tuskegee Machine might take legal action, Du Bois sought to amass as much evidence as he could to back his claims, appealing to Trotter, who presumably contacted Hopkins, for any information he had (Du Bois, "Letter"). The letter reveals that in 1903 Hopkins, who wrote a sizeable percentage of the fiction and nonfiction appearing in the *Colored American Magazine*, served as its de facto editor in chief, and went on speaking tours to promote the journal, earned a mere $7 a week. It was John C. Freund, a white man affiliated with a publication called *Musical Trades*, which had a smaller subscriber base than the *Colored American Magazine*, who undermined Hopkins's position at the magazine and eventually brought about its evisceration. Passing himself off as someone whose sole interest was helping the financially strapped journal, Freund began spending liberally. He paid for a dinner for twenty people associated with the magazine and sent gifts of furs, money, and books to Hopkins. With the benefit of hindsight, Hopkins recognizes in the Trotter letter what Freund was really doing: "As I am not a woman who attracts the attention of the opposite sex in any way, Mr. Freund's philanthropy with regard to myself puzzled me, but knowing that he was aware of my burdens at home [Hopkins's mother was bedridden], I thought that he was trying to help me in his way. I was so dense that I did not for a moment suspect that I was being politely bribed to give up race work and principles and adopt the plans of the South for the domination of the Blacks" (241). Once the magazine was dependent upon him financially, Freund began making demands on Hopkins, mandating that she—a frequent if subtle critic of Washington (L. Brown 407–41; Knight; Wallinger 70–96)—write a letter of introduction to the president of Tuskegee for him and issuing the ultimatum that she reduce the emphasis on literature, drop "anything which may create offense," "stop talking about wrongs and a proscribed race," and eliminate articles about the Philippines (243). It was just a matter of time before Hopkins's tenure at the magazine and thus its engagement with the empire abroad and at home would come to an end. In May 1904, Fred Moore, one of Washington's subordinates, bought the journal, moved it to New York from its strong base of support in Boston, and in September of that year fired Hopkins. Fifteen months later, she made a public address at the ceremony commemorating the centennial of the birth of the pioneering abolitionist William Lloyd Garrison in which she affiliates herself with preceding generations of freedom fighters, particularly the founders of the nation: "I am a daughter of the Revolution, you do not acknowledge black daughters of the Revolution but we are going to take that right" (355). In another instance, deliberate or accidental, of her frequently unruly voice being silenced, the opening paragraph containing this memorable statement, as Dworkin notes (357), was deleted when the speech was published in the pamphlet *The Anti-slavery Cause of Today* in 1906.

African American writers who came of age after the Civil War, such as Hopkins, were acutely aware of the courageous efforts of the generation that came before them, particularly the abolitionists, black and white, efforts that greatly contributed to the demise of slavery and the acquisition of citizenship rights for U.S. blacks. They were also fully cognizant of the inexorable erosion of those rights that began in earnest in the 1870s and accelerated during the decades that followed. In addition, these writers were confronted with deliberate falsifications of their history, namely, images of contented, dependent, backward, servile, and bestial blacks appearing in plantation fiction, southern rhetoric, and the scientific racism of the day. In response, Hopkins, at the *Colored American Magazine*, pursued an ambitious neo-abolitionist course designed to highlight the contrast between the era of Douglass and the era of Washington and to inspire blacks and whites to recommit themselves to the principle of freedom and justice for all.

A major component of this effort, the combination of her forty-three-thousand-word Famous Men of the Negro Race series (which, except for the concluding Booker T. Washington sketch, focuses on individual figures from previous generations) and her thirty-six-thousand-word Famous Women of the Negro Race series (comprising mainly communal portraits of members of Hopkins's generation), published in a total of twenty-three installments in the *Colored American Magazine* from November 1900 to October 1902, accounts for approximately half of Hopkins's nonfiction. In these writings, she frequently compares and contrasts the past and the present, asserting that the conditions that have been imposed on African Americans during her day amount to a new form of bondage. From the 1830s through the 1860s, there were white people who took risks and made personal sacrifices for the ideals on which the United States was founded. During the same period, black heroes and heroines emerged—abolitionists, such as Douglass, William Wells Brown,

Lewis Hayden, Charles Lenox Remond, and Sojourner Truth; Underground Railroad conductors, such as Harriet Tubman and Edwin Garrison Walker; literary artists, such as Douglass, Brown, and Frances Harper; and black soldiers in the tradition of Toussaint L'Ouverture, such as Sergeant William H. Carney. Since 1877 much has changed, Hopkins asserts. The party of Lincoln has abandoned African Americans, sacrificing principle for wealth and power, and white clubwomen have drawn the color line against their black sisters. Worse still, from Hopkins's perspective, many blacks have allowed themselves to be bribed by whites, surrendering their "manhood" in the process, and a "colored American" has appeared on the scene "who, having talent and opportunity to help build up, strengthen and succor us on our wearisome journey, deliberately adopts"—in contrast to the admirable, idealistic leaders of the past—"a policy of despair that will bind us down in a meaner bondage than that we have just escaped" ("Charles" 69). Clearly referring to the bargain Washington has made with the southern-led white power structure to keep blacks in submission and stifle agitation, Hopkins adds, "For such a one there seems no atonement unless, like Judas of old, he be moved to acknowledge his sin and go out and hang himself" ("Charles" 69). Without question this passage stands out as one of the most memorable references to betrayal in Hopkins's writings in the magazine.

Speaking of Hopkins's editorial vision for and many contributions to the magazine, C. K. Doreski observes in the pioneering essay "Inherited Rhetoric and Authentic History: Pauline Hopkins at the *Colored American Magazine*" (1996) that "thoroughly attuned to the intertextual power of the emulative matrix of the press, she knew that her historical portraits could gain power when read through the animated and often competing texts of each issue. She wrote in the certainty that her biographical texts would inform her fiction and social notes, even as they were informed by the larger textual whole" (72). Building on Doreski, Dworkin in his introduction to *Daughter of the Revolution* observes that the "intertextuality between the installments enables *Famous Men* to cohere as a unified series" (9). I would go further and argue that the Famous Men and Famous Women series, along with Hopkins's November 1902 sketch "Munroe Rogers," concerning a black man whom the attorney general of Massachusetts had recently turned over to North Carolina to face a bogus charge of arson, can be seen as functioning as a single unit.

Serving as a kind of epilogue to the two biographical series, the Rogers article begins by raising the subject of betrayal: "Who among the rejoicing millions could have been persuaded that in less than forty years from the day they celebrated—Emancipation day—this American people would have turned their backs upon the lessons of humanity learned in the hard school of sanguinary war, and repeated in their terrible acts exemplified by the surrender of Sims and Burns by a conservative North at the brutal demand of a domineering South!" (269). By referring to the cases of Thomas Sims and Anthony Burns, Hopkins makes clear that, in another disturbing parallel between her era and slavery, she regards Rogers as a latter-day fugitive slave. The Republican Party no longer "care[s] to" shoulder "a responsibility of its own making," the "South needs nothing less than a new moral code," and the "question of disenfranchisement has speedily resolved itself into one of serfdom; that means a gradual resumption of all the relations of slavery" (270). For these reasons, Hopkins, raising the prospect of interracial war in a manner somewhat reminiscent of Griggs's *Imperium in Imperio*, sees a revolution of some kind on the horizon: "If affairs remain as they are now in this unnatural and strained condition, where the manhood of both races is debased, the one by the consciousness of a wrong committed, the other of a wrong endured, there must come a revolution. The air breathes a spirit of restlessness which precedes self-defense. If some Toussaint L'Ouverture should arise!" (271). Careful readers of the *Colored American Magazine* would have recalled not only that the Famous Men series began with a profile of the leader of the Haitian Revolution but also that in the final installment she signals Washington's disloyalty to the race by identifying him with Napoleon, the man who betrayed Toussaint—all of which serves to suggest that blacks lack the heroic, inspiring leadership they need in this time of crisis. Nevertheless, in the Rogers piece she refuses to give up the fight, declaring, "Republics exist only on the tenure of being constantly agitated. We cannot live without the voice crying in the wilderness—troubling the waters that there may be health in the flow" (276). In another example of the intertextuality among the selections appearing in the *Colored American Magazine*, the imagery in this notable passage recalls that of Hopkins's serial novel *Winona*, which had just concluded its run in the magazine.

Empire, Slavery, and Piracy in "Talma Gordon"

In "Black Americans' Racial Uplift Ideology as 'Civilizing Mission': Pauline Hopkins on Race and Imperialism" (1993), Kevin Gaines asserts that Hopkins and other turn-of-the-twentieth-century U.S. black writers and public intellectuals "who considered themselves opposed to racism," including Harper,

Anna Julia Cooper, Alexander Crummell, and Du Bois, employed "a patriarchal, metaracist discourse" amounting to "ideological collusion with discriminatory ideologies and practices" (450). According to Gaines, because uplift assumes racial hierarchies that dovetail with the imperialist notion of a civilizing mission, "the preoccupation of many black leaders with racial uplift as a sign of respectability restricted possibilities for effective resistance" (450). Focusing on Hopkins's novel *Of One Blood; or, The Hidden Self* (serialized in the *Colored American Magazine* between 1902 and 1903) and her ethnographic series *The Darker Races of Mankind*, which appeared in the *Voice of the Negro* in 1905 after her termination from the *Colored American Magazine*, Gaines chides Hopkins for adopting a "deferential posture . . . to the received terms of dominant racial ideologies" (434), for being "too grounded in evangelical sentiment" (444), and for relying on proimperialist sources in "her own ethnological accounts of various peoples" (447). Widely praised, often cited, and rarely questioned, Gaines's article has dominated discussions of Hopkins and empire. Only recently has Colleen O'Brien in "'Blacks in all Quarters of the Globe': Anti-imperialism, Insurgent Cosmopolitanism, and International Labor in Pauline Hopkins's Literary Journalism" (2009) challenged readings of Hopkins by Gaines and others that cast her as a deeply religious figure who accepted much of the civilizationist rhetoric, racist science, and the expansionist fervor of the day. Citing Hopkins's fiction and especially her nonfiction as well as articles appearing in the *Colored American Magazine* during her tenure on such subjects as Oceola, Cuba, and the Philippine resistance leader and novelist José Rizal, O'Brien characterizes Hopkins as a U.S. black woman writer and editor who contested "Anglo-masculine national identity," "protested lynching," advocated an "insurgent rather than [a] cultural cosmopolitanism," "critiqued white territorial expansion," and "located heroism among righteous rebels like Toussaint" (248, 249, 267). It is indeed unfortunate that heretofore no scholar has offered a detailed reading of "Talma Gordon" in the context of empire, particularly as the story demonstrates neither the preoccupation with evangelicalism nor the use of secondhand, proimperialist sources that Gaines criticizes Hopkins for in connection with *Of One Blood* and *The Darker Races*.

Perhaps because it operates on several levels, "Talma Gordon" has attracted the attention of critics in pursuit of a variety of scholarly agendas. Although Hazel Carby does not analyze the story extensively in her landmark study *Reconstructing Womanhood: The Emergence of the Black Woman Novelist* (1987), she does connect it and Hopkins's first novel, *Contending Forces* (1900), to the legacy of colonialism, aptly describing "Talma Gordon" as the writer's "most concentrated revision of an imperialist history" (135). It is surprising that Gretchen Murphy, an insightful reader of texts relating to U.S. expansion, has recently taken issue with this reading. Regarding the tale's ending as "unresolved" on the subject of the effects of empire abroad (111), Murphy, who approvingly cites Gaines's article, asserts that Carby "overstates" her point "that 'Talma Gordon' is an anti-imperialist story" in "her otherwise successful effort to recover Hopkins as a political thinker with a global perspective" (250). Other critics, meanwhile, have overlooked or downplayed the tale's response to imperialism, focusing instead on issues of race and gender or on the role that detection plays in the story. Werner Sollors devotes three pages of his encyclopedic book about miscegenation (*Neither Black Nor White Yet Both: Thematic Explorations of Interracial Literature* [1997]) to "Talma Gordon," stressing the "tale of the *Natus Aethiopus* [i.e., a light-complected woman giving birth to a dark-skinned child], which forms the core" of Hopkins's story (73). In a 2006 essay entitled "'The Case Was Very Black against' Her: Pauline Hopkins and the Politics of Racial Ambiguity at the *Colored American Magazine*," Sigrid Anderson Cordell argues that the tale epitomizes Hopkins's difficult position as a writer seeking to expose the oppression of black women in a journal partly beholden for its continued existence on white readers and white, male financial backers. In *The Web of Iniquity: Early Detective Fiction by American Women*, published in 1998, Catherine Nickerson reads "Talma Gordon" at some length, linking it to the Lizzie Borden case and detective fiction by U.S. white women. Others have discussed the story in connection with Hopkins's use of popular genres, especially detective fiction, to explore racial themes, and the anthologists Paula Woods and Otto Penzler have reprinted it as the first example of African American mystery writing.[1] Nickerson, Woods, and Penzler note the fact that the triple murder in the story constitutes a locked-room mystery, thereby hearkening back to the first modern detective story, Edgar Allan Poe's "The Murders in the Rue Morgue" (1841). Perhaps because of their reluctance to acknowledge fully the role of imperialism in the story, these and other scholars have failed to connect "Talma Gordon" to a second detective tale by Poe, "The Gold-Bug" (1843), which concerns the buried treasure of a notoriously bloody seventeenth-century pirate, thereby evoking the theme of empire.

Like Carby, in what follows I emphasize the pivotal position Hopkins assigns to U.S. imperialism in "Talma Gordon," which appeared in a journal that between 1900 and 1904 (when Hopkins played a major editorial role) featured several articles about Cubans and Filipinos, as well as fictional works set during the occupation of the Philippines by former African American U.S. Army captain Frank R. Steward. In doing so, however, I by no means wish to ignore or marginalize the roles miscegenation, the exploitation of black women, and detection play in the story. On the contrary, I hope to show that each of these four elements plays an integral role in this fiction, whose intricate structure reveals the interconnectedness of Anglo-Saxon "civilization," the imperial exploitation of subject peoples, slavery, amalgamation, racial intolerance, and piracy. To counter the self-congratulatory belief among whites that U.S. expansion in the wake of the victory over Spain in 1898 represents a new echelon in human advancement, Hopkins places two predations at the heart of the tale: slavery (including its legacies of sexual exploitation and amalgamation) in the United States and Western imperialism in the East Indies.

A discussion of imperialism frames the story, in which the Beacon Hill home of the renowned Dr. Thornton serves as the gathering place for twenty-five members of the elite white Canterbury Club to address the topic "Expansion; Its Effect upon the Future Development of the Anglo-Saxon throughout the World" (271). A politician approvingly cites the wealth an overseas empire will bring the United States, and a noted theologian eagerly extols the missionary opportunities. Everyone seems convinced except for the host, who asserts that amalgamation will undoubtedly be a consequence of expansion, a possibility that no one else in the room has considered. Although he asserts that miscegenation "will occur among all classes, and to an appalling extent," Thornton does not categorically oppose the practice, supporting it "most emphatically when they possess decent moral development and physical perfection, for then we develop a superior being in the progeny born of the intermarriage. But if we are not ready to receive and assimilate the new material which will be brought to mingle with our pure Anglo-Saxon stream, we should call a halt in our expansion policy" (272–73). To illustrate his point, the physician proceeds to narrate the history of the Gordons, a family tracing its lineage back to the Pilgrims. Thornton's tale recounts how the beautiful, blond-haired, blue-eyed Talma is acquitted of the murders of her father, stepmother, and stepbrother, and it contains two shocking surprises: the father, Captain Gordon, disinherits Talma and her sister Jeannette because their mother has been revealed to be one-sixteenth black, and a East Indian known as Simon Cameron eventually confesses to using a secret passageway known only to Gordon's sailors to commit the murders in order to avenge the rapacious captain's cold-blooded killing of Cameron's father. Hopkins's story concludes with one final twist when the doctor introduces the Canterbury Club to his wife, who proves to be none other than Talma Gordon.

Carby discusses three revelations in the story, each of which relates to a distinct mystery: Gordon's revelation of the black ancestry of the first Mrs. Gordon and thus Talma and Jeannette (a racial mystery); Cameron's revelation that it is he who cut the throats of Gordon, his second wife, and their son to avenge the killing of his father (a murder and pirate mystery); and Thornton's revelation that he is married to Talma Gordon (a romantic or marital mystery). Sollors, Nickerson, and Cordell, meanwhile, see four layers in the story (although only the first two explicitly spell these out): 1) the frame narrative (i.e., the opening discussion of expansion and the surprise about Thornton's marriage at the end), which surrounds 2) Thornton's story about the Gordon murder case, in which he quotes 3) Jeannette's letter to Talma that includes 4) Captain Gordon's revelation that his infant son by the first Mrs. Gordon had black features and his subsequent discovery that the grandmother of Talma and Jeanette was an octoroon impregnated and abandoned by a white man. Although Carby fails to account for all the layers of the story, she grapples with the solution to the murder mystery more fully than Sollors and Cordell, who, because of their interests in miscegenation and the exploitation of black women respectively, do not include Cameron's confession in their analyses of the structure of the story. Nickerson, in contrast, does devote some attention to Cameron, yet fails to do complete justice to this narrative thread because her primary concern is the link between the story and the Lizzie Borden case.

I agree that there are indeed four layers to the story; however, unlike Nickerson, who uses the image of Chinese boxes (193), I believe the story more closely resembles a palimpsest in the sense that the layers are interpenetrating rather than discrete. Carby, Sollors, Cordell, and Nickerson do not note that Cameron's story, like Jeannette's letter, has two layers to it: there is his confession of the murders as well as the story of Gordon's killing of his father (perpetrated so that only the captain would know the location of the buried treasure) and the knowledge of a secret passageway within Gordon's mansion, both of which he presumably gets from his mother. Thus, I contend that the story has a second four-part structure, parallel to the one identified by Sollors, Cordell, and Nickerson: 1) the opening frame narrative and the revelation about Thornton's marriage at the end that surrounds 2) Thornton's story of the Gordon murders, which contains 3) Cameron's confession of his triple murder that includes 4) the story of his father's murder and the information about the secret entrance to the Gordon mansion that Cameron receives from his mother. In other words, there are in fact two parallel plots—the racial plot *and* the pirate plot—at the heart of the story, which can thus be diagrammed as follows:

> [3a. Jeannette's letter [4a. Gordon's revelations]]]

1. Frame [2. Thornton's story

> [3b. Cameron's confession [4b. Mother's revelations]]]

At first glance, it might appear that this diagram simply reflects the three mysteries cited by Carby, that is the frame (1) solves the romantic/marital mystery while Thornton's story (2) by quoting Jeannette's letter (3a) and Cameron's confession (3b) holds the key to both the racial and the murder mystery. Further reflection, however, reveals how inadequately such an overview accounts for the complexity and interconnectedness of the story. In addition to solving the romantic/marital mystery at the tale's conclusion, the frame (1) introduces the topic of Anglo-Saxon "civilization" through the Canterbury Club, whose members represent the most successful and, according to the social Darwinism and racist science of the day, the highest stage of development humankind has thus far achieved. By means of the club's topic of discussion, the frame (1) also introduces the subject of imperialism, which Carby stresses in her reading. Through the question that Thornton poses to the club—"Did you ever think that in spite of our prejudice against amalgamation, some of our descendents, indeed many of them, will inevitably intermarry among those far-off tribes of dark-skinned peoples, if they become a part of this great Union" (272)—the frame (1) also introduces the topics of amalgamation and racial intolerance. At the same time, however, Thornton's marriage to Talma Gordon can be seen as an instance of racial tolerance that contrasts with the prevailing intolerance of the era.

If we direct attention to the story that Thornton then tells about the Gordons (2), we see that it, too, concerns Anglo-Saxon "civilization," imperialism, and racial intolerance. Thornton reveals, first, that the "Gordons were old New England Puritans who had come over on the 'Mayflower'" (274), thereby linking Captain Gordon to the supposedly high level of advancement epitomized by the members of the Canterbury Club. Second, he reveals that Gordon and his ancestors were for many generations engaged in the imperial enterprise of "the East India trade" (274). Third, Thornton's story also records the reaction of Talma Gordon's one-time love interest, Edward Turner, to the news that she is thirty-one parts white and one part black: "God! Doctor, but this is too much. I could stand the stigma of murder, but add to that the pollution of Negro blood! No man is brave enough to face such a situation" (288)—a statement demonstrating that in the United States in the late 1800s even the smallest percentage of African ancestry represented a greater taint than the most heinous of criminal acts.

Turning to Jeannette's written and Cameron's oral confession (3a and 3b) that Thornton proceeds to divulge, we find that vengeance and intolerance characterize both. Jeannette tells the story of Gordon's intolerant act of disinheriting his daughters because of their ancestry. At the same, however, her letter (3a) also reveals her own plan to murder her father—significantly by means of "the old East Indian dagger" (287)—only to find, as she puts it, "that my revenge had been forestalled" (288) because someone—namely, the East Indian Cameron—has gotten to the captain first. Cameron's confession (3b), of course, concerns his successful act of vengeance against Captain Gordon. Tellingly, Thornton's reaction to this man, who comes to him as a patient, unveils an intolerant side of the doctor that conflicts with or at least qualifies the portrayal of him in the frame. On first mentioning Cameron, Thornton says, "Seldom have I seen so fascinating and wicked a face. . . . He was an enigma to me; and his nationality puzzled me, for of course I did not believe his story of being English" (280–81). Later, as the dying man begins his confession, he tells the doctor, "Cameron is not my name," to which Thornton replies, echoing his earlier statement, "I never supposed it was" (288). Because Cameron identifies himself as an East Indian and yet has adopted, albeit not completely successfully, an Anglo-Saxon identity, the implication is that he may himself be a product of miscegenation. If this is indeed the case, then it links the long-standing imperial East Indian trade, in which generations of the Gordons were involved, with amalgamation. As Thornton explicitly states to the Canterbury Club in the story's opening, he approves of race mixture in some instances and not in others.

As noted, both Jeannette and Cameron pass along shocking information they have learned from other sources. Captain Gordon's revelations (4a), which Jeannette includes in her letter, attest to not only her father and his second wife's intolerant treatment of Jeannette and Talma because of their ancestry but also to the sexual exploitation and amalgamation that resulted from slavery in the United States, which Cordell stresses in her reading. Gordon explains that after the birth of his mulatto son he sought enlightenment from his first wife's parents:

> I sent for Mr. and Mrs. Franklin, and then I learned the truth. They were child-less. One year while on a Southern tour, they befriended an octoroon girl who had been abandoned by her white lover. Her child was a beautiful girl baby. They, being Northern born, thought little of caste distinction because the child showed no trace of Negro blood. They determined to adopt it. . . . They made Isabel their heiress, and all went well until the birth of your brother. Your mother and the unfortunate babe died. This is the story which, if known, would bring dire disgrace upon the Gordon family. (286–87)

Captain Gordon indicates, like Turner when he hears the news about Talma, that no revelation—not even, presumably, his own acts of piracy and murder—could be more damning in the late nineteenth-century United States than the knowledge that some black blood runs in the veins of one or more of the illustrious Gordons.

Like Jeannette's letter, Cameron's confession includes information he received from his only surviving parent (4b). His mother, either as she lies dying or sometime earlier, tells Cameron the story of Gordon's killing of her husband perpetrated so that the captain alone would know the location of the treasure. After admitting that he killed the Gordons, Cameron explains why:

> There is many a soul crying in heaven and hell for vengeance on Jonathan Gordon. Gold was his idol; and many a good man walked the plank, and many a gallant ship was stripped of her treasure, to satisfy his lust for gold. His blackest crime was the murder of my father, who was his friend, and had sailed with him for many a year as mate. One night these two went ashore together to bury their treasure. My father never returned from that expedition. His body was afterward found with a bullet through the heart on the shore where the vessel stopped that night. It was a custom among pirates for the captain to kill the men who helped bury the treasure. Captain Gordon was no better than a pirate. An East Indian never forgets, and I swore by my mother's deathbed to hunt Captain Gordon down until I had avenged my father's murder. (289)

The second half of this statement bears an unmistakable resemblance to the ending of "The Gold-Bug." After the eccentric detective William Legrand, his black servant Jupiter, and the unnamed narrator recover a treasure chest containing millions of dollars worth of gold, we learn through Legrand that the seventeenth-century pirate William "Captain" Kidd killed the men who helped him bury the booty so that only he would know its location: "It is clear that Kidd—if Kidd indeed secreted the treasure, which I doubt not—it is clear that he must have had assistance in the labor. But this labor concluded, he may have thought it expedient to remove all participants in his secret. Perhaps a couple of blows with a mattock were sufficient, while his coadjutors were busy in the pit; perhaps it required a dozen—who shall tell?" (348). Cameron's mother also informs her son about the secret passageway in the Gordon mansion that Cameron later uses to commit the murders. Her story not only underscores the link between the Gordons and imperial exploitation but also equates the captain with piracy and murder.

Taken as a whole, Hopkins's intricately constructed narrative equates Anglo-Saxon "civilization" with piracy and a lust for gold and categorizes slavery in the United States as a byproduct of imperial rapacity that resulted in amalgamation and racial intolerance. By extension, then, amalgamation and intolerance constitute the legacy that Anglo-Saxon "civilization" has transmitted—by means of imperialism *and* slavery—to late nineteenth- and early twentieth-century U.S. expansion. The name Hopkins chooses for the title character and her family serves to reinforce these connections.[2] As Hopkins would note in her Famous Men sketch "Senator Blanche K. Bruce" published in the *Colored American Magazine* ten months after "Talma Gordon," the sea captain "Nathaniel Gordon was convicted of piracy in the United States District Court in the city of New York, for having fitted out a slaver, and shipped nine hundred Africans at Congo with a view of selling them as slaves" (87). In February 1862, the Maine-born Gordon became the only person from the United States ever hanged for slave trading (Soodalter 1). The statement from Ron Soodalter's *The Hanging of Captain Gordon: The Life and Trial of an American Slaver* (2006), emphasizing northern complicity in the highly profitable southern-based slave system, which serves as this chapter's second epigraph, comes close to being a gloss for "Talma Gordon." The content and bifurcated fourfold structure of Hopkins's story argue that turn-of-the-twentieth-century U.S. expansion should be seen as a new name for a long-standing practice of exploitation that has resulted in slavery, amalgamation, and racial intolerance. The people advocating and undertaking this piratical imperial enterprise, moreover, smugly—and falsely—

consider themselves to be the most highly developed intellectual and moral beings humankind has yet produced.

In "Talma Gordon" Hopkins produces, as Carby suggests but no other critic has fully acknowledged or sought to establish in detail, one of the most profound denunciations of empire appearing in a literary text by an African American author, significantly complicating Gaines's reading of her (and her contemporaries) as proimperialist. Similar to Sutton Griggs and James Weldon Johnson, Hopkins's position on expansion was far from stable. Though notably different from that of U.S. whites, the stance of African American writers and public intellectuals in the late 1800s and early 1900s vis-à-vis imperialism depended on a variety of factors, including the genre, audience, setting, venue, and political and cultural moment of, as well as the presence or absence of U.S. black soldiers in, the individual text.

Notes

Introduction. Empire at Home and Abroad

1. The names that have been applied to the period tend to be negative; some of these are temporal, such as the age of lynching, the age of Jim Crow, the age of accommodation, and the post-Reconstruction era, while others are spatial, e.g. the nadir and the Valley of Sorrows. For Charles Chesnutt, who lived long enough to observe and comment on—but did not actively participate in—the Harlem Renaissance, his writings appeared "a generation too soon" ("Remarks" 514), during a period he dubbed "postbellum-pre-Harlem," a phrase that entails a slippage between time and space.

2. Whereas I refer to "prejudice against color," Love uses the word "racism" and explains at some length why he does (14–17).

3. See "In Honor of the Soldiers," F. Steward, "Colored Soldiers," and T. Steward, "Thrift."

4. A memoir published in 1952 by his sister Eugenia, who served as president of the United Daughters of the Confederacy in the 1930s, recounts that he was given the nickname "Plato" after being seen while on KP duty stirring the pot with one hand and reading from a copy of the philosopher's works, in Greek, in the other (Lamar 32).

5. For example, both Pérez in *The Spanish* and Foner prefer the names "Spanish-American-Cuban War" and "Philippine-American War." For more on the names used to describe the conflict, see Pérez, *The War* 158n48, and Gianakos 3.

6. In 1892, a year after arriving in New York City, Arturo Alfonso Schomburg, born in San Juan, Puerto Rico in 1875, helped to found Las Dos Antillas, an organization lobbying for Cuban and Puerto Rican independence from Spain. Following the deaths of Martí, with whom he had taught high school in Manhattan, and Maceo, Schomburg withdrew from political activism. See "Biographical Note."

7. Hoganson points out that Filipinos were stereotyped in three ways—as savages, as children, and, in the case of the men, as less virile than white American males (135–37).

8. See Gatewood, *Black* and "*Smoked*," Kaplan chap. 4, and Stanford 85. For the reaction of the black press to U.S. imperialism during this period, see Marks.

9. On the subject of U.S. black soldiers' experiences in the Philippines, see Ngozi-Brown.

Chapter One. *Cuban Generals, Black Sergeants, and White Colonels: The African American Poetic Response to the Spanish-Cuban-American War*

1. For extended discussions on the relationship between gender and U.S. imperialism at the turn of the twentieth century, see Bederman, Hoganson, and Lears.

2. As noted in the introduction in conjunction with the Steward and Blount families, the Civil War and its aftermath often influenced white and black attitudes toward war and expansion at the turn of the twentieth century.

3. The subtitle reads: "Being a Brief, Comprehensive Review of the Negro's Participation in Wars of the United States: Especially Showing the Valor and Heroism of the Negro Soldiers of the Ninth and Tenth Cavalries, and the Twenty-fourth and Twenty-fifth Infantries of the Regular Army; as Demonstrated in the Decisive Campaign around Santiago de Cuba, 1898, when these Soldiers Crowned Themselves with a Halo of Unfading Glory."

4. See also Hoganson 131.

5. See Kaplan 133.

6. The murder of Baker plays a key role in Sutton Griggs's *Imperium in Imperio*.

7. An apprentice to William Lloyd Garrison at the *Liberator* at a young age and a cousin of and mentor to Pauline Hopkins, Smith (1830–95) became known as Boston's black poet laureate and received high praise for his verse from William Wells Brown (L. Brown 86; Hopkins, "Elijah" 278–79, 283). Several of his poems celebrate black and white abolitionists, including Garrison, Frederick Douglass, Lewis Hayden, William C. Nell, and Charles Sumner. In the "Song of the Liberators," the speaker assures Cuba that its cries for freedom have been "heard / Throughout our wide dominions," that "the souls of men are stirred," and that "rising in their manhood, / They shout from sea to sea, / 'Destruction to the tyrants! / Fair Cuba shall be free!'" (qtd. in Hopkins, "Elijah" 280). Clearly Smith, who had actively worked to bring slavery to an end in his own country, saw a compelling connection between the long-suffering Cubans and the past and present conditions of African Americans, a connection that figures in U.S. black poetry published in the late 1890s and the first years of the new century.

8. I have not been able to locate a copy of the 1899 edition of McGirt's first book of poetry. Thus, it is only my assumption that "The Memory of Maceo" was included in the first edition of this volume.

9. For more information about the book and the legend recounted in Temple's "epic," including the current site of the Columbus bell, see "Ringing Columbus' Bell."

10. The poem may have been inspired by journalist Murat Halstead's account of women in the Cuban forces in *The Story of Cuba: Her Struggles for Liberty*, published in 1896, which refers to the "Amazons" (147) who participated in the liberation fight.

11. Coffin's statement anticipates the sentiment expressed by Pauline Hopkins in her preface to *Contending Forces* (1900) and echoed by John Wesley Grant in his preface

to *Out of Darkness* (1909) and Otis Shackelford in his preface to *Lillian Simmons* (1915).

12. For a reading of Harper's "Maceo," along with her earlier poem "The Death of Zombi," in a transnational context, see Callahan.

13. Several white authors wrote poems about black soldiers in Cuba, some of which patronize black troops in the process of praising them. See, for example, B. M. Channing's "The Negro Soldier" and George E. Powell's "The Nigger Ninth on San Juan Hill."

14. Sutton Griggs develops this theme in detail in his novel *The Hindered Hand* (1905).

15. In the James Weldon Johnson Papers at Yale University's Beinecke Library, "The Color Sergeant" appears in a handwritten notebook, dated 1899–1904, in a different form from the published version. At the bottom of this version, Johnson has inscribed the date "1898," suggesting that he may have written the poem in that year and then copied it into the notebook in 1899 or sometime later. In the Johnson Papers, the handwritten version of the poem, dated 1899 and entitled "The Color Sergeant: Tenth U.S. Cavalry: At San Juan," has an "a" for "the" in line 1, "gallant" for "sable" in line 3, "fort-crown'd" for "fort-crowned" in line 5, a semicolon rather than a comma at the end of line 7, "was" for "grew" in line 9, "tho" for "though" in line 11, "maker" for "Maker" in line 16, "rank or name" for "honor or rank" in line 17, "Yet still" for "But, still" in line 18, and "But true to God and duty" for "Yet true, in death, to his duty" in line 20.

16. See Kaplan 134, Cashin et al., and E. A. Johnson.

17. The "Here and There" section of the July 1903 issue of the *Colored American Magazine* attributes another statement to "President Roosevelt" that contradicts even more starkly what he wrote in *Scribner's*: "I know of the bravery of the Negro soldier. He saved my life at Santiago, and I have had occasion to say so in many articles and speeches. The Rough Riders were in a bad position, when the Ninth and Tenth Cavalry came rushing up the hill, carrying everything before them. The Negro soldier has the faculty of coming to the front when he is needed most. In the Civil War he came up 4,000 [sic] strong, and I believe he saved the Union" (532). I have not been able to locate the original source for this passage. However, in 1905 a similar statement was reprinted in William A. Sinclair's *The Aftermath of Slavery: A Study of the Condition and Environment of the American Negro* (315). In his 1899 *History of Negro Soldiers in the Spanish-American War*, Edward A. Johnson reprinted another positive comment Roosevelt made about the Ninth and Tenth regiments: "The Spaniards called them 'Smoked Yankees,' but we found them an excellent breed of Yankees. I'm sure I speak the sentiments of officers and men in the assemblage when I say that between you and the other cavalry regiments exists a tie which we trust will never be broken" (39).

18. A second controversial aspect of the *Scribner's* article was Roosevelt's contention that black troops "are, of course, peculiarly dependent upon their white officers" (149), which served to justify the army's practice of not, except in highly unusual cases, appointing African Americans at a rank above second lieutenant, a policy that was much resented by black soldiers and the black public. In his rebuttal to Roosevelt, Holliday expresses his support for the *Richmond Planet's* slogan, which had been embraced by

the *New York Age*, "No officers. No soldiers" (97). In other words, U.S. blacks should not serve their country unless there were black officers to lead them.

19. As I note in chapter 4, Johnson's early, unpublished prose piece "The War Catechism," from which the second epigraph to this chapter is taken, makes clear that he knew the power of patriotic symbols to stir the imagination.

20. In *Playing in the Dark: Whiteness and the Literary Imagination*, Toni Morrison states of Poe, "We can look to 'The Gold-Bug' and 'How to Write a Blackwoods Article' (as well as *Pym*) for samples of the desperate need of this writer with pretensions to the planter class for the literary techniques of 'othering' so common to American literature: estranging language, metaphoric condensation, fetishizing strategies, the economy of stereotype, allegorical foreclosure; strategies employed to secure his characters' (and his readers') identity" (58).

21. The association between Legrand's Newfoundland and his dialect-speaking and malaprop-spouting black servant Jupiter in "The Gold-Bug" may also anticipate the connection between Marse Chan's dog and Sam in Page's story. Additionally, the narrator's statement about Amasa Delano in Melville's *Benito Cereno* (1855) is worth noting: "In fact, like most men of a good, blithe heart, Captain Delano took to negroes, not philanthropically, but genially, just as other men to Newfoundland dogs" (71).

Chapter Two. Wars Abroad and at Home in Sutton E. Griggs's Imperium in Imperio *and* The Hindered Hand

1. Unrelentingly pessimistic, *Overshadowed* tells the story of the Job-like trials and sad demise of the tragic mulatta Erma Wysong. In stark contrast, *Unfettered* claims that when the protagonist's "plan" for solving the race problem is implemented it enjoys remarkable success, vastly improving conditions for not only African Americans but also blacks across the globe. Gloom, however, pervades the next book, *The Hindered Hand*, which graphically depicts the lynching of an innocent black couple, includes a woman literally driven insane by the South's pursuit of racial purity, and concludes with one of the protagonists leaving for Liberia, where he will strive to provide a refuge for U.S. blacks denied their citizenship rights in the land of their birth, should this prove necessary. If the pessimism of the fourth novel recalls that of the second, the optimism of Griggs's final fiction resembles that of the third. Like *Unfettered*, *Pointing the Way* envisions a solution to the race problem, this one engineered by a coalition of talented blacks and enlightened whites that begins in one southern city and spreads throughout the nation.

2. Perhaps Elder has come as close as anyone has to summing up the writer's fiction: "Sutton Griggs's novels are literary collages, part propagandist blueprint for political action, part gothic romance of the maze and morass of miscegenation, and part symbolic description of the conditions threatening the internal and external life of the 'New Negro' of the turn of the century" (69).

3. Whereas Gloster, Frazier, Winter, and Knadler regard Griggs as an anti-Bookerite in his novels, Bone and Elder see him supporting Washington's policies.

4. Griggs also addresses the political, physical, and judicial assaults on U.S. blacks in *The One Great Question: A Study of Southern Conditions at Close Range*, published by Orion in 1907, a fifty-eight-page nonfiction tract that characterizes the South generally—and Nashville in particular—as "repressionist" and quotes passages from his own fiction that he claims were based on events he witnessed personally or were widely documented.

5. Although it does not specifically address the Spanish-Cuban-American or the Philippine-American War, as three of the other novels do, *Overshadowed* (1901) links the situation of U.S. blacks to that of people of color throughout the world. Erma's husband, Astral Herndon, buries her at sea rather than on U.S. soil, proclaiming himself "A CITIZEN OF THE OCEAN" instead of the country of his birth and asserting that "this title shall be entailed upon my progeny unto all generations, until such time as the shadows which now envelop the darker races in all lands shall have passed away, away and away" (217). The epilogue holds out the faint hope that Erma and Astral's son shall inspire "the Negro" to "emerge from his centuries of gloom" (219).

6. With the exception of James Robert Payne's 1983 essay "Afro-American Literature of the Spanish-American War," critics had not addressed connections between Griggs's novels on the one hand and the Spanish-Cuban-American War and U.S. expansion on the other until Susan Gillman's *Blood Talk: American Race Melodrama and the Culture of the Occult* (2003), Stephen Knadler's "Sensationalizing Patriotism: Sutton Griggs and the Sentimental Nationalism of Citizen Tom" (2007), which is reprinted in *Remapping Citizenship and the Nation in African-American Literature* (2010), and Caroline Levander's "Sutton Griggs and the Borderlands of Empire" (2010). In their extended readings of all five of Griggs's novels, Moses, Winter, and Elder do not address U.S. imperialism. The first two make no mention of the Spanish-Cuban-American and Philippine-American wars, and the third only briefly addresses the latter in connection with *Unfettered*. Moreover, one recent scholar, John David Smith, dubiously asserts that Griggs "advocated both American imperialism abroad and the establishment of a black empire at home" (54) in "'My Books Are Hard Reading for a Negro': Thomas Dixon and His African American Critics, 1905–1939" (2009).

7. Biographical information on Griggs remains sketchy. Most of the published chronologies of his life, including that in the 2003 Modern Library edition of *Imperium*, contain inaccuracies. Randolph Meade Walker's 1990 Memphis State University dissertation "The Metamorphosis of Sutton E. Griggs: A Southern Black Baptist Minister's Transformation in Theological and Sociological Thought during the Early Twentieth Century" offers reliable information but focuses on the latter half of the writer's career. Finnie D. Coleman's *Sutton E. Griggs and the Struggle against White Supremacy* (2007), the only published monograph devoted exclusively to the author, provides many tantalizing tidbits about Griggs's life, but its documentation leaves much to be desired.

8. The dedication reads, in part, as follows: "*The one dear life, in all the on going of time, I shall / Be allowed to live upon this planet, came to me / Within the borders of the imperial state of Texas. Whatever others / may say, shall I not love her? Well, I do*" (v).

9. Seeing the prospect of the Civil War on the horizon, Douglass nevertheless

adamantly asserts that he does not wish to behold the devastation this would entail: "I do not know but the spirit of rapine and plunder, so rampant in America will hurry her on to her own destruction. I hope it will not, for although America has done all a nation could do to crush me . . . yet, I trust in God, no ill may befall her. I hope she will yet see that it will be her duty to emancipate the slaves" (118).

10. For information on Morgan, see Upchurch.

11. It is not clear whether Johnson's plan may have inspired Griggs's *Imperium* or vice versa. In *The History of Black Baptists*, Leroy Fitts states that Johnson first proposed the "Texas Movement" in the early 1890s (247). Others, including A. Briscoe Koger, who wrote a 1957 biographical sketch of Johnson, assert that the "National Texas Purchase Movement" occurred after 1900. Koger describes Johnson's proposal as "unworkable" but goes on to note that "as fantastic as it may appear, however, several organizations endorsed the plan and sought information and advice about its workings" (16).

12. As George P. Marks documents, the African American press frequently connected the sinking of the *Maine* and the lynching of Baker, as does "Negroes Who Protect American Rights Abroad Must Be Protected at Home," a letter addressed to the U.S. Senate that was drafted following "a mass meeting of colored citizens" at Boston's Faneuil Hall on February 28, 1898, "to protest against the murder of the colored postmaster of Lake City, S.C." (199–200).

13. See Levander, "Confederate."

14. Additionally, the proposed but swiftly rejected option of mass emigration of U.S. blacks to Africa discussed by the Imperium targets the Congo Free State with the intent either to take the colony away from the Belgians by force or to purchase it from King Leopold, a plan that foreshadows Harry Dean's early twentieth-century dream of buying Portuguese East Africa for the establishment of a African American–led Ethiopian empire recounted in his 1929 autobiographical work *The Pedro Gorino*.

15. In "Literary Garveyism: The Novels of Reverend Sutton E. Griggs" (1979) Wilson Moses expounds upon Gayle's statement. See also Logan 360.

16. M. Giulia Fabi notes in *Passing and the Rise of the African American Novel* (2001) that Griggs consistently opposes the irresponsible actions of the privileged, fair-skinned Bernard with "the self-discipline that Belton has painfully had to acquire in his life as a lower-class, visibly black person" (54).

17. Some scientists held such notions. For example, the *Handbook for the Ship's Medicine Chest* by George W. Stoner, published at the direction of the U.S. surgeon general (first edition 1900, second edition 1904), quotes the theory that "the relative immunity of the negroes [to yellow fever] is to be attributed to the lively and quite specific activity of their skin, distinctly evidenced by the odor" (13).

18. At the turn to the twentieth century, U.S. academics such as Franklin Giddings and Harry H. Powers regarded Slavic people as the chief threat to Anglo-Saxon supremacy in the years to come (Gossett 312–14; Kramer 1334). Such fears diminished in the wake of Japan's defeat of Russia. A series of articles by Jack London, a correspondent during the Russo-Japanese War, stoked fears of an impending "yellow peril," and in 1910

he would publish a science fiction story about the use of biological warfare by "white" nations to wipe out the population of a surging China.

19. As T. G. Steward reports in *The Colored Regulars*, the black Twenty-Fourth Infantry regular army regiment lost one-third of its men to the disease when it was tasked with caring for the sick at a yellow fever hospital in Siboney during the summer of 1898 (222; see also Crosby 102). Espinosa has this to say on the topic: "Whether people of African descent actually enjoyed a somewhat lesser susceptibility to yellow fever remains a matter of controversy. Some historians claim that it was this innate resistance to yellow fever that led plantation owners in the southern North American colonies and in the Caribbean to increasingly favor African slavery over other available forms of labor" (127).

20. According to Cunningham, each regiment had twenty-four black lieutenants and one black chaplain, but all of the commanding officers were white.

21. As newspapers such as the *Chicago Broad Ax* noted, a few black soldiers were promoted after the defeat of Spain, but they lost their commissions when their regiments were mustered out (Marks 137–38).

22. For a discussion of the relationship between narrative and polemic in *The Hindered Hand* and *Unfettered*, see Gruesser, *Black* 24–33.

23. For information on Blackburn, see Steers, *Blood on the Moon*, Bell, *Mosquito Soldiers*, Steers, ed., *The Trial*, Singer, "A Fiend in Gray," and Haines, "Did a Confederate Doctor Engage in a Primitive Form of Biological Warfare," as well as the *New York Times* articles "Yellow Fever Plot" and "The Great Fever Plot."

24. For a discussion of Dixon's novel in connection with U.S. expansion, see Murphy 58–76.

25. Gossett 322–28, Kramer, and Jacobson, *Special Sorrows* 188–91 discuss the short-lived "rapprochement" between Britain and the United States that began in 1898 to which Ellwood refers. Another of the contemporaneous events cited by Ellwood is "the rise in the present day of a poet of the whole English speaking people" (207), a reference to Rudyard Kipling, whose poem "The White Man's Burden," written on the occasion of the takeover of the Philippines and sent to his friend Theodore Roosevelt prior to its publication, served as a moral justification for U.S. overseas expansion.

Chapter Three. Black Burdens, Laguna Tales, and "Citizen Tom" Narratives: African American Writing and the Philippine-American War

1. See, for example, the contrasting interpretations of the poem by Love and Brantlinger. The former questions whether it is the "classic exhortation to empire" many claim it to be, citing its "churning irony and cynicism" and the "dark prophecy of the fate of the imperialists" at its conclusion, which is "hardly an appeal to the glories of empire" (6). The latter, noting that Kipling wrote to Theodore Roosevelt urging him to push for annexation, states, "Kipling may or may not have felt that America was already assuming the role of imperial leadership that had heretofore belonged to England, but the

message of 'The White Man's Burden' is unmistakable: America should do so, at least in the Philippines" (188).

2. A short time later, Marlow distinguishes British imperialism from that of the other European powers, stating that it is "good to see at any time" Great Britain's colonial possessions on a map "because one knows that some real work is done there" (199).

3. Some white writers rejected Kipling's assertions of Anglo-Saxon enlightenment and altruism in the light of conditions facing U.S. blacks at the turn to the twentieth century. In "The Black Man's Burden" (1905), for example, Unitarian minister John White Chadwick invokes African American military service in responding to Kipling's poem:

> Take up the black man's burden!
> He helped to share your own
> On many a scene by battle-clouds
> Portentously overblown;
> On Wagner's awful parapet,
> As late where Shafter's plan
> Was for the boys to take the lead,
> He showed himself a man. (9–16)

Here Chadwick invokes not only the Fifty-Fourth Massachusetts regiment during the Civil War but the actions of U.S. black soldiers in the war against Spain.

4. On this subject, see, for example, Jacobson, *Special* 210–14.

5. Using the Kiplingesque pseudonym "Gunga Din," black socialist Hubert Harrison published a materialist parody entitled "The Black Man's Burden (A Reply to Rudyard Kipling)" directed primarily at British rather than U.S. imperialism. Published during World War I, the fifty-six-line, seven-stanza poem contends that "Teuton trained efficiency" will render Anglo-Saxon "hope for nought" (23–24). A few years later, another parody entitled "The Black Man's Burden," in this case by veteran African American journalist T. Thomas Fortune, appeared in one of Marcus Garvey's publications. Harrison and Fortune's poems and Bruce's essays indicate that Kipling's poem continued to be a flashpoint for U.S. black indignation years after its initial publication.

6. In 1910, Bruce wrote a short, openly anti-imperialist article entitled "The White Man's Burden," in which he describes Anglo-Saxons as obsessed, conceited, ignorant of history, and contemptibly laughable. Addressing one of the premises of Kipling's poem, he declares the supposedly "altruistic aims" of white men "in the countries of black, brown, and red men" to be, in fact, "to control the natural resources of these countries and enrich" themselves "by exploiting these darker races and their wealth-producing products." Moreover, he predicts that the "white man's burden, self-imposed, will break his back if he is not relieved of it" (97–98). See also Bruce's "White Man's Idea of Heaven."

7. The first version, the one analyzed here, was published as "The Burden of Black Women" in November 1907 issue of *Horizon*; a slightly different version, also entitled "The Burden of Black Women," appeared in the November 1914 issue of *The Crisis*; inclusive of some revisions, the poem, retitled "The Riddle of the Sphinx," was used as

an intertext in Du Bois's *Darkwater* in 1920, and in 1963 a slightly altered version was printed in *The ABC of Color*, a collection of Du Bois's writings.

8. For information about Ethiopianism, see Drake, Moses, *Golden*, Sundquist, and Gruesser, *Black*.

9. For readings of Du Bois's poem, see Sundquist 582–83 and Gilman and Weinbaum, introduction.

10. Susan Gillman quite appropriately terms *Unfettered* "Griggs's most political novel" (105).

11. During the election of 1900, mainstream anti-imperialists explored the possibility of launching a third party (Schirmer 202), and in June 1900 a proposal was floated to form a National Afro-American Party with a staunch anti-imperialist plank (Marks 173, 209–11).

12. For the use of similar language, see, for example, the writings of Du Bois, Hopkins, and Bruce. For a discussion of racist science and social Darwinism, see Lears 90–100 and Gossett, esp. 144–75 and 310–38. U.S. black writers and public intellectuals, including Griggs himself, often countered the lowly (and often doomed) status to which the era's racist discourse consigned peoples of African descent by invoking Ethiopianism's cyclical theory of races.

13. The play on the word "expansion" Warthell makes in this passage resembles the one Ellwood makes on the word "race" in *The Hindered Hand* as he hastily leaves Liberia upon learning that Tiara is available to him (273).

14. For a discussion of Griggs's use of Africa in *Unfettered* and *The Hindered Hand*, see Gruesser, *Black* 24–33.

15. "Gugus" is a racial epithet; it appears in Steward's first two Laguna stories as well as in letters he wrote about the Philippines.

16. See "He Prefers Hell to United States," "Turner Denies He Cursed Flag," and Redkey.

17. In addition to his novel, Gilmore wrote poetry, dramatic works, and song lyrics. See Gilmore, *Souvenir*.

18. Given the fact that the novel refers to *Othello* on three separate occasions, casting Henderson as the general, Freda as Desdemona, and, by extension, the jealous schemer Fairfax as Iago, there may be a distant echo of the epithets "inhuman dog" and "Spartan dog" that Roderigo and Lodovico hurl at the villain in act 5 of Shakespeare's tragedy in this passage.

Chapter Four. Annexation in the Pacific and Asian Conspiracy in Central America in James Weldon Johnson's Unproduced Operettas

1. For a useful article about the position of cigar factory "lectors" (who were hired, fired, and paid not by management but by the workers themselves) explaining the dynamic nature of their relationship with the workers, see Pérez, "Reminiscences."

2. All but lost amid the recent criticisms that have been directed at the novel is the precedent Johnson establishes by depicting his home state as a transnational location.

Subsequent writers, notably Zora Neale Hurston in *Their Eyes Were Watching God*, portray Florida in a similar manner. Hurston sets her most famous novel in various Florida locations, including Eatonville, Jacksonville, and the Everglades, the last of which annually attracted migrant workers from other parts of the state, Georgia and places further north, and the Caribbean, especially the Bahamas, in the early twentieth century. The transnational dimensions of the Everglades section of the novel complicate the black versus white dynamic that, along with various gender considerations, has been the focus of scholarship on *Their Eyes Are Watching God*. African American criticism, especially that by men when the novel was first published, has tended to read the book in the light of race relations in the United States from the time of the Civil War to the period between the two world wars. Such an approach, however, fails to account for Hurston's decisions to set the novel in a liminal location, Florida, particularly the Everglades, and employ a liminal figure, Janie, as the protagonist. Hurston not only includes Bahamans and Native Americans, as well as U.S. whites and blacks, but also information relating to the devastating hurricane of 1928, which affected Canada, the United States, and the Caribbean, into the story.

Much has been made of the courtroom scene in the penultimate chapter of the novel, specifically the contrast between, on the one hand, the sympathy shown to Janie by the white doctor, sheriff, jury, and spectators for having to shoot her deranged and dying husband and, on the other, the desire of the black community to see her punished for taking Tea Cake's life. Yet, viewed from a transnational perspective, the trial functions as the last of a series of at least six instances in which people from different nations, "races," classes, castes, and genders come into conflict from the start of chapter 14, when Tea Cake and Janie arrive in "de muck," until the opening of chapter 20, when she returns to Eatonville. Read strictly in the context of black-white relations, Janie's momentary alienation from the black community and affiliation with white people in the all-important courtroom scene may indeed appear problematic. Looked at in the transnational context of Florida and the Everglades, however, it must be seen as part of a larger pattern of difference, prejudgment, and misunderstanding rather than a single, defining instance. For the connection between *Their Eyes Are Watching God* and the hurricane of 1928, as well as the novel's relevance to the devastation wrought by Hurricane Katrina, see Cartwright. For a discussion of the Bahaman presence in Hurston's novel, see Bone.

3. In *Along This Way*, Johnson uses the title *Toloso* to refer to the comic opera he initially wrote with his brother in 1899 (originally entitled *The Royal Document* and then renamed *Tolosa; or, The Royal Document*, which, in later versions written with Bob Cole, became *The Fakir* and *The Czar of Czam*). For the sake of convenience, in this chapter I use *Toloso* to refer to this project generally.

4. For biographical information on Johnson, see Levy, Fleming, Carroll, Beavers, and Seniors.

5. Johnson's opinion of his native city soured, however. He describes the Jacksonville of the time at which he wrote his autobiography as "one hundred per cent Cracker town" (*Along* 45).

6. For information on the racial dynamics of the Chicago World's Fair, see Bederman 31–41.

7. By not traveling with *The Shoo-Fly Regiment*, which toured extensively and later had a run on Broadway, Johnson was spared the financial burden of the show when it bogged down in the South. In *Along This Way*, he explains that, as a large, black-run production, *The Shoo-Fly Regiment* could not get bookings at first-class venues and thus proved untenable (240). Compounding the problem, as Reid Badger notes, it was scheduled to be performed in three Texas cities and elsewhere in the Southwest in the wake of the 1906 Brownsville incident, which resulted in three companies of African American soldiers, several of whom had served in Cuba and the Philippines, being dishonorably discharged en masse by Roosevelt (33). Such was the outcry of blacks over the president's action that Johnson was seriously considered for a more prominent consular posting, that in Nice, France, although the appointment never came (*Along* 250–51).

8. Roosevelt not only praised and thanked Johnson for the tune "You're All Right, Teddy" and appointed him consul in Latin America, but, in 1912, at the request of his friend Columbia professor Brander Matthews, who served as a kind of mentor to Johnson and wrote the introduction to *Fifty Years and Other Poems*, Roosevelt, as indicated in the first epigraph to this chapter, read and commented on *Ex-Colored Man*, even though he refused to endorse it publicly. His assessment, which suggests that he may have assumed the book was a memoir rather than a novel, indicates that, if nothing else, *Ex-Colored Man* forced Roosevelt to face his conflicted feelings about U.S. race relations. See Taubenfield 175.

9. Allen Woll provides a somewhat different synopsis, reporting that *The Shoo-Fly Regiment* "centers on Hunter Wilson . . . , a young graduate of Tuskegee Institute who is about to become a teacher. But the Spanish-American War erupts, and Hunter decides to defend his country. His patriotic zeal pleases his friends and neighbors, but his sweetheart, Rose Maxwell . . . , feels that Hunter should remain at home. In the final scene of the first act, Rose returns Hunter's engagement ring. Hunter is sent to the Philippines, where he leads an attack on an enemy fortress. . . . He returns triumphantly to his Alabama home, and Rose finally agrees to marry him" (23). Seniors, however, reports that Hunter Wilson was a janitor at Lincolnville and the focus of a humorous subplot in which he marries the Village Pride (a stock minstrel character typically portrayed by a man and thus akin to Tyler Perry's Madea), who has ten children. Although in the absence of a surviving libretto, it is hard to know for certain, the discrepancy between Seniors's and Woll's overviews of the operetta may be attributable, at least in part, to changes that were made to it over the two-year period, 1906 to 1908, during which it was performed. Woll describes the plot as "somewhat hackneyed by modern standards" (23); however, as Seniors makes clear, what was not typical, in an era of so-called coon shows was the portrayal of educated, patriotic blacks engaged in romantic situations. The *Indianapolis Freeman* hailed the musical as "perhaps the most ambitious effort yet attempted by a colored company," both for its theme and its humorous satire of African American vanity, social pretension, and imitation of the white elite (qtd. in Krasner 136).

10. Lacking the satirical bite of Ade's Stories of Benevolent Assimilation columns, which highlight the injustice and absurdity of the Philippine occupation by chronicling Washington Conner's comically unsuccessful attempts to convince the Kakyak family of the benefits of adopting the beliefs and practices of U.S. whites, *The Sultan of Sulu* focuses on a single ironic aspect of U.S. policy in the Philippines: the fact that slavery and polygamy were practiced in Moro, one of the few places in the islands to welcome U.S. rule.

11. Johnson Papers, box 75, folder 456.

12. Johnson Papers, box 75, folder 458.

13. Johnson Papers, box 74, folders 449 and 438.

14. Johnson Papers, box 74, folder 427.

15. Johnson Papers, box 75, folders 444, 445, and 446.

16. In his *Autobiography*, Roosevelt designates the building of the Panama Canal as his single greatest foreign policy achievement and vigorously defends the steps he took to make it possible. (See the chapter "The Monroe Doctrine and the Panama Canal" 443–71.) Although at least one historian doubts that Zelaya tried to interest the Japanese in building a canal (Bermann 150), Johnson states that he was briefed by his superiors about "secret negotiations with Japan for the acquisition of the Nicaraguan route" in 1908 and that a copy of the Zelaya's "letter broaching the matter was in the hands of the State Department" (*Along* 288). Furthermore, he emphasizes the importance that the United States placed on the threat of a canal across Nicaragua and argues that security concerns rather than financial considerations largely determined U.S. policy in the region (288–89).

17. London's war correspondence and "The Yellow Peril" are reprinted in *Jack London Reports*. "The Unparalleled Invasion," which appeared in *McClure's Magazine* in 1910, was republished in London's collection *The Strength of the Strong*. See also Reesman 13–54, 101–3, and 121–22, Sharp, Berkove, and Lye.

18. Skinner's comical ancestry also provides the occasion for digs at Democrats, especially William Jennings Bryan. There are additional references to Roosevelt in Johnson's lyrics for Skinner's song "When I Am Czar of Czam," which mentions a "strenuous life" and "Racial Suicide." See Johnson Papers, box 74, folder 439.

Coda. Pauline Hopkins, the Colored American Magazine, *and the Critique of Empire Abroad and at Home in "Talma Gordon"*

1. In my anthology *A Century of Detection: Twenty Great Mystery Stories* (2010), I do the same but stress the role that expansion plays in the story and note the link between "Talma Gordon" and "The Gold-Bug" (341).

2. Hopkins frequently named her fictional characters after people from history. The notoriously corrupt Simon Cameron served for a year as Lincoln's first secretary of war before being forced to resign.

Works Cited

Ade, George. *George Ade's "Stories of 'Benevolent Assimilation.'"* Ed. Perry E. Gianakos. Quezon City, Philippines: New Day, 1985.

———. *The Sultan of Sulu: An Original Satire in Two Acts*. New York: Russell, 1903.

"All Negro Regiments to Go to Philippines." *New York Times* 6 January 1907.

Allen, John Henry. "Rings upon the Pike." *For the Love of Liberty: African American Soldiers in the Post War Years, 1900–1916*. By Anthony Powell. 102–3. http://issuu.com/dakarinteractive/docs/love_of_liberty_3/search.

Andrews, William. "Liberal Religion and Free Love: An Undiscovered Afro-American Novel of the 1890s." *MELUS* 9.1 (1982): 23–36.

"Anti-imperialist Resolutions, Black Citizens of Boston." *The Philippines Reader: A History of Colonialism, Neocolonialism, Dictatorship, and Resistance*. Ed. Daniel B. Schirmer and Stephen Rosskamm Shalom. Boston: South End, 1986. 31–32.

Appiah, Kwame Anthony. *In My Father's House: Africa in the Philosophy of Culture*. New York: Oxford University Press, 1992.

Bacote, Clarence A. "Negro Proscriptions, Protest, and Proposed Solutions in Georgia, 1880–1908." *Journal of Southern History* 25.4 (1959): 471–98.

Badger, Reid. *A Life in Ragtime: A Biography of James Reese Europe*. New York: Oxford University Press, 1995.

Barr, Alwyn. *Black Texans: A History of African Americans in Texas, 1528–1995*. Norman: University of Oklahoma Press, 1996.

Bauer, Ralph. "Hemispheric Studies." *PMLA* 124.1 (2009): 234–50.

Beadle, Samuel Alfred. "Lines." 1899. *African-American Poetry of the Nineteenth Century: An Anthology*. Ed. Joan R. Sherman. Urbana: University of Illinois Press, 1992. 465–66.

Beavers, Herman. "Johnson, James Weldon." *The Oxford Companion to African American Literature*. Ed. William L. Andrews, Frances Smith Foster, and Trudier Harris. New York: Oxford University Press, 1997. 404–6.

Bederman, Gail. *Manliness and Civilization: A Cultural History of Gender and Race in the United States, 1880–1919*. Chicago: University of Chicago Press, 1995.

Bell, Andrew McIlwane. *Mosquito Soldiers: Malaria, Yellow Fever, and the Course of the American Civil War*. Baton Rouge: Louisiana State University Press, 2010.

Berkove. Lawrence J. "A Parallax Correction in London's 'The Unparalleled Invasion.'" *American Literary Realism* 24.2 (1992): 33–39.

Bermann, Karl. *Under the Big Stick: Nicaragua and the United States since 1848*. Boston: South End, 1986.

"Biographical Note." Arthur A. Schomburg Papers. Schomburg Center for Research in Black Culture, New York Public Library. http://www.nypl.org/archives/3953.

Blisard, F. X. "Tarzan versus Tarzan." Pt. 1. *ERBzine* 0291. http://www.erbzine.com/mag2/0292.html.

Blount, James H., Jr. *The American Occupation of the Philippines, 1898–1912*. New York: Putnam, 1912.

———. "Philippine Independence When?" *North American Review* 18 January 1907, 135–49.

———. "Philippine Independence Why?" *North American Review* 21 June 1907, 365–77.

Bold, Christine. "Where Did the Black Rough Riders Go?" *Canadian Review of American Studies* 39.3 (2009): 273–97.

Bone, Martyn. "The (Extended) South of Black Folk: Intraregional and Transnational Migrant Labor in *Jonah's Gourd Vine* and *Their Eyes Were Watching God*." *American Literature* 79.4 (2007): 753–79.

Bone, Robert. *The Negro Novel in America*. Rev. ed. New Haven, Conn.: Yale University Press, 1965.

Bowser, J. Dallas. "Take Up the Black Man's Burden." *Colored American* (Washington, D.C.) 8 April 1899, 1.

Bradley, James. *The Imperial Cruise: A Secret History of Empire and War*. New York: Little, Brown, 2009.

Brantlinger, Patrick. "'The White Man's Burden' and Its Afterlives." *English Literature in Transition, 1880–1920*, 50.2 (2007): 172–91.

Brazley, Stella A. E. "The Colored Boys in Blue." *The Spanish-American War Volunteer*. 2nd ed. Ed. W. Hilary Coston. Middleton, Pa.: n.p., 1899. 81.

Brown, Lois. *Pauline Elizabeth Hopkins: Black Daughter of the Revolution*. Chapel Hill: University of North Carolina Press, 2008.

Bruce, John E. "The Stronger Nations vs. the Weaker Nations." *Voice of the Negro* April 1905, 256–57.

———. "The White Man's Burden." Ca. 1910. *The Selected Writings of John Edward Bruce: Militant Black Journalist*. Ed. Peter Gilbert. New York: Arno, 1971. 97–100.

———. "The White Man's Idea of Heaven." *Colored American* (Washington, D.C.) 22 December 1900, 11.

———. "Why Talk of the White Man's Burden?" *Colored American* (Washington, D.C.) 25 February 1899, 1.

Callahan, Monique-Adelle. "Translations of Transnational Black Icons in the Poetics of Frances Harper: Brazil's Zumbi and Cuba's Maceo." *Loopholes and Retreats: African American Writers and the Nineteenth Century*. Ed. John Cullen Gruesser and Hanna Wallinger. Muenster: Lit, 2009. 59–80.

Carby, Hazel V. *Reconstructing Womanhood: The Emergence of the Afro-American Woman Novelist.* New York: Oxford University Press, 1987.

Carroll, Anne E. "James Weldon Johnson (1871–1938)." *Harlem Speaks: A Living History of the Harlem Renaissance.* Ed. Cary D. Wintz. Naperville, Ill.: Sourcebooks, 2007. 343–60.

Cartwright, Keith. "'To Walk with the Storm': Oya as the Transformative 'I' of Zora Neale Hurston's Afro-Atlantic Callings." *American Literature* 78.4 (2006): 741–67.

Cashin, Herschel V., et al. *Under Fire with the Tenth U.S. Cavalry.* 1899. Salem, Mass.: Ayer, 1969.

Chadwick, John White. "The Black Man's Burden." 1899. *Later Poems.* Boston: Houghton, 1905. 115–17.

Channing, B. M. "The Tenth at Quasina." *Baptist Home Mission Monthly* November 1898, 375.

"Character Sketch: Mr. Rudyard Kipling: The Banjo Bard of Empire." *Review of Reviews* 15 April 1899, 318–27.

Chesnutt, Charles. "Remarks of Charles Waddell Chesnutt, of Cleveland, in Accepting the Spingarn Medal in Los Angeles." *Charles W. Chesnutt: Essays and Speeches.* Ed. Joseph R. McElrath, Robert C. Leitz III, and Jesse S. Christie. Stanford, Calif.: Stanford University Press, 2002. 510–15.

Coffin, Frank B. *Coffin's Poems and Ajax's Ordeals.* Little Rock, Ark.: The Colored Advocate, 1897.

———. "Maceo—Cuba's Liberator." Coffin 71–75.

———. "Preface." Coffin 5–6.

Coleman, Finnie D. *Sutton E. Griggs and the Struggle against White Supremacy.* Knoxville: University of Tennessee Press, 2007.

Conrad, Joseph. *Heart of Darkness. Blackwood's Magazine* February 1899, 193–220.

Cordell, Sigrid Anderson. "'The Case Was Very Black against' Her: Pauline Hopkins and the Politics of Racial Ambiguity at the *Colored American Magazine.*" *American Periodicals* 16.1 (2006): 52–73.

Crosby, Molly Caldwell. *The American Plague: The Untold Story of Yellow Fever, the Epidemic That Shaped Our History.* New York: Berkley, 2006.

Cunningham, Roger D. "The Black 'Immune' Regiments in the Spanish-American War." *The Army Historical Foundation.* http://www.armyhistory.org/ahf2.aspx?pgID=877&id=145&exCompID=56.

Damon, Woolford. "Twenty-Third Annual Session of the National Negro Baptist Convention at Philadelphia." *Colored American Magazine* November 1903, 778–93.

Dasenbrock, Reed Way. "Intelligibility and Meaningfulness in Multicultural Literature in English." *PMLA* 102.1 (1987): 10–19.

Davis, Daniel Webster. "The Black Woman's Burden." *Voice of the Negro* July 1904, 308.

Dean, Harry. *The Pedro Gorino.* Boston: Houghton, 1929.

Doreski, C. K. "Inherited Rhetoric and Authentic History." *The Unruly Voice: Rediscovering Pauline Elizabeth Hopkins.* Ed. John Cullen Gruesser. Urbana: University of Illinois Press. 1996. 71–97.

Douglass, Frederick. "Texas, Slavery, and American Prosperity: An Address Delivered in Belfast, Ireland, on January 2, 1846." *The Frederick Douglass Papers: Series One—Speeches, Debates, and Interviews.* 5 vols. New Haven, Conn.: Yale University Press, 1979. 1:118.

Douglass, Lewis H. "Black Opposition to McKinley." 1899. Foner 2:824–25.

Drake, St. Clair. *The Redemption of Africa and Black Religion.* Chicago: Third World, 1970.

Du Bois, W. E. B. "The Burden of Black Women." *Horizon* 2 (November 1907): 3–5.

———. "The Color Line Belts the World." 1906. *W. E. B. Du Bois on Asia.* Ed. Bill V. Mullen and Cathryn Wilson. Jackson: University of Mississippi Press, 2005. 33–34.

———. *Dark Princess: A Romance.* New York: Harcourt, 1928.

———. Letter to Oswald Garrison Villard. 24 March 1905. *African American Political Thought, 1890–1930: Washington, Du Bois, Garvey, and Randolph.* Ed. Cary D. Wintz. Armonk, N.Y.: Sharpe, 1996. 98–102.

———. "Negro Art and Literature." 1924. Sundquist, *Oxford* 311–24.

———. "The Present Outlook for the Dark Races of Mankind." 1900. Sundquist, *Oxford* 47–54.

———. *The Souls of Black Folk.* 1903. Sundquist, *Oxford* 97–240.

Dunbar, Paul Laurence. "The Conquerors: The Black Troops in Cuba." *The Collected Poetry of Paul Laurence Dunbar.* Ed. Joanne M. Braxton. Charlottesville: University Press of Virginia, 1993. 112–13.

Dworkin, Ira, ed. *Daughter of the Revolution: The Major Nonfiction of Pauline E. Hopkins.* New Brunswick, N.J.: Rutgers University Press, 2007.

Elder, Arlene. *The "Hindered Hand": Cultural Implications of Early African-American Fiction.* Westport, Conn.: Greenwood, 1978.

"Elihu Root on the Negro Problem." *Harper's Weekly* 21 February 1903, 306–7.

Espinosa, Mariola. *Epidemic Invasions: Yellow Fever and the Limits of Cuban Independence, 1878–1930.* Chicago: University of Chicago Press, 2009.

Fabi, M. Giulia. *Passing and the Rise of the African American Novel.* Urbana: University of Illinois Press, 2001.

Faust, Drew Gilpin. "Telling War Stories: The Civil War and the Meaning of Life." *New Republic* 30 June 2011. http://www.tnr.com/article/essay/magazine/89638/civil-war-remembrance.

Federal Writers' Project. *Florida: A Guide to the Southernmost State.* 1937. New York: Oxford University Press, 1973.

Fitts, Leroy. *The History of Black Baptists.* Nashville, Tenn.: Broadman, 1985.

Fitz, Earl E. "In Quest of 'Nuestras Américas' or Inter-American Studies and the Dislocation of the Traditional 'American' Paradigm or (with Apologies to José Martí and Stanley Kubrick) How I Learned to Stop Worrying and Love Academic Change." *AmeriQuests* 14.2 (2004). ejournals.library.vanderbilt.edu/ameriquests.

Fleming, Robert E. *James Weldon Johnson.* Boston: Twayne, 1987.

Foley, Neil. *The White Scourge: Mexicans, Blacks, and Poor Whites in Texas Cotton Culture.* Berkeley: University of California Press, 1999.

Foner, Philip S. *The Spanish-Cuban-American War and the Birth of American Imperialism.* 2 vols. New York: Monthly Review Press, 1972.

Fortune, T. Thomas. "The Black Man's Burden." 1921. *African Fundamentalism: A Literary and Cultural Anthology of Garvey's Harlem Renaissance.* Ed. Tony Martin. Dover: Majority, 1991. 241–42.

Foster, Frances Smith, ed. *A Brighter Coming Day: A Frances Ellen Watkins Harper Reader.* New York: Feminist Press, 1990.

Franklin, James T. "Battle of Manila." *Jessamine Poems.* 1900. World's Fair edition. 1900. African American Perspectives: Pamphlets from the Daniel A. P. Murray Collection, 1818–1907. Library of Congress. http://memory.loc.gov/ammem/aap/aaphome.html.

Frazier, Larry. "Sutton E. Griggs's *Imperium in Imperio* as Evidence of Black Baptist Radicalism." *Baptist History and Heritage* 35.2 (2000): 72–91.

Fullinwider, S. P. *The Mind and Mood of Black America.* Homewood, Ill.: Dorsey, 1969.

Gaines, Kevin. "Black Americans' Racial Uplift Ideology as 'Civilizing Mission.'" Kaplan and Pease 433–55.

Garvey, Marcus. "African Fundamentalism." 1925. *Marcus Garvey: Life and Lessons.* Ed. Robert A. Hill and Barbara Bair. Berkeley: University of California Press, 1987. 3–6.

Gates, Henry Louis, Jr., and Jennifer Burton, eds. *Call and Response: Key Debates in African American Studies.* New York: Norton, 2011.

Gates, Henry Louis, Jr., and Nellie Y. McKay, eds. *The Norton Anthology of African American Literature.* 2nd ed. New York: Norton: 2004.

Gatewood, Willard B. *Black Americans and the White Man's Burden, 1898–1903.* Urbana: University of Illinois Press, 1975.

———, ed. *"Smoked Yankees" and the Struggle for Empire: Letters from Negro Soldiers, 1898–1902.* Urbana: University of Illinois Press, 1971.

Gayle, Addison. "The Harlem Renaissance: Towards a Black Aesthetic." 1970. *The Addison Gayle Reader.* Ed. Nathaniel Norment Jr. Urbana: University of Illinois Press, 2009. 71–80.

Gianakos, Perry E. Introduction. Ade 1–8.

Gillman, Susan. *Blood Talk: American Race Melodrama and the Culture of the Occult.* Chicago: University of Chicago Press, 2003.

Gillman, Susan, and Ayls Eve Weinbaum. "Introduction: W. E. B. Du Bois and the Politics of Juxtaposition." *Next to the Color Line: Gender, Sexuality, and W. E. B. Du Bois.* Ed. Susan Gillman and Ayls Eve Weinbaum. Minneapolis: University of Minnesota Press, 2007. 1–33.

Gilmore, F. Grant. *The "Problem": A Military Novel.* 1915. New York: AMS, 1969.

———. *Souvenir and Visitor's Guide: History and Development of the American Negro within the Last Half-Century.* 1926. *Black Biographical Dictionaries, 1790–1950.* Alexandria: Chadwyck-Healey, 1987.

Gloster, Hugh M. Preface. *Imperium in Imperio.* By Sutton E. Griggs. New York: Arno, 1969. iii–viii.

Gossett, Thomas F. *Race: The History of an Idea in America.* Dallas: Southern Methodist University Press, 1975.

Grant, John Wesley. Preface. *Out of the Darkness; or, Diabolism and Destiny.* Nashville, Tenn.: National Baptist Publishing Board, 1909. 7–9.

"The Great Fever Plot." *New York Times* 26 May 1865.

Griggs, Sutton E. *The Hindered Hand; or, The Reign of the Repressionist.* 1st ed. 1905. Miami, Fla.: Mnemosyne, 1969.

———. *The Hindered Hand; or, The Reign of the Repressionist.* 3rd rev. ed. 1905. New York: AMS, 1969.

———. *Imperium in Imperio.* 1899. New York: Modern Library, 2003.

———. *The One Great Question.* Philadelphia: Orion, 1907.

———. *Overshadowed.* Nashville, Tenn.: Orion, 1901.

———. *Pointing the Way.* Nashville, Tenn.: Orion, 1908.

———. *The Story of My Struggles.* Memphis, Tenn.: National Public Welfare League, 1914.

———. *Unfettered.* Nashville, Tenn.: Orion, 1902.

———. *Wisdom's Call.* Nashville, Tenn.: Orion, 1911.

Gruesser, John Cullen. *Black on Black: Twentieth-Century African American Writing about Africa.* Lexington: University Press of Kentucky, 2000.

———, ed. *A Century of Detection: Twenty Great Mystery Stories, 1841–1940.* Jefferson: McFarland, 2010.

Guy, Lulu Baxter. "The Black Man's Burden." *Cleveland (Ohio) Journal* 26 December 1903.

Haines, J. D. "Did a Confederate Doctor Engage in a Primitive Form of Biological Warfare? The Northern Press Thought So." *America's Civil War* 12.4 (1999): 12–13.

Halstead, Murat. *The Story of Cuba, Her Struggles for Liberty: The Cause, Crisis and Destiny of the Pearl of the Antilles.* Chicago: Cuba Libre, 1896.

Harper, Frances. "Burdens of All." Foster 390.

———. "'Do Not Cheer, Men Are Dying,' Said Capt. Phillips, in the Spanish-American War." Foster 388–90.

———. "Maceo." Foster 374–76.

Harrison, Hubert. "The Black Man's Burden." 1915. Harrison 390–91.

———. *A Hubert Harrison Reader.* Ed. Jeffrey B. Perry. Middleton, Conn.: Wesleyan University Press, 2001.

"He Prefers Hell to United States." *Atlanta (Ga.) Constitution* 16 February 1906, 5.

"Here and There." *Colored American Magazine* July 1903, 532.

Hoganson, Kristen L. *Fighting for American Manhood: How Gender Politics Provoked the Spanish-American and Philippine-American Wars.* New Haven, Conn.: Yale University Press, 1998.

Holliday, Presley. Letter to the editor of the *New York Age.* 11 May 1899. Gatewood, *"Smoked"* 92–97.

Hopkins, Pauline E. "Charles Lenox Remond." 1901. Dworkin 63–69.

———. "Club Life among Colored Women." 1902. Dworkin 178–84.

———. "Elijah William Smith: A Colored Poet of Early Days." 1902. Dworkin 277–84.

———. Letter to William Monroe Trotter. 16 April 1905. Dworkin 238–48.

———. "Munroe Rogers." 1902. Dworkin 269–76.

———. Preface. *Contending Forces: A Romance Illustrative of Negro Life North and South.* 1900. New York: Oxford University Press, 1988.

—. "Senator Blanche K. Bruce." 1901. Dworkin 87–93.

—. "Sergeant William H. Carney." 1901. Dworkin 70–76.

—. "Some Literary Workers." 1902. Dworkin 140–46.

—. "Talma Gordon." *Colored American Magazine* October 1900, 271–90.

Horne, Gerald. *The White Pacific: U.S. Imperialism and Black Slavery in the South Seas after the Civil War.* Honolulu: University of Hawaii Press, 2007.

Hurston, Zora Neale. *Their Eyes Were Watching God.* 1937. New York: HarperCollins, 1990.

Imes, B. A. "Sergeant Berry." Cashin et al. 281–83.

"In Honor of the Soldiers." *Colored American* (Washington, D.C.) 14 September 1901, 5.

Jacobson, Matthew Frye. *Barbarian Virtues: The United States Encounters Foreign Peoples at Home and Abroad, 1876–1917.* New York: Hill and Wang, 2001.

—. *Special Sorrows: The Diasporic Imagination of Irish, Polish, and Jewish Immigrants in the United States.* Cambridge, Mass.: Harvard University Press, 1995.

Jackson, Miles M., ed. *They Followed the Trade Winds: African Americans in Hawaii.* Honolulu: University of Hawaii Press, 2004.

James, Jennifer C. *A Freedom Bought with Blood: African American War Literature from the Civil War to World War II.* Chapel Hill: University of North Carolina Press, 2007.

Johnson, Edward A. *History of Negro Soldiers in the Spanish-American War, and Other Items of Interest.* Raleigh, N.C.: Capital, 1899.

Johnson, H. T. "The Black Man's Burden." 1899. Gatewood, *Black* 183–84.

Johnson, James Weldon. *Along This Way: The Autobiography of James Weldon Johnson.* New York: Viking, 1933.

—. "And the Greatest of These Is War." *Fifty Years and Other Poems.* 1917. Johnson, *Complete Poems* 90–91.

—. *The Autobiography of an Ex-Colored Man.* 1912. New York: Hill, 1960.

—. "The Color Sergeant (On an Incident at San Juan Hill)." *Fifty Years and Other Poems.* 1917. Johnson, *Complete Poems* 123.

—. "The Color Sergeant: Tenth U.S. Cavalry: At San Juan." Johnson Papers, Beinecke Library, Yale University, box 83, folder 642, notebook 8, p. 15.

—. *The Complete Poems.* Ed. Sondra Kathryn Wilson. New York: Penguin, 2000.

—. "El Presidente; or, The Yellow Peril." Johnson Papers, Beinecke Library, Yale University, box 75, folders 444, 445, and 446.

—. Lyrics to *The Shoo-Fly Regiment.* Johnson Papers, Beinecke Library, Yale University, box 74, folder 427.

—. "NAACP Testimonial Dinner Speech." 1930. Johnson, *Selected Writings* 123–28.

—. "Ode to Florida." Ca. 1890–95. S. K. Wilson 188–89.

—. "The Royal Document." Johnson Papers, Beinecke Library, Yale University, box 75, folder 456.

—. *The Selected Writings of James Weldon Johnson.* Vol. 2, *Social Political, and Literary Essays.* Ed. Sondra Kathryn Wilson. New York: Oxford University Press, 1995

—. "Tolosa, or the Royal Document." Johnson Papers, Beinecke Library, Yale University, box 75, folders 457, 458, and 459.

———. "The War Catechism." Johnson Papers, Beinecke Library, Yale University, box 73, folder 385.

———. "Why Latin-America Dislikes the United States." 1913. Johnson, *Selected Writings* 195–97.

Johnson, James Weldon, and Bob Cole. "The Czar of Czam." Johnson Papers, Beinecke Library, Yale University, box 74, folders 438 and 439.

———. "The Fakir." Johnson Papers, Beinecke Library, Yale University, box 75, folders 449 and 450.

Jun, Helen H. "Black Orientalism: Nineteenth-Century Narratives of Race and Citizenship." *American Quarterly* 58.4 (2006): 1047–66.

Kaplan, Amy. *The Anarchy of Empire in the Making of U.S. Culture.* Cambridge, Mass.: Harvard University Press, 2003.

Kaplan, Amy, and Donald E. Pease, eds. *Cultures of U.S. Imperialism.* Durham, N.C.: Duke University Press, 1993.

Kellman, Steven G. "Imagining Texas as Black Utopia." Review of *Imperium in Imperio*, by Sutton E. Griggs. *Texas Observer* (Austin, Tex.) 27 February 2004.

Knadler, Stephen. *Remapping Citizenship and the Nation in African American Literature.* New York: Routledge, 2010.

———. "Sensationalizing Patriotism: Sutton Griggs and the Sentimental Nationalism of Citizen Tom." *American Literature* 79.4 (2007): 673–99.

Knight, Alisha R. "Furnace Blasts for the Tuskegee Wizard: Revisiting Pauline Hopkins, Booker T. Washington, and the *Colored American Magazine*." *American Periodicals* 17.1 (2007): 41–64.

Knowles, Frederic Lawrence. *A Kipling Primer.* Boston: Brown, 1899.

Koger, A. Briscoe. *Dr. Harvey Johnson—Pioneer Civic Leader.* Baltimore, Md.: n.p., 1957.

Kramer, Paul A. "Empires, Exceptions, and Anglo-Saxons: Race and Rule between the British and the United States Empires, 1880–1910. *Journal of American History* 88.4 (2002): 1315–53.

Krasner, David. *Resistance, Parody, and Double Consciousness in African American Theatre, 1895–1910.* New York: St. Martin's, 1997.

Lamar, Dolly Blount. *When All Is Said and Done.* Athens: University of Georgia Press, 1952.

Lamon, Lester C. *Black Tennesseans, 1900–1930.* Knoxville: University of Tennessee Press, 1977.

Landers, Jane. *Black Society in Spanish Florida.* Urbana: University of Illinois Press, 1999.

Lasch, Christopher. "The Anti-imperialists, the Philippines, and the Inequality of Man." *Journal of Southern History* 24.3 (1958): 319–31.

Lears, Jackson. *Rebirth of a Nation: The Making of Modern America, 1877–1920.* New York: Harper, 2009.

Levander, Caroline F. "Confederate Cuba." *American Literature* 78.4 (2006): 821–45.

———. "Sutton Griggs and the Borderlands of Empire." *American Literary History* 22.1 (2010): 57–84.

Levander, Caroline F., and Robert S. Levine, eds. *Hemispheric American Studies*. New Brunswick, N.J.: Rutgers University Press, 2008.

Levy, Eugene. *James Weldon Johnson: Black Leader, Black Voice*. University of Chicago Press, 1973.

Lewis, David Levering. *W. E. B. Du Bois: The Fight for Equality and the American Century, 1919–1963*. New York: Holt, 2000.

Logan, Rayford W. *The Betrayal of the Negro: From Rutherford B. Hayes to Woodrow Wilson*. New York: Collier, 1972.

London, Jack. "The Unparalleled Invasion." 1910. *The Strength of the Strong*. New York: Macmillan, 1914. 71–100.

———. "The Yellow Peril." 1904. *Jack London Reports: War Correspondence, Sports Articles, and Miscellaneous Writings*. Ed. King Hendricks and Irving Shepard. New York: Doubleday, 1970. 340–50.

Long, Richard A. "A Weapon of My Song: The Poetry of James Weldon Johnson." *Phylon* 32.4 (1971): 374–82.

Love, Eric T. L. *Race over Empire: Racism and U.S. Imperialism, 1865–1900*. Chapel Hill: University of North Carolina Press, 2004.

Lye, Colleen. *America's Asia: Racial Form and American Literature, 1893–1943*. Princeton, N.J.: Princeton University Press, 2005.

Marks, George P., III, ed. *The Black Press Views American Imperialism (1898–1900)*. New York: Arno, 1971.

Mason, Lena. "A Negro in It." *Twentieth Century Negro Literature; or, A Cyclopedia of Thought on the Vital Topics Relating to the American Negro*. Ed. D. W. Culp. Toronto: Nichols, 1902. 447–48.

McCaskill, Barbara, and Caroline Gebhard, eds. *Post-Bellum, Pre-Harlem: African American Literature and Culture, 1877–1919*. New York: New York University Press, 2006.

McGirt, James Ephraim. "Avenging the Maine." *Avenging* 9–14.

———. *Avenging the Maine, A Drunken A. B., and Other Poems*. 2nd ed. Raleigh, N.C.: Edwards, 1900.

———. "In Love as in War." *The Triumphs of Ephraim*. Philadelphia: n.p., 1907. 63–76.

———. "The Memory of Maceo." *Avenging* 15.

———. "The Siege of Manila." *Avenging* 16–19.

———. "The Siege of Santiago." *Avenging* 20–21.

———. "The Stars and Stripes Shall Never Trail the Dust." *Avenging* 22–24.

McSherry, Patrick. "Casualties during the Spanish American War." Spanish American War Centennial. http://www.spanamwar.com.

McWilliams, Tennant S. "James H. Blount, the South and Hawaiian Annexation." *Pacific Historical Review* 57.1 (1988): 25–46.

Melville, Herman. *Benito Cereno*. 1855. *Melville's Short Novels*. Ed. Dan McCall. New York: Norton, 2002. 34–102.

———. *Moby-Dick*. 1851. 2nd ed. Ed. Hershel Parker and Harrison Hayford. New York: Norton, 2002.

Middleton, Michael A. "Michael A. Middleton's Remarks, Missouri Bar Annual Meeting, October 20, 2003." Office of the Deputy Chancellor, University of Missouri-
Columbia. http://deputychancellor.missouri.edu/speeches/MoBar2003.html.

Miller, Albert G. *Elevating the Race: Theophilus G. Steward, Black Theology, and the Making of an African American Civil Society, 1865–1924*. Knoxville: University of Tennessee Press, 2003.

Miller, Stuart Creighton. *"Benevolent Assimilation": The American Conquest of the Philippines, 1899–1903*. New Haven, Conn.: Yale University Press, 1982.

Mitchell, Michele. *Righteous Propagation: African Americans and the Politics of Racial Destiny after Reconstruction*. Chapel Hill, N.C.: University of North Carolina Press, 2004.

Morrison, Toni. *Playing in the Dark: Whiteness and the Literary Imagination*. New York:
Vintage, 1993.

Moses, Wilson Jeremiah. *The Golden Age of Black Nationalism, 1850–1925*. New York:
Oxford University Press, 1988.

———. "Literary Garveyism: The Novels of Reverend Sutton E. Griggs." *Phylon* 40.3
(1979): 203–16.

Mullen, Bill V. *Afro-Orientalism*. Minneapolis: University of Minnesota Press, 2004.

Murphy, Gretchen. *Shadowing the White Man's Burden: U.S. Imperialism and the Problem of the Color Line*. New York: New York University Press, 2010.

"National Afro-American Party." 1900. Marks 209–11.

The National Geographic Visual Atlas of the World. Washington, D.C.: National Geographic Society, 2008.

"Negroes Who Protect American Rights Abroad Must Be Protected at Home." 1898.
Marks 199–200.

Ngozi-Brown, Scot. "African-American Soldiers and Filipinos: Racial Imperialism, Jim
Crow and Social Relations." *Journal of Negro History* 82.1 (1997): 42–53.

Nickerson, Catherine R. *Web of Iniquity: Early Detective Fiction by American Women*.
Durham, N.C.: Duke University Press, 1998.

Nwankwo, Ifeoma C. K. "The Promises of U.S. African American Hemispherism: Latin
America in Martin Delany's *Blake* and Gayl Jones's *Mosquito*." Levander and Levine
187–205.

O'Brien, Colleen. "'Blacks in all Quarters of the Globe': Anti-imperialism, Insurgent
Cosmopolitanism, and International Labor in Pauline Hopkins's Literary Journalism." *American Quarterly* 61.2 (2009): 245–70.

"Offered to Pay All the Philippine Indemnity." *New York Times* 16 May 1902.

Oh, Seiwoong. "Cross-Cultural Reading Versus Textual Accessibility in Multicultural
Literature." *MELUS* 18.2 (1993): 3–16.

Ontal, Rene G. "Fagen and Other Ghosts: African Americans and the Philippine-
American War." *Vestiges of War: The Philippine-American War and the Aftermath of
an Imperial Dream, 1899–1999*. Ed. Angel Velasco Shaw and Luis H. Francia. New
York: New York University Press, 2002. 118–33.

Page, Amanda M. "The Ever-Expanding South: James Weldon Johnson and the Rhetoric
of the Global Color Line." *Southern Quarterly* 46.3 (2009): 26–46.

Page, Thomas Nelson. "Marse Chan: A Tale of Old Virginia." *Century Magazine* April 1884, 932–42.

Payne, James Robert. "Afro-American Literature of the Spanish-American War." *MELUS* 10.3 (1983): 19–32.

Penzler, Otto, ed. *Black Noir: Mystery, Crime, and Suspense Fiction by African-American Writers*. New York: Pegasus, 2009.

Pérez, Louis A., Jr. *Cuba: Between Reform and Revolution*. 2nd ed. New York: Oxford University Press, 1995.

———. "Reminiscences of a *Lector*: Cuban Cigar Workers in Tampa." *Florida Historical Quarterly* 53.4 (1975): 443–49.

———. *The Spanish-Cuban-American War, 1878–1902*. Pittsburgh, Pa.: University of Pittsburgh Press, 1983.

———. *The War of 1898: The United States and Cuba in History and Historiography*. Chapel Hill: University of North Carolina Press, 1998.

Peterson, Carla L. "Commemorative Ceremonies and Invented Traditions: History, Memory, and Modernity in the 'New Negro' Novel of the Nadir." McCaskill and Gebhard 34–56.

Petry, Elizabeth. *Can Anything Beat White: A Black Family's Letters*. Jackson: University of Mississippi Press, 2005.

Poe, Edgar Allan. "The Gold-Bug." 1843. *The Selected Writings of Edgar Allan Poe*. Ed. G. R. Thompson. New York: Norton, 2004. 321–48.

Powell, George E. "The Charge of the 'Nigger Ninth' on San Juan Hill." Edward A. Johnson 35–38.

Rampersad, Arnold. *The Art and Imagination of W. E. B. Du Bois*. Cambridge, Mass.: Harvard University Press, 1976.

———. "Griggs, Sutton E[lbert]." *Dictionary of American Negro Biography*. Ed. Rayford W. Logan and Michael R. Winston. New York: Norton, 1982. 271.

Redkey, Edwin S. "Bishop Turner's African Dream." *Journal of American History* 54.2 (1967): 271–90.

Reef, Catherine. "Carney, William Harvey." *African Americans in the Military*. Rev. ed. New York: Facts on File, 2010. 60–62.

Reesman, Jeanne Campbell. *Jack London's Racial Lives: A Critical Biography*. Athens: University of Georgia Press, 2009.

Riehle, Dave. "'300 Afro-American Performers': The Great Cuba Pageant of 1898; St. Paul's Citizens Support the Struggle for Civil Rights." *Ramsey County History* 33.4 (1999): 15–20.

"Ringing Columbus' Bell." *Library Company of Philadelphia: 1994 Annual Report*. Philadelphia: Library Company, 1995. 36–37.

Roberts, Brian Russell. "Passing into Diplomacy: U.S. Consul James Weldon Johnson and *The Autobiography of an Ex-Colored Man*." *Modern Fiction Studies* 52.2 (2010): 290–316.

Robinson, Michael C., and Frank N. Schubert. "David Fagen: An Afro-American Rebel in the Philippines, 1899–1901." *Pacific Historical Review* 44.1 (1975): 68–83.

Roosevelt, Theodore. *The Rough Riders*. 1899. New York: Scribner's 1902.

———. *Theodore Roosevelt: An Autobiography*. 1913. New York: Scribner's, 1920.

"Roosevelt to Colored Men." *New York Times* 15 October 1898, 2.

Root, Elihu. "The Union League Club." 1903. *Miscellaneous Addresses*. Ed. Robert Bacon and James Brown Scott. Cambridge: Harvard University Press, 1917. 123–27.

Schirmer, Daniel B. *Republic or Empire: American Resistance to the Philippine War*. Cambridge, Mass.: Schenkman, 1972.

Seniors, Paula Marie. *Beyond "Lift Every Voice and Sing": The Culture of Uplift, Identity, and Politics in Black Musical Theater*. Columbus: Ohio State University Press, 2009.

Seraile, William. *Voice of Dissent: Theophilus Gould Steward (1843–1924) and Black America*. New York: Carlson, 1991.

Shackelford, Otis M. Preface. *Lillian Simmons; or, The Conflict of Sorrows*. 1915. New York: AMS, 1975. 7–10.

Sharp, Patricia B. "The Great White 'Race Adventure': Jack London and the Yellow Peril." *Crossing Oceans: Reconfiguring American Literary Studies in the Pacific Rim*. Ed. Noelle Brada-Williams and Karen Chow. Hong Kong: Hong Kong University Press, 2004. 89–97.

Sinclair, William A. *The Aftermath of Slavery: A Study of the Condition and Environment of the American Negro*. Boston: Small, 1905.

Singer, Jane. "A Fiend in Gray." *Washington Post* 1 June 2003.

Smethurst, James. "'Those Noble Sons of Ham': Poetry, Soldiers, and Citizens at the End of Reconstruction." *Hope and Glory: Essays on the Legacy of the Fifty-Fourth Massachusetts Regiment*. Ed. Martin H. Blatt, Thomas J. Brown, and Donald Yacovane. Amherst: University of Massachusetts Press, 2001. 168–87.

Smith, J. Clay, Jr. *Emancipation: The Making of the Black Lawyer, 1844–1944*. Philadelphia: University of Pennsylvania Press, 1993.

Smith, John David. "'My Books Are Hard Reading for a Negro': Tom Dixon and His African American Critics, 1905–1939." *Thomas Dixon Jr. and the Birth of Modern America*. Ed. Michelle K. Gillespie and Randal L. Hall. Baton Rouge: Louisiana State University Press, 2006. 46–79.

Smith-Travers, Alice. "The White Man's Burden." *The Freeman* (Indianapolis, Ind.) 4 March 1899.

Sollors, Werner. *Neither Black Nor White Yet Both: Thematic Exploration of Interracial Literature*. New York: Oxford University Press, 1997.

Stanford, Karin L., ed. *If We Must Die: African American Voices on War and Peace*. Lanham, Md.: Rowman and Littlefield, 2008.

Stead, William T. *The Americanization of the World: The Trend of the Twentieth Century*. New York: Markley, 1901.

———. Commentary on "The White Man's Burden," by Rudyard Kipling. *Review of Reviews* 15 February 1899, 139.

Stecopoulos, Harilaos. "Up from Empire: James Weldon Johnson, Latin America, and the Jim Crow South." *Imagining Our Americas: Toward a Transnational Frame*. Ed.

Sandhya Skukla and Heidi Tinsman. Durham, N.C.: Duke University Press, 2007. 34–62.

Steers, Edward, Jr. *Blood on the Moon: The Assassination of Abraham Lincoln*. Lexington: University Press of Kentucky, 2001.

———. ed. *The Trial: The Assassination of President Lincoln and the Trial of the Conspirators*. Lexington: University Press of Kentucky, 2003.

Steward, Frank R. "Colored Officers." T. G. Steward 299–328.

———. "Colored Soldiers Again Show Prowess." *Colored American* (Washington, D.C.) 1 May 1901, 6.

———. "The Men Who Prey." *Colored American Magazine* October 1903, 720–24.

———. "Pepe's Anting-Anting: A Tale of Laguna." *Colored American Magazine* September 1902, 358–62.

———. "'Starlik': A Tale of Laguna." *Colored American Magazine* March 1903, 387–91.

Steward, Theophilus G. *The Colored Regulars in the United States Army*. Philadelphia: AME Book Concern, 1904.

———. "Thrift among Soldiers." *Colored American* (Washington, D.C.) 12 January 1901, 3.

Stoner, George W. *Handbook for the Ship's Medicine Chest*. 2nd ed. Washington, D.C.: GPO, 1904.

Sundquist, Eric J., ed. *The Oxford W. E. B. Du Bois Reader*. New York: Oxford University Press, 1996.

———. *To Wake the Nations: Race in the Making of American Literature*. Cambridge: Harvard University Press, 1993.

Swift, John N. "Jack London's 'Unparalleled Invasion': Germ Warfare, Eugenics, and Cultural Hygiene." *American Literary Realism* 35.1 (2002): 59–71.

Tal, Kali. "'That Just Kills Me': Black Militant Near-Future Fiction." *Social Text* 20.2 (2002): 65–91.

Taubenfeld, Aviva F. *Rough Writing: Ethnic Authorship in Theodore Roosevelt's America*. New York: New York University Press, 2008.

Temple, George Hannibal. "The Cuban Amazon." *The Epic of Columbus' Bell and Other Poems*. Reading, Pa.: Reading Eagle, 1900. 44–46.

Thompson, Era Bell. "Veterans Who Never Came Home." *Ebony* October 1972, 104–15.

Tillman, Katherine Davis Chapman. "The Black Boys in Blue." *Recitations*. 1902. *The Works of Katherine Davis Chapman Tillman*. Ed. Claudia Tate. New York: Oxford University Press, 1991. 188–89.

Torruella, Juan. *Global Intrigues: The Era of the Spanish-American War and the Rise of the United States to World Power*. San Juan: La Editorial Universidad de Puerto Rico, 2007.

Tucker, David M. *Black Pastors and Leaders: Memphis, 1819–1972*. Memphis: Memphis State University Press, 1975.

Turner, Henry McNeal. "The American Flag." 1906. *Respect* 196–99.

———. "The Negro and the Army." 1899. *Respect* 184–85.

———. "The Philippine Insurrection." 1900. *Respect* 186–87.

———. *Respect Black: The Writings and Speeches of Henry McNeal Turner*. Ed. Edwin S. Redkey. New York: Arno, 1971.

"Turner Denies He Cursed Flag." *Atlanta (Ga.) Constitution* 24 February 1906, 3.

Upchurch, Thomas Adams. "Senator John Tyler Morgan and the Genesis of Jim Crow Ideology, 1889–1891." *Alabama Review* 57 (April 2004): 110–31.

Walker, Randolph Meade. "The Metamorphosis of Sutton E. Griggs: A Southern Black Baptist Minister's Transformation in Theological and Sociological Thought during the Early Twentieth Century." PhD diss., Memphis State University, 1990.

Wallinger, Hanna. *Pauline Elizabeth Hopkins: A Literary Biography*. Athens: University of Georgia Press, 2005.

Washington, Booker T. *Up from Slavery*. 1901. New York: Barnes and Noble, 2003.

Washington, Booker T., N. B. Wood, and Fannie Barrier Williams. *A New Negro for a New Century*. 1900. New York: Arno, 1969.

Wegener, Frederick. "Charles W. Chesnutt and the Anti-imperialist Matrix of African-American Writing, 1898–1905." *Criticism* 41.4 (1999): 465–93.

Welch, Richard E. *Response to Imperialism: The United States and the Philippine-American War, 1899–1902*. Chapel Hill: University of North Carolina Press, 1979.

Wheeler, Joseph. Introduction. Cashin et al. xii–xv.

White, Charles Fred[erick]. *The Plea of the Negro Soldier and a Hundred Other Poems*. Easthampton, Mass.: Enterprise, 1908.

Wilson, William Huntington. "The Return of the Sergeant." *Harper's Weekly* 15 September 1900, 871–73.

Winter, Molly Crumpton. *American Narratives: Multiethnic Writing in the Age of Realism*. Baton Rouge: Louisiana State University Press, 2007.

Woll, Allen. *Black Musical Theatre: From Coontown to Dreamgirls*. Baton Rouge: Louisiana State University Press, 1989.

Woods, Paula. *Spooks, Spies, and Private Eyes: Black Mystery, Crime, and Suspense Fiction*. New York: Doubleday, 1995.

Wright, Richard. *The Color Curtain: A Report on the Bandung Conference*. New York: World, 1956.

X-Ray. "Charity Begins at Home." *Colored American* (Washington, D.C.) 18 March 1899, 4.

"The Yellow Fever Plot." *New York Times* 16 May 1865.

Yglesias, Jose. "Martí in Ybor City." *José Martí in the United States: The Florida Experience*. Ed. Louis A. Peréz Jr. Tempe: Arizona State University Center for Latin American Studies, 1995. 103–14.

Index

abolitionism, 22, 43, 115–16, 128n7
accommodationism, 48, 113, 116–17
activism, as tactic, 57, 101
Ade, George: Fables in Slang, 105; Stories of Benevolent Assimilation, 105, 138n10; *The Sultan of Sulu*, 105, 111
African American press: Philippine-American war and occupation, 8, 63–64, 87, 118, 127n8; Spanish-Cuban-American war, 11, 35, 132n12. *See also* Fortune, T. Thomas; Hopkins, Pauline
African ancestry, hidden, 92–93, 121, 123–24
Aguinaldo, Emilio, 13, 20
American Law Enforcement League, 23
American Negro Academy, 1, 68
anti-imperialism: black, 14, 69, 74–75, 94, 105–8, 134n6; white, 4, 9, 13, 14, 67, 105, 135n11. *See also* imperialism, responses to
antiwar sentiments, 68, 102–3
Appiah, Kwame Anthony, 4
armed resistance, proposals for, 40, 46–47, 50, 56, 117
Asians, images of: among blacks, 63–64, 65, 87, 89; Hawaiians, 2, 4, 10; among whites, 4, 10, 13–14, 105, 127n7. *See also* Filipinos
Asian supremacy, fears of, 53, 109–11, 132–33n18

Asian women: and black men, 85–86; sexual exploitation of, 77–82, 86, 95, 108
Autobiography of an Ex-Colored Man, The (Johnson, J. W.), 5, 23, 97–98, 99, 103

Baker, Frazier (lynching victim), 23, 46, 132n12
Battle of Manila, 12
battle standard. *See* flag, U.S.
Beadle, Samuel Alfred, 29–30, 31, 32, 56
Beyond "Lift Every Voice and Sing" (Seniors), 97, 104, 111
biological warfare, 41, 53–54, 58, 109–10, 133n18, 133n23
Birth of a Nation, The (Griffith), 4
Blackburn, Luke Pryor, 58, 133n23
"Black Man's Burden, The" (Chadwick), 134n3
"Black Man's Burden, The" (Fortune), 69, 134n5
"Black Man's Burden, The" (Johnson, H. T.), 63, 68, 69
Black Man's Burden Association, 14
black military regiments, 33–34, 90; in Civil War, 20, 134n3; in Cuba, 55, 76, 100, 128n3, 129n13, 129n17, 133n19. *See also* military service
black orientalism, defined, 63

153

black women: in "The Burden of Black Women," 71–73, 94, 134n7; positive images of, 25, 72–73, 115; sexual exploitation of, 56–57, 71–72, 92, 93, 119, 124

Blount, James H., Jr., 9, 10

Blount, James H., Sr., 9

Bold, Christine, 20, 21, 35

Bradley, James, 3

Brantlinger, Patrick, 66, 68, 133n1

Brazley, Stella A. E., 24, 27, 33

Brooks, Gwendolyn, 113

Brown, William Wells, 20, 22, 24, 115, 128n7

Brownsville incident, 84, 94, 137n7

Bruce, John Edward, 64, 68–69, 134nn5–6, 135n12

Bryan, William Jennings, 14, 66, 102, 138n18. *See also* election of 1900

Buffalo Soldiers, 90

"Burden of Black Women, The" (Du Bois), 71–73, 94, 134n7

Burns, Anthony, 117

Burroughs, Edgar Rice, 67

Burton, Jennifer, 5

Carby, Hazel, 118–19, 121–22, 126

Carnegie, Andrew, 13, 66

Carney, William H. (sergeant in Civil War), 20, 30, 36, 56, 90, 115–16

Cashin, Herschel V., 21, 85

Chadwick, John White, 134n3

Channing, B. M., 129n13

Chesnutt, Charles, 39, 127n1

Chicago World's Fair, 101, 137n6

"Citizen Tom" (image of black servility), 48, 83–94; in Gilmore's writings, 83, 87–92; in McGirt's writings, 84–87

Coffin, Frank B., 25–26

Cole, Bob, 4, 16, 101, 108, 109, 136n3

Cole and Johnson Brothers, 97, 104, 106

"Colored Officers" (Steward), 8

"colors." *See* flag, U.S.

"Color Sergeant, The" (Johnson, J. W.), 30–33, 35, 38, 56, 68, 103

Conrad, Joseph, 67

Cooper, Anna Julia, 25, 118

Cordell, Sigrid Anderson, 119, 121, 124

Crummell, Alexander, 118

Cuba: and American public attitudes, 12, 22; independence of, 24–30; racial equality in, 98. *See also* military service; Spanish-Cuban-American war

Cuban women, 24–25, 128n10

Davis, Jefferson, 58

Davis, Richard Harding, 37, 91

Dean, Harry, 132n14

disenfranchisement, 4, 40, 44, 93. *See also* oppression, economic and social, in United States

Dixon, Thomas, Jr., 4, 41, 54, 59, 60, 131n6, 133n24

Doreski, C. K., 116

Dos Antillas, Las, 127n6

Douglass, Frederick: as abolitionist, 115–16, 128n7; and Cuba, 22, 25; and Johnson, James Weldon, 101; patriotism of, 131–32n9; and Texas, 43

Du Bois, W. E. B.: and Asian supremacy, 110; "The Burden of Black Women," 71–73, 94, 134n7; and Johnson, James Weldon, 101; and race chauvinism, 1, 118; and U.S. imperialism, 2, 4, 11, 96, 111; and Washington, Booker T., 114; and "The White Man's Burden," 64, 68, 71–73; writings of, 134–35n7

Dunbar, Paul Laurence, 29, 31, 39, 76, 101

Dworkin, Ira, 114, 115, 116

Elder, Arlene, 40, 130n2

election of 1900, 14, 74, 75, 135n11

emancipation, 40, 74, 131–32n9

Emancipation Day (Juneteenth), 44, 117

emigration of blacks: outside United States, 40–45, 57, 76, 87, 94, 130n1, 132n14; within United States, 16, 42, 44, 45–46

Equiano, Olaudah, 71

Ethiopianism, 68, 72, 135n8

expansionism. *See* anti-imperialism; imperialism, responses to

Fabi, M. Giulia, 50, 132n16
Fables in Slang (newspaper column, Ade), 105
Famous Men of the Negro Race series (Hopkins), 115
Famous Women of the Negro Race series (Hopkins), 115
Faust, Drew Gilpin, 10
Filipinos: compared with oppressed groups in United States, 41, 67, 70, 74, 91; oppression of, 15, 77; and "Talma Gordon," 119–20. *See also* Asians, images of; Asian women; Gilmore, F. Grant; McGirt, James Ephraim; Steward, Frank R.
Finlay, Carlos, 55
flag, U.S.: in battle, 20, 30–33, 38, 56; as symbol of hypocrisy, 15, 56, 83–84, 103. *See also* Turner, Henry McNeal
Florida, 135–36n2. *See also* Jacksonville, Fla.
Fortune, T. Thomas, 45, 69, 87; "The Black Man's Burden," 69, 134n5
Freund, John C., 114

Gaines, Kevin, 3, 117–18, 119, 126
Garnet, Henry Highland, 22
Garrison, William Lloyd, 115, 116, 128n7
Garvey, Marcus, 47, 69, 134n5
Gates, Henry Louis, 5
Gebhard, Caroline, 5
Gillman, Susan, 59, 131n6, 135n10
Gilmore, F. Grant: "Citizen Tom" narrative of, 83, 87–92; and domestic race chauvinism, 4, 84, 88, 93, 94; and Philippine occupation, 64–65, 89–90; *The "Problem,"* 65, 83, 84, 88, 92–93, 94; writings of, 135n17
"Gold Bug, The" (Poe), 36, 119, 124, 130nn20–21, 138n1
Gordon, Capt. Nathaniel, 123–25
Grajales, Antonio Maceo, 12, 23–28, 33, 127n6

Griffith, D. W., 4
Griggs, Sutton E., 39–60; biographical information, 42, 131n7; and black oppression, 40, 74–76, 131n4; and Philippine occupation, 64–65, 74; and Spanish-Cuban-American war, 53, 56, 57, 60, 131n6; and Washington, Booker T., 40, 130n3. *See also Hindered Hand, The; Imperium in Imperio; Unfettered*
Guantánamo Bay, 12

Haiti, 4, 5, 8, 27, 28, 98, 117
Harlem Renaissance, 127n1
Harper, Frances: as abolitionist, 115–16, 128n7; and Cuba, 22, 25; and imperialism, 117–18; "Maceo," 24, 25, 27–28, 68; and "The White Man's Burden," 64, 68, 70–71, 73
Harrison, Hubert, 134n5
Hawaii, annexation of, 6, 9, 44, 105, 112
Hawaiians, 2, 4, 10
Hayden, Lewis, 116, 128n7
Hindered Hand, The (Griggs), 16, 41, 49, 51–60, 65; and Africa, 135n14; and domestic oppression, 129n14, 130n1; mentioned, 39–40, 73, 109, 135n13
Holsey, Bishop Lucius H., 45
Hopkins, Pauline: and accommodationism, 116–17; criticism of, 117–18; as editor of *The Colored American Magazine*, 76–77, 113–17; and imperialism, 2–3, 118–19, 126; and Washington, Booker T., 113, 114
—works of: "Munroe Rogers," 116–17; "Talma Gordon," 2–3, 117–26; *Winona*, 117
Howells, William Dean, 67
Hurricane Katrina, 136n2
Hurston, Zora Neale, 136n2

images of blacks, negative, 21–22, 36–38, 59, 115; "Citizen Tom," 48, 83–94. *See also* military service images of blacks, positive, 25, 49, 72–73, 84, 104, 137n9; of black women, 25, 72–73, 115. *See also* military service

imperialism, responses to: black versus white, 3, 4, 120, 126; inconsistency among blacks, 5–7, 64, 97, 99; support for, black, 76, 87; support for, white, 4, 66. *See also* anti-imperialism

Imperium in Imperio (Griggs), 41–51, 60, 65, 128n6, 132n11; mentioned, 5, 39, 52, 57, 58, 73, 117

insanity and oppression, 57, 130n1

interracial marriage, 84–87, 91, 119–23

interracial tolerance, 68–71, 122

Jacksonville, Fla., 23, 99–100, 101, 136n5

James, Jennifer C., 11, 13, 21, 84

Jim Crow. *See* oppression, economic and social, in United States

Johnson, Harvey, 45

Johnson, Henry Theodore, 64, 68; "The Black Man's Burden," 63, 68, 69

Johnson, James Weldon: biographical information, 99–102, 105, 109, 136n4; diplomatic service of, 97, 98, 101–2, 137n8; as educator, 101, 102; and imperialism, 98–99, 103, 104–9; papers of, at Yale University, 129n15, 138nn11–15; political activism of, 101
—works of: *The Autobiography of an Ex-Colored Man*, 5, 23, 97–98, 99, 103; "The Color Sergeant," 30–33, 35, 38, 56, 68, 103; musical dramas, 97, 99, 101–12, 137nn8–9; poetry, 31, 103; *El Presidente; or, The Yellow Peril*, 103, 104, 105, 108, 109–11; *Toloso*, 99, 103, 104, 105–9, 111

Johnson, J. Rosamond. *See* Johnson, James Weldon

Jun, Helen H., 63, 64

Juneteenth (Emancipation Day), 44, 117

Kaplan, Amy, 3, 19, 36–37, 89

Kipling, Rudyard, 59, 133n25, 133–34n1. *See also* "White Man's Burden, The"

Knadler, Stephen, 5, 40, 48, 49, 83, 131n6

Knowles, Frederic Lawrence, 66

Koger, A. Briscoe, 132n11

Langston, John Mercer, 22

Lasch, Christopher, 4

Latin Americans, 22, 102, 109–11. *See also* Cuba

Levander, Caroline F., 5, 22, 42, 47, 49–50, 131n6

Levine, Robert S., 3

Lewis, David Levering, 72

Lodge, Henry Cabot, 66

London, Jack, 109, 132–33n18, 138n17

Long, Richard A., 31

Love, Eric T. L., 6

lynching: denunciation of, 26, 101, 118; in fiction, 52, 98, 101, 130n1; mentioned, 93, 111, 127n1. *See also* Baker, Frazier

"Maceo" (Harper), 24, 25, 27–28, 68

Maceo, Antonio. *See* Grajales, Antonio Maceo

Maine (battleship), 12, 132n12

"Marse Chan" (Page, T. N.), 21–22, 36–38, 85, 130n21

Martí, José, 12, 127n6

McCaskill, Barbara, 5

McGhee, Frederick, 23

McGirt, James Ephraim, 3–4, 24, 26–27, 83; biographical information, 26; "Citizen Tom" narrative of, 84–87; and domestic race chauvinism, 94; and Philippine war and occupation, 64–65, 84–85

military service: accusations of black cowardice in, 11, 20–21, 94; black heroism in, 20, 32–33, 56, 84–91, 93–95, 103; black veterans, 16, 31, 41, 56, 60, 108 (*see also* Brownsville incident); limits to black advancement in, 11, 31, 93, 129n18, 133nn20–21; opportunities for black advancement in, 8, 14, 21, 94; and positive self-image for blacks, 11, 21, 65; racial integration in, 88–89.

See also flag, U.S., in battle; Roosevelt, Theodore; San Juan Hill, Battle of
Miller, Joaquin, 22
miscegenation. *See* interracial marriage
Moore, Fred, 114
moral inferiority of whites, 71–72, 78, 87, 89, 125, 134n6. *See also* whites, treason among
moral superiority of blacks, 73, 86, 87, 90, 91–92
Morgan, John T., 9, 44
Morrison, Toni, 130n20
Mullen, Bill V., 96
multicultural misunderstandings, 78–80
"Munroe Rogers" (Hopkins), 116–17
Murphy, Gretchen, 3, 21, 67–68, 81, 82, 119
musical compositions by African American composers, 24, 36. *See also* Johnson, James Weldon: works of: musical dramas

NAACP, 76, 102, 105
National Afro-American Party, 14, 135n11
National Association for the Advancement of Colored People. *See* NAACP
National Negro Anti-Expansion, Anti-Imperialist, Anti-Trust, and Anti-Lynching League, 14
National Negro Baptist Convention, 41
Negro Society for Historical Research, 69
Norton Anthology of African American Literature, 3, 52

O'Brien, Colleen, 118
oppression, economic and social, in United States, 33, 60, 93, 101, 127n1. *See also* disenfranchisement; lynching; segregation
Othello, parallels with, 86, 89, 135n18

Page, Amanda M., 97, 98
Page, Thomas Nelson, 22, 91; "Marse Chan," 21–22, 36–38, 85, 130n21

Panama Canal, 56, 109, 138n16
Payne, Bishop Daniel, 25
Payne, James Robert, 31–32, 88, 90, 131n6
Peterson, Carla, 93
Philippine-American war and occupation: and black advancement, 8, 84–85; black ambivalence about, 64–65, 74, 77–82, 118; black deserters in, 14, 77, 87; black opposition to, 14–15; race chauvinism in U.S. military in, 14; span of, 12–13
plantation literature, 21, 36–38, 48, 59, 83, 115. *See also* "Marse Chan"
Platt amendment, 12
Poe, Edgar Allan, 36, 119, 130n20; "The Gold Bug," 124, 130n21, 138n1
poetry by African American writers, 22, 24–33, 38. *See also* Johnson, James Weldon
Ponce, Ricardo Rodriguez, 100
Powell, George E., 129n13
Presidente, El (Johnson, J. W.), 103, 104, 105, 108, 109–11
"Problem," The (Gilmore), 65, 83, 84, 88, 92–93, 94

race chauvinism: and Asians, 4, 10, 13–14, 105, 109–11, 127n7; and Latin America, 22, 102, 109–11; as science, 6, 75, 111, 115, 122, 135n12
race loyalty versus patriotism, 6, 48, 49, 68
racism. *See* race chauvinism
Rampersad, Arnold, 40, 71–72
Reconstruction, era of, 7, 9, 10, 23, 36, 92
Remond, Charles Lenox, 116
Rizal, José, 118
Roberts, Brian Russell, 97, 99
Roosevelt, Theodore: fictional representations of, 88–89, 110; and Panama Canal, 138n16; praise of black military service, 34–35, 129n17; and Turner, Henry McNeal, 83; and "The White Man's Burden," 66. *See also* San Juan Hill, Battle of

San Juan Hill, Battle of: accusations of
black cowardice in, 12, 19–20, 33, 34,
94; black heroism in, 29, 34, 56, 104
Santiago, Cuba, battle at, 12, 23, 28, 33,
128n3, 129n17
Scarborough, William Saunders, 45,
76, 87
Schomburg, Arturo Alfonso, 12, 68, 127n6
segregation, 4, 22, 44, 51, 100–101, 111.
See also oppression, economic and
social, in United States
Seniors, Paula Marie, 97, 103–4, 111, 137n9;
Beyond "Lift Every Voice and Sing," 97,
104, 111
Shoo-Fly Regiment, The. See Johnson,
James Weldon: works of: musical
dramas
Sims, Thomas, 117
Slavic challenge to Anglo-Saxon
supremacy, 52–53, 59, 109–10, 132n18
Smith, Elijah W., 24, 128n7
Smith-Travers, Alice, 69–70
social Darwinism. *See* race chauvinism:
as science
Sojourner Truth, 115–16
solidarity among people of color, 49, 65,
97, 131n5, 136n2
Spanish-Cuban-American war, 11,
28–35, 56, 57. *See also* military service;
Roosevelt, Theodore; San Juan Hill,
Battle of
spirituality, appeals to, 27, 68, 69, 70–71, 73
Stead, William T., 66–67, 76
Stecopoulos, Harilaos, 97, 98–99
stereotypes. *See* Asians, images of; images
of blacks, negative; Latin Americans;
race chauvinism
Steward, Frank R., 7–10; biographical
information, 8, 76; and U.S.
imperialism, 64, 82
—works of: "Colored Officers," 8; Laguna
short stories of, 76–82, 120
Steward, Theophilus G., 7–8
Stories of Benevolent Assimilation
(Ade), 105, 138n10

sultan of Sulu, 15
Sultan of Sulu, The (Ade), 105, 111

Taft, William Howard, 110
"Talma Gordon" (Hopkins), 2–3, 117–26
Temple, George Hannibal, 24–25, 26,
128n9
Texas, 16, 41–47, 51, 132n11
Tillman, Katherine Davis Chapman,
29, 33
Toloso (Johnson, J. W.), 99, 103, 104,
105–9, 111
Torruella, Juan, 12, 13
Toussaint L'Ouverture, 28, 33, 116, 117, 118
Treaty of Paris, 13
Trotter, William Monroe, 77, 113, 114
Tubman, Harriet, 115–16
Turner, Henry McNeal, 14–15, 45, 55, 56,
83–84, 135n16

Unfettered (Griggs): critique of, 39,
133n22, 135n10; and imperialism, 41,
65, 74, 76, 94; and race chauvinism, 75,
130n1, 131n6, 135n14
United Daughters of the Confederacy,
127n4
Universal Negro Improvement
Association, 69

veterans. *See* military service
Victoria, Queen, 59
virility of black men, 86, 88

Walker, Edwin Garrison, 115–16
Washington, Booker T.: and
accommodationism, 48, 113, 116; and
Griggs, Sutton E., 40; and Johnson,
James Weldon, 101; and Roosevelt,
Theodore, 111–12; and Turner, Henry
McNeal, 83–84
Wheatley, Phillis, 71
Wheeler, Maj. Gen. Joseph, 21, 85
white immorality and inferiority, 71–72,
78, 87, 89, 125, 134n6. *See also* whites,
treason among

"White Man's Burden, The" (Kipling), 16, 133n25; black responses to, 64–65, 68–73, 83, 94; and oppression of U.S. blacks, 69–70; parodies of, 64, 66, 67–70, 94, 134n5; white responses to, 66–68

whites, treason among, 38, 53, 56, 58, 88, 90, 92

white women, race chauvinism among, 116

Williams, Fannie Barrier, 34

Wilson, William Huntington, 20, 21

Wilson, Woodrow, 4

Winona (Hopkins), 117

"Wizard of Tuskegee." *See* Washington, Booker T.

Woll, Allen, 137n9

women: Cuban, 24–25, 128n10; white, 116. *See also* Asian women; black women

Wood, N. B., 34

yellow fever, 51–52, 53–56, 132n17, 133n19

"yellow peril." *See* Asian supremacy, fears of

Yglesia, José, 23

Zelaya, José Santos, 109, 138n16